KU-503-260

# EARLY TO SCHOOL

## Four Year Olds in Infant Classes

**Shirley Cleave**

**and**

**Sandra Brown**

# NFER-NELSON

Published by The NFER-NELSON Publishing Company Ltd,
Darville House, 2 Oxford Road East,
Windsor, Berkshire SL4 1DF, UK

First published 1991

© 1991 Shirley Cleave and Sandra Brown

All rights reserved, including translation. No part of this publication may
be reproduced or  transmitted in any form or by any means, electronic or
mechanical, including photocopying, recording or duplication in any
information storage and retrieval system, without permission in writing
from the publishers.

Phototypeset by David John Services Ltd, Maidenhead, Berkshire.
Printed in Great Britain by Billings & Sons Ltd, Worcester.

ISBN 07005 1269 1

Code 8508 02 4

HERTFORDSHIRE
LIBRARY SERVICE

| No. H30 441 725 / |  |  |
| Class 372.24'1 |  |  |
| Supplier BC | Price £12.50 | Date 11/91 |

# Acknowledgements

We welcome the opportunity to thank everyone involved in this NFER-funded project. We are especially grateful to all those LEAs, college and schools who gave up precious time to talk with us and answer our questions. We are particularly indebted to the in-service providers who allowed us to attend their sessions, the teachers and their colleagues who tolerated us in their classrooms and the children who so good-naturedly let us look on at their activities.

Special thanks are due to our advisory group, Lesley Abbott, Solveig Morris and John Stannard, for their wisdom, guidance and support thoughout the research. We are also grateful to our colleagues at NFER: Judy Bradley for directing the project; Lesley Saunders and Caroline Sharp for their helpful comments on our draft report; and Janet May-Bowles and her library team for keeping us well supplied with documentation throughout the study.

Finally, we wish to record our appreciation of our secretary, Iris Ashby, for her unfailing good humour, and Pauline Pearce, Dorothy Merritt, Maura Stock, Moci Carter and Jane Westing for their patience in processing the many drafts of this report.

# Contents

*Bold type within the text indicates the main principles that have
been drawn from the study and are included in 'A Framework for
Action' (Chapter 12).*

# PART ONE

## Setting the Scene

The growing practice of admitting children to infant classes soon after their fourth birthday has given rise to concern that their needs should be appropriately provided for. What are the educational needs of these younger pupils and what does this mean for the schools they attend?

# 1 Introduction

This book reports the findings of the project *The Educational Needs of Four Year Olds*. The research was funded and carried out by the National Foundation for Educational Research (NFER) from January 1988 to February 1990, and continued the Foundation's longstanding interest in the field of early years education.

The project, staffed by two full-time researchers, was set up in response to the growing practice of admitting children under five to infant classes, and to widely expressed fears that the primary school curriculum was inappropriate to their needs. Over the last decade, many local education authorities (LEAs) have changed their policies to admit children to school below the statutory starting age. When the project began, 62 per cent of four year olds were in infant or primary classes compared with 15 per cent in nursery schools and classes (GB.DES, 1990a). The study was particularly concerned with children admitted to mainstream classes in infant or primary schools at the beginning of the year in which they become five. Many of these new entrants, therefore, embark on their full-time school careers at barely four years of age.

The research coincided with plans for the introduction in September 1989 of the National Curriculum Key Stage 1 for children aged five to seven. This, together with proposals for National Assessment at the age of seven, was expected to strengthen demands for early admission so that all children should have three full years of infant schooling.

The study was not intended to advocate the placement of young children in infant rather than nursery classes. However, given that many four year olds were now in school, the study set out to consider how their needs could best be provided for. The project had three aims:

❀ to identify what the educational needs of four year olds were believed to be, with particular regard to a developmentally appropriate curriculum;
❀ to describe ways in which these needs might be met in the context of the infant or primary school;
❀ to draw out the common principles which could inform policy and practice for young children in school, and to provide a framework, with examples of good practice, which would assist teachers working with four year olds and inform courses in initial and in-service training.

The research was divided into two stages. The first stage was designed to explore perceptions of appropriate provision and practice for children around the age of four. A wealth of literature and documentation (particularly that published from 1985 to 1989) was studied, and early years specialists at all levels of the education service were consulted. At this stage a total of 80 professionals, chosen because they were known to have paid particular attention to the issue of early admission, were interviewed about the educational needs of four year olds and how these needs should be met. The interviewees included 60 early years specialists drawn from 15 teacher training establishments (universities, polytechnics and colleges of higher education) and the advisory service in 15 LEAs; and a selection of headteachers, teachers, nursery nurses, education officers and pre-school providers. Views were explored on needs associated with the young child's development, appropriate practice in meeting these needs, the difficulties of providing adequately in schools, the changes that needed to be made and the support required to sustain such changes. While there was a large measure of consensus at this stage, the data also highlighted some of the gaps and tensions in the theory of early childhood education.

Also at this stage, LEAs with policies of admitting children to school at rising-five or earlier were approached for any guidelines they might have produced for teachers of four year olds. A total of 24 authorities supplied guidelines to the project. Some had been written originally for nursery teachers, some were for 'early years' teachers and others had been prepared specifically for infant teachers with four year olds in their classes. Several LEAs had conducted pilot studies or evaluations of their early admissions policy and these, together with a number of teachers' dissertations on the subject, were studied where they were made available to the research team.

All the information gathered at this stage was drawn together in a paper entitled 'Professionals' views of appropriate provision and practice for four year olds in school' (unpublished) and presented on request to the government's Committee of Inquiry into Provision for the Under Fives whose terms of reference included looking at 'quality, continuity and progression', with particular attention to 'quality'. The data also formed the basis of the project's interim publication *Four Year Olds in School – Meeting their Needs* (Cleave and Brown, 1989).

The second stage of the research focused on the translation of these precepts into actual practice. Interviewees recommended a number of primary, infant and first schools which they judged to have achieved a measure of success in trying to provide appropriately for four year olds; a selection of these were visited by the team. The sample was selected to include schools that were large and small, rural and urban, with and without a nursery, and having a range of social and ethnic groups. All the infant classes admitted four year olds annually at the start of the school year, and some of these classes spanned an age range of three or four years.

Initial one-day visits were made to 33 classes (32 infant classes and one nursery/infant unit) in 18 schools in 11 LEAs in England and Wales. Four of the schools had a nursery class for three year olds, each of which was visited at this stage. Preliminary interviews were held with headteachers and class teachers to obtain information about their organization, entry procedures, parental involvement, the monitoring of children's progress, changes made or planned and any support received. Ten of the schools were then selected for further visits and seven of these were re-visited several times more for in-depth study. Visits took place across three terms to give the researchers the opportunity to note aspects of progression during the children's first year of infant schooling.

The purpose of the follow-up visits was to gather information on positive aspects of the schools' provision for four year olds. This was done by means of semi-structured interviews and observations. Schedules were developed which directly addressed the research questions arising from the first stage. These included admission arrangements, staffing, the organization and use of space, equipment and materials, activities, teaching approach, the monitoring and recording of progress, roles and relationships, and support.

Observations were made on each visit and in-depth interviews were held with headteachers, class teachers and, where appropriate, nursery nurses, non-teaching assistants, parent helpers and others working in the classroom. Curriculum coordinators and a number of parents and governors were also interviewed. In addition, views were sought informally from some of the youngest children. To gain a wider perspective in the LEAs in which the schools were situated, interviews were held with advisers and personnel from other services (special needs, medical and social services as appropriate) and education officers and elected members with a particular interest or involvement in early years education. Because perceptions of 'appropriateness' were firmly rooted in nursery education, two exemplary nursery schools in two other authorities were visited. At that time in-service courses were proliferating, so four very different initiatives were selected for study: a one-day curriculum 'circus', two part-time courses and a cluster of ongoing support groups for early years teachers. Participants were later followed up by questionnaire and selected visits to see how they were implementing new ideas in their schools.

None of the infant classes visited in the study matched up to ideal provision and practice in *all* respects, but each had particular strengths to which special attention had been paid. All the schools had focused on at least one aspect and had had to make considerable adjustments to provide suitably for their youngest pupils. Some wished to make further changes to meet more adequately the needs of these children. However, each school contributed to a fuller picture of what can and should be done if children are admitted to infant classes below the statutory age.

Most of the professionals interviewed in the study were adamant that four year olds should *not* be in infant classes. However, they felt that the situation was here to stay and therefore they should do their best to try to improve it. A substantial minority of interviewees considered that it was irrelevant whether the child was in a nursery or infant class as long as provision was *appropriate*. They felt that early admission was acceptable provided that it was done properly. They stressed the importance of *quality*: there was nothing wrong with admitting young children to school *per se*, 'It's what happens when they get there that matters'. What educationists believe should happen when the children get there forms the substance of this report.

Chapter 2 describes the background to the research and considers what the educational needs of four year olds are. Part 2 (Chapters 3, 4, 5 and 6) discusses appropriate practice in meeting these needs and Part 3 (Chapters 7, 8 and 9) describes the provision required both to meet children's needs and to facilitate suitable practice. Part 4 (Chapters 10 and 11) considers the sources of support which can help sustain good practice and provision, and the final chapter (Chapter 12) draws out the main principles of practice, provision and support to form a framework for action in meeting the needs of four year olds in infant classes (see Figure 1.1).

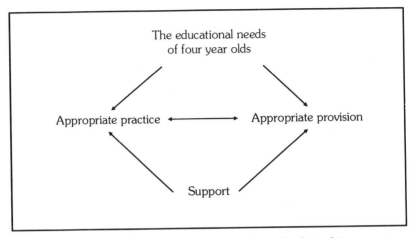

**Figure 1.1: A model of the findings described in this report.**

# 2 The Needs of Four Year Olds

This chapter describes the context and basis of the study. It considers why four is the particular age in question, whether the needs of four year olds can really be distinguished from those of other age-groups, what these needs are broadly believed to be and what this implies for schools admitting younger pupils.

## Why is Four the Age at Issue?

Children in this country start school earlier than children in most of Europe and the USA. Compared with France, Denmark and Italy, for example, where school starts at five-and-a-half to six-and-a-half, and the majority of states in the USA, where children are admitted at six, seven or even eight, the admission age in England and Wales is low. By law, children must start school the term following their fifth birthday. In practice, however, most children are now starting school when they are four.

Gradually over the last few years, early admission has become the rule rather than the exception. This change has coincided with falling rolls in many primary schools, an insufficiency of nursery places to meet the demand and increasing pressure from the parents that their children should have three full years in the infant school. Surveys carried out by the NFER in 1983 (Cleave et al., 1985) and 1986 (Sharp, 1988) showed that more and more LEAs were changing their policies in favour of admitting younger children to school. By 1986, only eight of the 90 LEAs responding to the survey retained a policy of admitting children at statutory age. Depending on whether admission is termly, twice yearly or annually, it is possible for the starting age to vary from just four to five years four months. However, the most widespread policy is to admit children at the beginning of the year in which they are five. This means that some children start school when barely 48 months old.

By January 1988 when our study began, the majority of four year olds were in infant classes rather than in nursery schools and classes. Those children who, by virtue of their age, would normally be eligible for nursery education were now being admitted to primary education with its entirely different traditions, resourcing and organization, and this in turn has given rise to widespread concern about appropriate

practice for these younger pupils. This concern is not without foundation. As recent research has clearly demonstrated (Sharp, 1988; Bennett and Kell, 1989), younger children are often admitted to school
without adequate planning and resourcing, and in an article on the
subject Bennett is led to conclude that 'authorities must provide more
appropriate funding, staffing and curriculum support' (Bennett, 1989).

Four year olds in school have increasingly become a focus of attention as awareness of the issues has spread. Conferences have been
held, and many words have been spoken and written on the subject. A
number of research initiatives, such as the Small Authorities Project
(SMAP), which ran from 1985 to 1988 (Bennett, 1987), and studies
by Stevenson (1987) and Ghaye and Pascal (1988), have been carried
out in specific LEAs. Several authorities that recently established a
policy of early admission have carried out their own evaluation of their
schemes, while others have set up pilot projects to consider the feasi-
bility of introducing it. Early admission has also proved popular as a
subject of dissertations by teachers taking advanced courses of study.

In 1988, a House of Commons Select Committee was set up to
look at educational provision for the under-fives. The Select Committee recommended that:

No further steps should be taken by LEAs towards introducing
three and four year olds into inappropriate primary school settings.
Policies in LEAs of annual (September) entry for four year olds into
school should be explicitly subject to the availability of appropriate
provision and should normally be for part-time places. (House of
Commons, 1988, para. 7.13)

The government replied that it shared the committee's view that
where four year olds are receiving education in infant classes, full account must be taken of their needs. The reply went on to say that it
was an intention of the new LEA Training Grants Scheme (LEATGS),
under which INSET for teachers of these children would be a priority
from April 1989, to ensure a wider understanding of those needs.
The government also set up a committee of inquiry, chaired by the
then education minister Angela Rumbold, to look at 'quality, continuity and progression' in provision for the under-fives. Their report
(GB.DES, 1990b) recommends that reception classes with four year
olds should have more generous ratios of staff with early years training, and should offer an appropriate range of activities and a curriculum capable of being adapted to the needs of the children. The report
stresses that unless these conditions are fulfilled, 'there is a risk that
young children in reception classes will receive limited benefit from
their early educational experiences' (para. 201).

Provision for four year olds in reception classes has recently come under the scrutiny of Her Majesty's Inspectorate (HMI). The Senior Chief Inspector of Schools, in his annual report (GB.DES, 1989a) said: 'Education and care in nursery schools and classes are often good, but in reception classes both frequently give cause for concern although there are signs of improvement' (para. 8). The timely HMI publication *The Education of Children Under Five* (GB.DES, 1989b) states that, although in some primary classes there is excellent practice with under-fives, in most cases 'the curriculum is not as well matched to their educational needs as it should be' (para. 7).

While there is considerable agreement among educationists about what is considered *inappropriate* for four year olds in school, there has until very recently been remarkably little written on the subject of what is *appropriate* for these children. However, there are signs both in the UK and abroad of an increasing awareness of the need to clarify an appropriate curriculum for children below school age. In the UK, for example, the HMI document (ibid.) and the NCB curriculum pack (Drummond *et al.*, 1989) provide practical guidance for those working with under-fives. A similar concern is reflected in the Northern Ireland Curriculum Council's 'Principles of Nursery Education', which are listed in a new set of guidelines for teachers of three and four year olds; and in the USA, in the position statement produced by the National Association for the Education of Young Children (NAEYC) (Bredekamp, 1986) on developmentally appropriate practice for four and five year olds.

Many professionals share the view that nursery education offers the best model for appropriate provision for four year olds. This is supported by recent HMI surveys, which found that 'children under five in nursery schools and classes generally receive a broader, better balanced curriculum than those of the same age in infant and first school classes' (GB.DES, 1990d). On the other hand, some professionals argue that not all nursery practice is good and that perhaps the best of nursery *and* primary practice should be combined in the reception class.

At the time of writing (1990), concern that four year olds should have learning experiences appropriate to their needs is mounting as the National Curriculum gets under way. Although children under five are officially not eligible to start on the National Curriculum, there has been uncertainty about what would happen to those four year olds who are in classes containing older pupils. There are fears that both the National Curriculum and National Assessment at seven will put additional pressure on younger children to embark too soon on more formal learning.

The National Curriculum has been welcomed by some early years professionals as providing the incentive for a long overdue reappraisal of curricula and assessment procedures throughout the nursery and infant stages; and there have been deliberate efforts (for example, Early Years Curriculum Group, 1989) to examine how good practice in the early years links with the requirements of the National Curriculum.


## Can the Needs of Four Year Olds Be Distinguished?

Concern for the needs of four year olds in school raises the question of whether the needs of this age group can really be distinguished from the needs of younger or older children. How far is it meaningful to refer to the needs of four year olds as distinct from, say, three or five year olds?


### Four as a Distinct Age and Stage

Asked whether they could say what the educational needs of four year olds are, most of the professionals interviewed in the study said yes, they could. They regarded four year olds as a distinctive group whose early admission to school makes them a special case deserving special consideration. Compared with five year olds, children of four years are much younger, since they have had only four-fifths of the life-span, and it is important to remember this when admitting them to a school system which is oriented towards older children.

There is a considerable body of opinion to support this view. Government documents have acknowledged that a distinction should be made between younger four year olds and children around five years. Indeed, *Better Schools* (GB.DES, 1985a) stated that: 'it is unrealistic to expect a teacher simultaneously to provide an appropriate education for younger four year olds and for children of compulsory school age' (para. 126). HMI have also made their views clear. For example, inspector Ron Weir, addressing an NFER conference in 1988, said: 'Four is a distinctive age and stage – the needs of children of this age are distinctive and if the curriculum is to respond effectively it also needs to change and become distinctive. The curriculum will need to respond to the characteristics of the four year old as a learner.' This reinforces the statement made by staff inspector Brenda Staniland to the NAHT Conference two years earlier: 'There has to be a clear understanding of the needs of four year olds and what the range of these might be when the different developmental characteristics of four year olds...are taken into account.'

The notion that four year olds may have different developmental needs from older children is taken up in a recent report from the British Association for Early Childhood Education (BAECE), which states that pupils admitted early to school should have 'a curriculum which

takes account of the developmental needs of four year old children'
(McCail, 1989).

However, some of the people we interviewed added that, although
they agreed that the needs of this age group *could* be distinguished, it
is important to remember that individual children are at different
stages, and that some four year olds are more like three year olds
while others are like five and six year olds. A number of professionals
stressed the point that their concern for the four year olds did not
mean that they believed they had 'got it right for the five, or even the
six and seven year olds'. In other words, concern should be for early
years education in general as well as for one year-group in particular.

**The Early Years Continuum**

A substantial minority of interviewees took the view that the needs of
four year olds cannot be distinguished because the early years are a
period of continuous development that should be considered as a
whole. For some, the period in question meant from three to five
years, for others from two to six years or even from birth to seven
years. This variety is reflected in the literature. For example, Curtis
(1986) and Dowling (1988) concentrate on the years from three to
five, whereas Bruce (1987) covers the range from birth to seven. The
NAEYC statement (Bredekamp, 1986) groups four year olds with five
year olds.

It is important to remember that the age of four is part of a continuous period of rapid growth and development which begins before
birth and does not slow down until after the age of six. Perhaps what
is required is an awareness of continuity and progression throughout
the early years and *at the same time* an understanding of the needs
of children at certain stages in the continuum. As one headteacher
said of children admitted early to school, 'It is important to realize that
these younger children are not being immature. They are being four.'

# What Are the Needs of Four Year Olds Believed to Be?

All the evidence in this project, from the study of the literature and
LEA guidelines to the interviews, observations and INSET initiatives,
points to the fact that young children's educational needs are usually
articulated in terms of the typical characteristics of the age range and
the requirements needed to cater for them. In general, statements
about four year olds' needs range across the physical, cognitive, social
and emotional aspects of development, all of which are closely interrelated. Individually, statements differ in what they include. For example,

some refer to the more universal needs such as love, security, praise and recognition, while others ignore these and concentrate on needs that they believe to be directly related to learning, such as sensory experiences and language development. By drawing all these statements together, we obtain a broad picture of what typical four year olds are like and what they need in order to develop normally. These may be summarized as follows.

## Physical Development

✿ Four year olds are physically active and energetic. They need space both indoors and out in which to move freely, to let off steam and be spontaneous.

✿ Motor development is at an important stage. They need opportunities to practise both gross and fine motor skills and coordination, and to test themselves physically in a safe environment.

✿ Energy tends to occur in bursts, so they also need space in which to withdraw and rest or be quiet.

## Cognitive Development

✿ Typical four year olds are mentally active, with an enthusiasm for mastering a wide range of practical skills and competencies. They need stimulus through new experiences, and the opportunity to practise and consolidate what they have already experienced. They need to express themselves in a wide variety of ways with a rich selection of materials.

✿ They deal in concrete first-hand experiences rather than abstractions, and therefore they need a broad range of activities that allows them to explore, investigate and make sense of the world.

✿ They are beginning to hypothesize and reason, so they need opportunities for trial and error, to test hypotheses and solve problems. They want to find out and experiment, and they need to see that there are lots of ways of doing things rather than just one 'right' way. They need to be able to make mistakes without fear of failure.

✿ Four year olds still live very much in the present. They need to do things now and to talk about them now. They are questioning and curious, and they need to ask questions and to discuss what they are doing while they are doing it.

✿ Children in this age group show considerable variation in learning styles and exhibit a particularly wide range of competencies. This means that account must be taken of children as individuals, and a variety of teaching methods and materials employed.

✿   Because of the developmental range of the age group, four year olds need time to pursue activities at their own pace; they need time to get involved in an activity, develop it, reflect upon it and perhaps complete it.

## Social Development

✿   Four year olds still operate very much as individuals and therefore need a great deal of adult attention. Although they are becoming more aware of others, they are still preoccupied with self and with establishing their self-identity; they need to be addressed personally (by name) rather than as a group.

✿   They are learning to share and collaborate, and some are beginning to emerge as leaders. They need opportunities to interact with others in pairs and in small groups, although they may find large group situations difficult.

✿   At this age language is developing rapidly, so children need opportunities for interaction, dialogue and discussion with other children and with adults.

## Emotional Development

✿   Four year olds are emotionally less stable that five year olds, still prone to sudden changes of mood and seemingly irrational fears, but they are beginning to get a grip on themselves. They are gradually becoming less dependent on an adult in the sense that they are able to take some responsibility for their belongings and for servicing their own requirements. They therefore need opportunities to take responsibility for their activities, and to make choices and decisions.

✿   At the same time they need a certain amount of security; a safe environment in which to relax and get on with their activities; some kind of overall pattern to the day; clearly defined goals, together with freedom of choice in achieving these goals; and an atmosphere that promotes confidence and capability rather than failure.

# What Are the Implications for Schools?

## The Learning Environment

The evidence shows that statements about young children's educational needs are closely bound up with the developmental characteristics they normally exhibit. It is preciously because four year olds are like they are that they have certain needs. For example, because four year olds are physically active they need space indoors and out in which there are opportunities to develop their motor skills; because four year olds are individualistic they need high adult–child ratios, and so on. Thus, a description of these children's characteristics signals messages about the kind of learning environment and learning experiences believed to be appropriate to meet their developmental needs.

Most of the early years specialists interviewed in the study believed that the most appropriate learning environment for this age group is one based on an extension of good nursery practice. This view is also adopted in the guidelines provided by some authorities for their reception teachers. The problem is that schools are not normally resourced or staffed as generously as nurseries. Despite Select Committee recommendations (House of Commons, 1986) that suitable conditions for four year olds in infant classes 'should be fixed by the DES and should compare in all appropriate respects with the requirements for nursery classes' (para. 5.45), a study carried out by Sharp (1988) showed that infant classes with four year olds were usually bigger, did not often have ancillary help and many of the teachers were not trained or experienced in this age range.

During the present study, there have been signs that an awareness of these shortcomings is spreading and that conditions are being improved in some of the LEAs that admit children to school early. The contrast in the response of a four year old observed in a school where changes had been made clearly illustrates the benefits to the child (see pages 131-2). However, many schools still have a long way to go and more changes are needed if provision for these younger entrants is to be matched to their needs.

Professionals interviewed in the present study spelt out the areas in which they considered changes should be made. These included: the improvement of adult–child ratios; the organization of time, with special consideration to school 'fixtures' such as playtime, lunch and assembly; the location of the reception class and the organization of space indoors and out; the range and variety of suitable equipment and materials; the activities provided and the teaching approaches used. Also, schools should give special consideration to their admission arrangements so that children are eased in gently. In order to match learning experiences to children's needs, attention must be given to improving observation and record-keeping. The attitudes of teachers, headteachers, parents and the community at large need to become more sympathetic to and understanding of the necessity for these changes. Finally, if changes are to be made and sustained, teachers and their schools need support.

## The Need for Commitment

Throughout the study it has become increasingly clear that if such changes are to be successfully brought about there has to be commitment, not only by schools but by everyone involved, including the parents, the governing body, the LEA, the politicians and the community at large.

Drawing on all the data collected, the research team identified ten areas to which there has to be commitment if schools are to go some way towards providing more appropriately for their younger pupils. These are discussed, with examples, in the following chapters.

The ten areas of commitment are:

✿   Admission and entry procedures (Chapter 3);
✿   Organization of time (Chapters 3 and 5);
✿   Activities (Chapter 4);
✿   Teaching approach (Chapter 5);
✿   Monitoring and recording progress (Chapter 6);
✿   Organization of space (Chapter 7);
✿   Equipment and materials (Chapter 8);
✿   Staffing (Chapter 9);
✿   Roles and relationships (Chapters 3, 5 and 10);
✿   Support (Chapters 10 and 11).

# PART TWO

The typical needs and characteristics of four year olds have implications for the kinds of practice that encourage healthy development in children of this age. Schools therefore need to consider sensitive ways of treating younger children when settling them in, promoting their learning and evaluating their progress.

# 3 Admission and Entry

Starting school is an important time for children and their families. For the children it is a new experience and for the parents it may be the first contact they have with schools since being a pupil themselves. This chapter looks at the variety of provision offered prior to admission and the induction procedures developed. Examples are used to demonstrate the sensitive treatment that can be provided for children at the beginning of their school careers.

Even though legally children are not obliged to attend school until the term following their fifth birthday, many authorities are admitting younger children. A clear trend towards lowering the age of admission to school was identified by Sharp (1988). This trend seems to be continuing, with more schools admitting children soon after their fourth birthday. Recent developments suggest that some LEAs may still change their policy 'as an unexpected result of the Education Reform

Act' (*Teacher*, 1989). Early admission is believed to give children the opportunity to develop confidence and security before embarking on the National Curriculum, and can provide all children with an equal length of schooling before assessment at seven.

LEAs tend to adopt different policies of admitting children to school. There may be termly admission, biannual admission or annual admission for children of statutory age or younger. Some LEAs have a mixture of these policies, which leads to complex patterns of admission and differences in age at school entry of as much as a year and four months, depending on where the child lives. Decisions about early admission for children are often coloured by the availability of funding from the local authority or space available in the school. In some schools children have been admitted because of falling rolls rather than authority policy and in these cases children under five are not usually included in capitation allowances. Local Management of Schools (LMS) is also likely to affect such decisions with governors being concerned about attracting pupils to the school while at the same time being aware that funding for this age group may detract from resources needed elsewhere.

The issues discussed in this chapter, though pertinent for all children on entry to school, are even more important for the youngest children. Younger entrants in particular need sensitive understanding from the people responsible for and involved in admitting them to school. This includes representatives from the local authority, the governors, the headteacher, the class teacher, the nursery nurse or ancillary helper (if there is one) and the parents.

The first stage of the study identified areas to be considered if provision is to go some way towards being appropriate for these younger children at the beginning of their school careers. It is a critical stage in their life. **Transition from home to school and the arrangements made for their arrival and early days in school should be gradual processes that respond flexibly to individual needs and take children's pre-school experiences into account.***

Children arrive at school from a variety of different home backgrounds and with a range of experiences and abilities. These differences need to be acknowledged in the procedures for admission that are developed by the school.

## Home–School Links

In the LEA curriculum guidelines collected in the study, the home–school transition period is seen as a continuous and cumulative pro-

---

* Bold type indicates the main principles that have been drawn from the study and are included in 'A Framework for Action' (Chapter 12).

cess with the phrase 'starting where the child is and taking account of previous experience' occurring in various forms over and over again.

Professionals interviewed in the study considered it to be **essential to develop links with parents.** This could be achieved through a number of strategies. For example, home visits by the teacher, parents and children visiting the school, parents and teachers exchanging information and schools encouraging parents to become involved through extra-curricular activities, such as visiting the school bookshop or library.

These ideas are supported in research by Barrett (1986) who recommended closer links with pre-school provision and parents. HMI acknowledge that by this age 'children have already made major steps in learning' and 'parents play a crucial part in that early learning' (GB.DES, 1989b, para. 11). A successful partnership between home and school is paramount.

This relationship was encouraged in a number of ways by schools involved in the second stage of our study. There was a wide variety of well thought out induction programmes, attractively presented brochures or booklets and invitations to visit schools. Arrangements for pre-admission visits for parents, parents with the children and the children on their own were organized.

## Letters and Booklets

Personal letters inviting parents and children to visit are probably the first contact some families have with the school. Such letters invite parents to meetings or classroom visits and children to spend some time in the classroom and meet their teacher.

Booklets provided important introductions to involving and including parents in their child's induction to school. Nearly all the schools that were visited had an 'about our school' booklet. In a few cases reception children had produced booklets for new entrants but more usually the staff had selected the information to be included in the booklets. These were given to parents before their child entered school on one of the pre-admission meetings or the home visit. They were often produced on the school photocopier. Most documents included illustrations by children and the contents informed parents and children about the school, about the curriculum and about health and safety aspects.

The topics covered valuable information about the school, including the induction arrangements, class and staffing details, how parents could be involved, school procedures, such as the collection of dinner money or PE kit requisites, and any extra-curricular activities. Nearly every booklet obtained from schools in our study contained details to show parents how the children should be taught to form letters.

## Pre-admission Meetings and Visits

Visits of any kind were almost always carried out in the *summer* term but one of two schools delayed teachers' home visits or children's visits to school until the *autumn* term. Teachers said autumn term visits were less disruptive to the established reception class. Visits to the reception class before the long vacation often resulted in the child either forgetting or becoming worried during the period prior to admission to school. By arranging visits at the beginning of the school year there would be fewer children in the classroom and the children would meet their classmates in a quieter, calmer situation.

### *Meetings and visits for parents*

During the summer term prior to their child's admission, parents were invited to visit the school one or twice for a formal meeting. The most common practice was to invite them in to tour the school in the afternoon, although some schools favoured evening meetings so that parents with daytime jobs could attend. In the evening sessions the classroom was laid out to show parents the equipment and activities provided. Most meetings included information about the school's organization, routines and philosophy.

Some headteachers explained the language, reading and number activities the children would be doing. This sometimes included practical workshop sessions where parents were encouraged to 'try things out for themselves'. More often these sessions were held after admission and included parents of older children as well. A few schools used slides, photographs and videos of the reception children busily engaged in their activities to help explain the teaching approach adopted and the value of the activities offered. One parent commented that showing a video to new parents had 'made us very aware of the differences in children and the activities provided for them'.

Parents need to feel welcome and well-informed about the school and its organization, and sometimes booklets and formal visits were not considered to be enough. Opportunities for parents to ask questions and to share information about their child can help to promote mutually beneficial relationships between home and school. Some schools encouraged this by inviting parents in for individual interviews with the headteacher. Although this was time-consuming it was regarded by one headteacher as 'a valuable movement towards partnership and ascertaining the parents' perception of their child'. Other schools held informal talks. As one headteacher commented 'the *real* talk with new parents tends to happen over a cup of tea'. In this school the members of the parent teachers association (PTA) provided tea and helped answer parents' questions. A flexible approach had evolved over a number of years in another school: '...visits will often last throughout the week. Sometimes this is combined with a specific activity like a book week or maths week'.

*Visits for children with their parents*
Children also need to know about the school since they are, after all, the ones who will be attending! The first contact many children have is when they are invited to spend time in school with their parents. Gradually as the children gain confidence, they spend short times without their parents in the classroom.

Some schools had mother and toddler groups or playgroup meetings on the premises, which meant that some of the children were already familiar with the buildings that would become part of their daily life. Other schools encouraged parents to 'drop-in' with their child and perhaps visit the school library.

The fact that parents are expected to stay with the children on these occasions provides opportunities for the headteacher, early years coordinator or reception teacher to talk with the parents and children. Some authorities suggest that 'a minimum of three visits to the school will be needed'. In the schools in our study the four year olds usually visited for four or five afternoons during the summer term. Parents stayed for the first few sessions, gradually encouraging the children to stay on their own.

Sometimes these visits were found to be disruptive to the established reception class, particularly when outdoor areas were unavailable and new children arrived with mothers, toddlers and prams. Schools with large intakes found that, to avoid overcrowding, arrangements needed to be made to have fewer children in the class when new entrants were visiting. Attempts were made to keep visiting groups manageable by allocating extra help, such as nursery nurses, ancillary helpers or additional staffing, or by having 'invitation only' sessions that lasted throughout the week.

An informal atmosphere for the children and opportunities for parents to exchange information helped to develop good relationships between the home and the school and to make the children feel secure. Here is one example:

> The new entrants and their parents had visited the school the previous week. The parents were invited to the staffroom where the deputy headteacher talked to them over a cup of tea. They were then shown around the school and given time to see the various facilities and observe the activities offered to the children. The second afternoon, a week later, the parents brought the children into school after lunch and as soon as the children were settled parents were able to leave, returning to collect them at 3 o'clock.
>
> The head commented that 'we tend not to have any tears because the reception teacher and the nursery nurse arrange the

classroom so that all the children have things which appeal to them'. Older brothers and sisters were brought in from other classes to help the children settle. To avoid overcrowding some of the reception children went to visit the older children's classrooms. This gave them a chance to meet other teachers.

This system worked quite well, especially as only half of the children attended at a time, that is, 12 on Thursday afternoon and 12 on Friday afternoon. If parents wanted to stay all afternoon they were quite welcome to do so. The headteacher also commented that during these sessions the members of the PTA provided tea in the staffroom. On the second afternoon the headteacher and teachers were not present at tea, so that 'new' parents had an opportunity to talk to parents of existing pupils. This gave parents a chance to discuss the school and ask questions without feeling threatened or embarrassed.

### Visits for children on their own

Prior to starting infant school, children have had a wide range of experiences. At the age of four some children will be starting school straight from home, others will have attended playgroups, child-minders or nurseries or any combination of these, while others may have had a full-time placement in a nursery school or even a nursery class attached to the school. These experiences need to be taken into consideration when planning an induction programme for individual children. For some children with or without a previous nursery placement school can seem an 'alien place'. Sensitive treatment can help to prevent children from feeling like this. For example, in one school with no nursery:

the classroom was set up with practical and free choice activities. Construction toys were freely available as were the sand, water, dough, paint and, because the weather was fine, the outdoor play area. The mothers arrived in the classroom with their offspring and handed their child over to the nursery nurse or teacher, older brother or sister, or a friend in the reception class. Each child had someone 'special' welcoming them and the older children enjoyed being with the young ones and showing them what to do.

The children settled very well and took part in most activities. Both the teacher and the nursery nurse were involved in the activities during which they watched the children, observed what they were doing and were alert for any signs of stress. When one child looked a little uncertain about approaching the dough table the teacher took her by the hand and sat down with her at the table. The child was then able to join in making pancakes.

In another school without a nursery:

> The new entrants are invited for the afternoon story time. The parents are encouraged to stay at first. The headteacher helps to keep the group small by taking some of the established reception class with the group of new entrants for a story. After two weeks the headteacher takes the reception children and leaves the new entrants with their 'new' teacher. In June the new entrants attend for a morning and afternoon session about a week apart. They spend the time with about six established reception class children and their teacher. Meanwhile the rest of the existing class pursue other activities elsewhere with the headteacher.

Pre-admission visits for children are much easier to organize if there is a nursery class or playgroup nearby, especially if good liaison has already been established. For example, in many cases where there was a nursery class on site the children were able to join in for regular sessions and selected assemblies, plays or stories. They were able to have three or four visits to the reception class in small groups, staying longer each time.

The staff of one school had given a great deal of thought to the transition from nursery to school. The nursery class children started their term a week later than the reception class, which enabled the nursery staff to spend the first week of the term with the new entrants in the reception class.

A particularly gentle start to school was observed in a small rural school:

> An early years unit had been formed in an open-plan classroom. The nursery children spent most of their time with the nursery nurse in the 'nursery end' while the reception teacher and the 5–7 year olds spent most of their time in activities at the other end of the classroom. When children were at an age to 'transfer' to school they spent time 'wandering between areas', enjoying the security of the nursery world and the challenges provided by the reception class. The teacher and nursery nurse also worked in both areas.

*Home visiting*

The professionals interviewed recommended that **new entrants and their families should be visited in their homes**. However, they were very aware of the limited time available to carry this out effectively. It was pointed out that home visits might be rushed because of the lack of non-contact time for teachers working with this age group. Often home visiting was reserved for 'special' circumstances and carried out in the teachers' own time.

Staff in schools visited by the project team expressed different views about arrangements for home visits. For example in some schools no home visiting arrangements were made because of 'lack of time', 'we are hoping to introduce them next year', 'they are not needed in the area' or 'they were done in the nursery'.

In other schools there were home visits for some children. This included home visits only for the children who were being admitted to the reception class without having attended the attached nursery. The nursery class children would have already been visited at home before admission to nursery. 'Special cases' identified by the health visitor were also visited by school staff.

Several headteachers were committed to the theory but found it practically difficult. For example, one headteacher attempted to visit children at home but found that the time constraints were prohibitive. Time was saved by visiting the mothers at the playgroups. Although this was not felt to be as satisfactory as home visiting, parents and children were being met 'on their own territory'.

In some instances where home visits had been tried teachers commented that it was not only a strain on their time but that they felt like 'an intruder'. In one school for example:

> Until recently the nursery nurses used to deliver letters about starting school to the children's homes. The headteacher is now encouraging the reception teacher to go, but this is difficult because she has to leave her current class with another teacher. She feels that her own class needs all the input she can give. A lot of the families who receive these letters decide to send their children to another school in the end and therefore it is a waste of valuable class teacher's time visiting those homes. She does not like calling on homes uninvited and she is not sure whether the parents approve. When the children visit the school with their parents they stay all the afternoon and she feels this is more worthwhile.
>
> At present the reception teacher visits homes when the children have been in her class for a while. She has contact with parents when they bring and fetch their children daily and this builds up a relationship. In special cases she may well approach them at home, she may take a sick child home or she may visit the home if invited. She said, 'Some parents invite you into their homes after a while anyway.'

In schools where there was a commitment to home visiting there was often a nursery on site or a high percentage of children for whom English was not their first language. These teachers tried to visit every home. In some schools the nursery closed a week early at the end of the summer term in order to free staff to go into homes to 'iron out any problems' that might occur. In other schools home visiting was possible because there was only a small number of new entrants or because staggered and part-time attendance by the children freed the teacher, and in some cases the nursery nurse, to do the visits.

This is how home visits were arranged in one school:

> The parents have already had a letter from the school asking for information about date of birth, brothers and sisters and so on, so the ground has been prepared. The teachers visit the local clinics to see if there are difficulties with children about to start school. Teachers also visit the playgroups and talk with the playgroup leaders over a cup of coffee. They feel this fosters good relationships with both the parents and the playgroups.
>
> Each family is given road safety leaflets, a booklet about the infant and nursery school and a leaflet showing how to help their children to write the letters of the alphabet. A nursery nurse and teacher visit the home taking with them the letter or form for admission, a puppet and a storybook. The teacher has time to talk to the parents while the nursery nurse plays with the child. The children are invited into the school on the Friday after the teachers have visited them and are admitted to school the following Monday. Parents may stay if they wish, it is an individual choice and teachers promise to telephone if there are any problems.
>
> The whole team commented that they enjoyed the home visits and felt that the shared starting-point was very valuable. They hoped to finish visiting homes and admitting children to school by half term. Adult–child ratios are kept low by involving parent-helpers while some of the staff are visiting homes.
>
> All this takes place in September rather than the previous term when numbers are high. As each visit lasts about half an hour teachers are able to visit three families in one morning. They commented that this is a significant event for the children: they talk all year about what happened at their home visit.

Interviewees recommended home visits so that close links with new entrants and their families could be developed. Practical difficulties often deterred all but the most committed staff from carrying them out.

*Contact with staff in pre-school settings*
The meetings teachers are able to arrange with staff in various types of pre-school provision depends on what is available and whether or not it is 'on-site'. Meetings can be formal or informal at regular or intermittent intervals. The more formal meetings tended to be where the headteachers and teachers visited the pre-school playgroup or nursery. Other more informal meetings were often carried out through personal contact with the playgroup or nursery by the recep-

tion teachers who would make visits if released from their teaching duties. Teachers commented that pre-school provision varies and by visiting they can begin to understand the experiences children have been offered.

## Admission and Entry Procedures

Meetings and visits prior to starting infant school can help to dispel some of the anxiety children and their families may feel. At this stage children need time and adult attention to help develop their sense of security in an environment that is only just becoming familiar to them. Professionals suggested that schools should consider adopting staggered entry patterns and part-time attendance policies because these enable 'a gradual introduction to school procedures and time to settle in'. Some schools have addressed these issues, identified constraints and attempted to implement procedures which take into account children's individual needs.

### A Staggered Start

Professionals who were interviewed felt that **a staggered starting date allows children to be admitted to school singly or in small groups**. This gave the adults time to be with the new entrants, to listen to them and evaluate their stage of development. The information gained could then be taken into account in subsequent curriculum planning.

In practice the length of time involved in admitting children can vary from a few hours or days to a period spanning several weeks. Usually the process is completed by half-term with the oldest children attending first. Much depends on the numbers of new entrants involved and the environment provided for them. It is important to inform parents that their children may not be attending school from the first day of term. This helps to avoid any misunderstanding or disappointment.

Most of the schools visited by the project team admitted children a few at a time. In small schools where there were only one or two new entrants it was much easier to give these children individual attention and to respond to their individual needs. However, most schools do not have such a small annual intake. In larger schools attempts were made to give individual attention to new pupils by arranging for children to start school in small groups. Group sizes varied according to the size of the intake in a particular year but attempts were made to keep the groups to four or five children. Often these were friendship groups based on information obtained at pre-admission meetings from parents or adults working with the children in their pre-school or nursery class settings.

There were numerous patterns of staggered admission to school. Occasionally the youngest were the first entrants because they were considered to be 'less able to cope with the noise and bustle of a large class'. However, when the period of admission extended over several weeks it was possible for some children to reach statutory age before it was their 'turn' to attend school.

The oldest children were usually admitted first. Here are some examples of the arrangements made by the schools:

- ✿ All new entrants were admitted full-time over two days at the beginning of September. This involved 12 children on the first day, the other 12 children on the second day and all 24 children on the following day. This was recognized by the teacher in a rural school as 'not ideal but bussing children in from outlying areas makes part-time attendance difficult'.

- ✿ A third of the class was admitted on Monday, another third on Tuesday and the rest on Wednesday. This arrangement was not what the teacher would have liked but it had been adopted because it was what the parents wanted.

- ✿ All new entrants were admitted during the course of one week. These children arrived in groups of two or three at half-hourly intervals and attended for the morning sessions only.

- ✿ Groups of five or six children were admitted on alternate days. This meant that if there was a large intake of children the youngest would not start attending until October.

- ✿ No new children were admitted to the infant school in the first few days of term so that by the time they arrived there was a reasonably settled atmosphere in the school. The oldest children started first and other groups joined in over a period of three weeks.

- ✿ Children were admitted to school over a two or three week period. Groups of four or five children were admitted every three days. Their time of arrival was negotiated with parents so that each child could receive an individual welcome.

- ✿ Where children had already been attending a nursery class part-time they continued to attend the reception class part-time for two weeks. An example of this is shown overleaf.

- ✿ Groups of eight children were admitted for either the morning or afternoon sessions over a three week period. An example is shown overleaf.

*Some children who had already been attending a nursery class part-time continued to attend the reception class part-time for two weeks. For example:*

| | |
|---|---|
| Week 1 | Monday. Nine children with autumn birthdays were admitted at 9.00 a.m. |
| | Tuesday. The autumn-born group arrived at 9.00 a.m. and were joined by the spring-born children at 10.00 a.m. |
| | Wednesday. Both the autumn- and spring-born children arrived in school at 9.00 a.m. and stayed all morning. |
| | Thursday. The summer-born children joined the existing group of children at 10.00 a.m. |
| | Friday. All groups attended from 9.00 a.m. |
| Week 2 | All the children attended for the morning only. |
| Week 3 | After negotiation with parents there was a gradual introduction to full-time attendance. |

*Groups of eight children were admitted for either the morning or the afternoon sessions over a three-week period. For example:*

| | |
|---|---|
| Week 1 | Eight children for the morning session, and eight different children for the afternoon session. |
| Week 2 | Eight new entrants joined the morning children and eight new entrants joined the afternoon children; this made two sessions of 16 children. |
| Week 3 | Eight new children joined the existing groups for the morning or afternoon session. |
| | There was a gradual introduction to full-time attendance after discussions between the teacher, headteacher and parents. |

**Figure 3.1: Examples of admission arrangements: sample timetables.**

Admitting small groups with time intervals in between allows the children to feel secure and become familiar with the environment. It enables the adults involved to give them more time. It was reported by one authority that 'several headteachers considered staggered admission to be very successful and said that they would extend the time scale for full-time attendance to the end of October in future'. Some teachers, however, believed that it was disruptive if entry was staggered over too great a period of time and parents, whose children attended nursery full-time, often expected similar provision to continue.

**Part-time Attendance**

In the 1986 NFER survey (Sharp, 1988) it was noted that only seven LEAs stipulated that admission for the youngest children *must* be part-time for at least the first half-term. A further 12 LEAs advised headteachers to admit younger children part-time at first. The SMAP team (Bennett, 1987) reported that schools admitting four year olds were making special arrangements with regard to part-time attendance for these younger children. In Ghaye and Pascal's study (1988) changes were made, which included part-time attendance for children with a flexible change to full-time attendance based on joint decisions between parents and teachers.

Discussion with interviewees in the present study revealed that **part-time attendance was considered to be appropriate practice.** It was suggested that the local authority should define the policy but that there should be enough flexibility for schools to respond to individual needs and that parents should have choice about enrolling their children.

There is a range of policies adopted by different authorities (see Sharp, 1988). The focus of the present study centred on authorities where children were admitted annually in the September after their fourth birthday. In some authorities four year olds were admitted as follows: autumn-born children attended full-time from September; spring-born children attended mornings only in the autumn term and transferred to full-time attendance in the spring term; summer-born children attended afternoons only in the autumn term, mornings only in the spring term and full-time for the summer term.

In other authorities, schools made their own arrangements and, where headteachers attempted to respond to individual needs, the child's pre-school experiences and the school's organization, a variety of part-time procedures evolved. For example, schools in our study:

✿ admitted children full-time almost straight away: this was often because of parental expectations, the transport difficulties of children in rural areas, or children attending nursery full-time prior to admission to school;

✿ admitted children part-time until they were of statutory age;

✿ admitted children part-time for two or three weeks; usually the youngest children attended the afternoon session;

✿ admitted children part-time for the first half-term;

✿ offered part-time attendance in the nursery unit and gradual transfer full-time to the reception class;

✿ offered part-time attendance which was totally flexible. The transition to full-time attendance was based on negotiation between parents, teachers and the headteacher. This depended on how well each child had settled into school and, in practice, most children were attending full-time after the October half-term. In special cases it could be as long as two terms.

It was emphasized by those who had given the process of starting school a lot of thought, that **the transfer from part-time to full-time attendance for these younger children should be negotiated** by the headteacher with the parents, after discussions with the teacher and sometimes the nursery nurse. Headteachers felt that there was often pressure from parents to admit children to full-time schooling earlier. One head resisted such pressure for early admission by 'putting it to them [the parents] that we are thinking of their children'.

Professionals in small schools thought that attending full-time almost immediately was not problematic because with small classes 'children are not trying to cope with pressures of a large school too soon'.

For some schools part-time attendance enabled them to cope with mixed-age classes. They were able to offer an 'infant-type curriculum' in the morning and a 'more nursery-type curriculum' in the afternoon. Transfer to full-time attendance was considered to be 'quite straightforward' because the children were already familiar with the environment, the teacher and the other children. Other teachers used the afternoon session when there were no children in school to visit new entrants in their homes.

These 'gentle starts' were perceived to be giving the children time to settle in. Teachers were able to 'give the child time and make them feel comfortable'. It also enabled attendance at lunch-time, often a difficult time for young children in school, to be delayed until children were feeling secure and confident in their new environment. Teachers commented that even after a period of part-time attendance it was clear that some of the 'younger' children were not able to cope with full-time education even in an informal, appropriate atmosphere.

## Grouping

Consideration should also be given to the organization of classes for the youngest children. Information from the guidelines and interviews suggested that these younger children need small classes. Some guidelines stressed that children of this age should 'not be in vertically grouped classes if it could possibly be avoided'.

Just as children arrive at school with a range of different pre-school experiences, so they find themselves in a variety of school settings. The organization of the class in which new entrants are placed will vary depending on the number of children involved and the staffing available. The youngest four year olds may be admitted to:

✿ a class of summer-born children;
✿ an early years unit which includes nursery-aged children;

❀ a year-group class;
❀ a vertically grouped class of four to five year olds;
❀ a vertically grouped class which spans an age range of more than two years.

### Summer-born classes

There are negative and positive arguments with regard to schools organizing children into age-related classes. If the youngest children are able to attend small classes with extra welfare assistance there can be more flexibility and informality to allow for the individuality of four year olds. Professionals in such schools feel it helps to avoid downward pressure from the National Curriculum and that teachers and parents are not as likely to respond to four year olds as though they are five year olds.

In practice, contrary to the advice offered in some curriculum guidelines, there was a move away from forming classes solely of summer-born children. Several reasons were given for this:

❀ It segregated the youngest children from the rest of the school, and thus they became isolated and regarded as 'the babies'.
❀ The children had no role models. Where classes had been arranged this way it was thought to be a mistake, since summer-born children still seemed less mature and less confident than the rest of the year group at middle infant level.
❀ Parents tend to compare the younger group with the older groups.
❀ Children for whom English is not their first language have less opportunities to practise their language with older children.
❀ There may be physical constraints, such as the availability of space, staffing allocation or a large intake of new entrants. In one school the headteacher said she would not split them into classes of winter- and summer-born children again because of the number of children, the space available and staffing ratios. It was not always the youngest children who found difficulties with coping in school.

Even in an authority where there was a well thought out policy, good support and guidance for headteachers and teachers as well as funding for schools, the headteachers had decided against repeating this type of organization because 'the youngest children need role models' and 'many of the youngest children were more able than those in the alternate group'.

### Early years units

Where possible, some schools had formed early years units incorporating the reception and nursery classes. They felt that this enabled them to adopt their own 'pre-approach', which they regarded as being so vital prior to the National Curriculum. It was less tempting to treat the four year olds as five year olds in these units and the teachers could work as a team. One school changed to an early years unit because they felt unhappy about their earlier attempts to satisfy the needs of the youngest children and their provision to cater for the range of skills at this stage. The teachers thought that the children were coming to formal skills too early in the year.

*Year-group classes*
Other schools with a large intake had two or three parallel reception classes and chose to allocate children to them at random, although sometimes headteachers gave attention to forming equal groups of girls and boys, mixing children with and without nursery experience, and grouping children speaking the same language so that no child was a language isolate. Often friendship groups were taken into consideration and for this the headteacher relied on information from playgroups and parents.

   Grouping across the year was considered to be advantageous because it 'improves peoples' attitudes' towards this age group and makes them part of the school instead of it being perceived as 'the baby class'.

*Vertically grouped classes*
For social, practical and educational reasons children in some schools were in vertically grouped classes spanning two or more years. For example, in small rural schools, this could not be avoided, but in others it had been organized this way to take account of new entrant numbers. Headteachers who had opted to arrange such classes considered that the 'older ones look after the little ones, explain things to them', and 'what the older children in the class do rubs off on the fours who also want to do it; it helps the youngest get on quicker'. To be in the same class for two years enabled good relationships to be developed and gave children a feeling of stability. However 'it's all right for four year olds to play but what about the others' was the view of one teacher. Some schools were returning to year grouping as a response to the demands of the National Curriculum. Other research (West et al., 1990) identifies teachers' concerns about four year olds in vertically grouped classes and the lack of models in nursery classes when there is an early admission policy.

   Decisions about grouping children are not always made on educational grounds. Often expediency prevails: numbers of children and staffing allocations are the deciding factors and these vary from year to year. One reception teacher stated she would be 'sorry to be having fours only next term because older ones are useful to help the younger ones. But I will be having a GA [general assistant] full-time instead of half-time. The classroom is a long way from the toilets, the oldest used to take the youngest, now the GA will have to do it for the first few weeks'.

# Settling In

The schools in the study were attempting to meet the needs of four year olds by recognizing them as individuals who are becoming more independent but still need security and adult attention. **A sensitive approach enables the youngest children to settle into school gradually**.

## School Routines

Organization can be improved by separating reception children from whole-school routines. There are considerable differences between nursery and reception classes in the organization of time. Extensive research (Cleave *et al.*, 1982; Bennett, 1987; Stevenson, 1988; McCail, 1989) found that, in general, the reception class had a more formal approach with timetable 'fixtures' like assembly, lunch, play and hall times. A flexible start to the day with time for children to choose and complete activities was more commonly found in other types of provision.

In the present study, curriculum guidelines favoured a flexible, calm start to the day and recommended that there should be sensitive treatment for these younger children with regard to assembly, lunch and playtimes.

*Beginning and end of the day*
The beginning and end of the school day can provide valuable opportunities for informal discussions with parents, but they can also be distressing times for some children. Many nursery classes have flexible beginnings and endings to their day or, if they are on a school site, stagger their times so that the youngest children can avoid the hustle and bustle of arrivals and mass exodus at home times. It also gives teachers a chance to welcome each child and parent.

LEA guidelines suggest that there should be a calm start to the day. To achieve this, all children and their parents must not be expected to arrive at once. If the daily arrival is organized flexibly, it will be unnecessary to have signals such as bells indicating the beginning of the school day. It will also be inappropriate for the children to sit down in one registration area. The legal requirements for registration can be carried out without calling a register and without interrupting children involved in an activity. For example, on arrival children can, with their parents' help, find their own name and hang it on a board. This makes it possible for the teacher to check who is present without formal registration procedures while providing opportunities for children to continue their involvement in activities with their parents.

Observation in one school revealed that two children had not yet settled and were anxious and upset at their parents' departure. These children had not been in a nursery and, although they had been attending school part-time for a while, they were finding the early part of the morning difficult. All the other children appeared to be quite happy waiting for large group registration and discussion time. Perhaps a flexible start, with a choice of activities for the children, would have averted the tears. The teacher would have been free to comfort the apprehensive children while the others could have been actively engaged rather than passively waiting for the teacher.

Some teachers felt that there were advantages when they had 'an open door policy' at each end of the day. Parents bringing children into the classroom could see 'what has been set out for the children' and 'they can stay as long as they want and do activities with the children'. However, it needs sensitive handling and other schools only encouraged parents to stay for a short while because they considered it was unnecessary when the children had already attended the nursery. Some parents had been found to dominate their child and one headteacher expressed concern that 'the child does not make friends with other children if stifled by the mother's presence'. Working parents may also find it difficult to stay if they do not have a flexible start themselves. One parent appreciated the consideration shown by the school but was aware of the reality of parting: 'After all, if your child gets upset you have to leave at some stage, and then the teacher will have to sort it out anyway.'

At the end of the day many schools found that by inviting the parents to collect the children from the classroom, 'valuable opportunities' were provided to exchange information and gave pre-school siblings a chance to see what happens in school. Even though it could present difficulties with transport arrangements or collecting other children, some schools staggered their leaving times. For example, an attempt to avoid the main school rush resulted in dismissing the youngest children ten minutes earlier than the other classes. They were escorted by the teacher to parents waiting in the playground. Elsewhere at the end of the day the mums, and a sprinkling of dads and grandparents, came in to the classroom to meet their children. One child proudly showed her mother a page of her writing that was on display.

*Assembly*

A flexible and sensitive approach to assembly should be encouraged. The needs of the youngest children can be taken into account because the act of worship may take place at any time during the school day and it does not necessarily involve the whole school. This means that assembly can fit in with the school organization and be attended by smaller groups or classes. The content can be more suitable and relevant for the age group attending. Four year olds should be able to enjoy an act of worship that matches their development.

Many young children find it difficult to cope with large groups of people and it was considered by some professionals and in some LEAs' guidelines to be inappropriate for these younger children to attend assembly. One document even reminded headteachers that four year olds were not of statutory age and were not therefore legally obliged to be included in school assemblies.

Conflicts can occur if reception class children are provided with a gentle start to the day but are also expected to attend whole-school assemblies. Sometimes the hall is situated some distance from the classroom and preparations to attend with young children can seem like a major expedition.

Assemblies, if they must be attended, should be short and the input should be appropriate. Children should be introduced to assembly gradually. It is an interesting contradiction that while 'large group' times are acknowledged to be difficult for young children, many nursery children have their first experience of school by attending 'special assemblies'.

In the schools visited by the project team there was a range of expectations with regard to assembly. By the summer term almost all children were happily involved. There had been special arrangements to introduce them gradually to whole-school assemblies. These included:

✿ assemblies not attended because the school aimed 'not to deal with children in large groups anyway' or 'the early years unit was exempt because the children were not of statutory age and the school did not have to respond to the Act' or it was 'dropped because of the span of languages or language development and intellectual needs of the children';

✿ assembly not attended for the first few, perhaps four or five weeks. Then short, special assemblies like birthday assemblies were attended. When the children were settled for these they attended school assemblies;

✿ separate assemblies held once a week for the reception children which included the nursery class;

✿ attending special assemblies from the beginning of the year; for example, weekly year-group assemblies which were based on themes;

✿ reception children attending *half* of each school assembly. This helped the staff, as well as the children, to feel part of the school;

✿ no special arrangements at all; this tended to be in schools where children had already been in a nursery class.

When children are introduced gradually and sensitively to assembly they feel they have valuable contributions to make. Even the shyest children can enjoy sharing their special assemblies with their peers. In some schools the reception classes took their turn in leading class assemblies once a term. These were based on themes they had covered during the previous weeks. The teacher commented, 'they do it very well'. Parents were invited to these assemblies. Teachers and nursery nurses were expected to attend.

*Lunchtimes*
Lunchtimes can prove difficult for some children because they may be presented with unfamiliar food and cutlery (Cleave *et al.*, 1982; Sharp, 1988; West *et al.*, 1990). The length of time children are expected to spend in the playground at lunchtime can be another stressful situation (Blatchford, 1989). Throughout this period the youngest children may find themselves in the care of adults with whom they are not familiar. Some of these difficulties can be avoided during the first part of the year by part-time attendance and children returning home at the end of the morning session or arriving at school for the afternoon after lunch.

Once the children attend full-time, schools adopt different strategies to meet the needs of the youngest children at lunchtimes. Those encountered in the present study included:
✿ enlisting the cooperation of parents and sending children home to lunch for at least two months after admission;
✿ inviting parents in to share school dinners;
✿ staff staying to lunch and eating with the children;
✿ children with packed lunches being able to go into lunch together and leave when they have finished;
✿ the youngest children eating earlier than the rest of the school. This enables them to have the playground to themselves for most of the dinner play;
✿ the youngest children eating with their teachers in a separate room, their own classroom perhaps;
✿ the reception class being served by dinner ladies although the rest of the school have a cafeteria system;
✿ for the first month children sitting with the teacher and then taking their turn in the cafeteria system;
✿ having a first year table with a 'third year monitor' on it to help the younger ones;
✿ having two sittings: either the oldest and youngest eat together or families are kept together.

As one teacher pointed out she rarely gets a break but, because the children are so young, she feels that they need her to sit with them to have lunch, even in the summer term. Other teachers in our study felt that lunchtime provides an opportunity to help the children with socializing skills. In a school where children were no longer accompanied by adults at the table it was considered to be a 'shame because a vital part of social development and language acquisition was lost'.

One headteacher explained:

> the reception classes are regarded as part of the whole school and it is a deliberate wish not to isolate them from the rest of the school. A compromise has been reached. For example, now that the reception children have been in the school for a while, they still have a separate playtime in the morning and afternoon. However, at lunchtime they play out with the older children, although the reception classes attend the first sitting for lunch so they are not out with all the children all the time.

It was commonly found that the long midday break was the most difficult time for all young children, particularly in the winter months. Filling the time in a bare playground can be stressful, and as one dinner lady said: 'it must seem strange to children that they have play equipment to use all morning but at lunchtime they have very little to do...'. Only a few schools had made flexible arrangements for lunchtime play. Children were given the choice of going out or staying in. They had large toys to play with or cushions to curl up on. These sessions were supervised by the nursery nurses or the dinner ladies.

The Select Committee suggest that: 'Playtime and lunchtime with a big group of older children can be overwhelming for three and four year olds, and they should be protected from this experience' (House of Commons, 1988, para. 7.10).

*Playtime*
Blatchford (1988) remarks on the barren environment provided by many school playgrounds and suggests that improvements should, and could, be made for all children, not just the youngest, at lunch and playtimes. One teacher in our study commented that playgrounds should become more attractive and stimulating areas, not just for the four year olds. A garden would be an improvement, with sand and water under cover outside. Large play equipment and wheeled toys for the use of younger children would be beneficial, but this kind of provision was usually reserved for nursery children.

Playtime can be a time of wasted opportunities for older children (*Times Educational Supplement*, TES, 14.7.89) and has long been identified as a difficult time for young children in school (Cleave *et al.*, 1982; Barrett, 1986; Sharp, 1988). There are often established procedures like 'lining up' so that large numbers of children can be moved at the same time safely from the classrooms to the playground. Once in the playground children can find that it is a time when they are surrounded by unfamiliar adults and children and that there are certain 'rules' imposed in the interests of safety and school management: for example, not being allowed into the classroom because of lack of adult supervision. Stevenson (1988) identifies the anomaly of interrupting children's play 'to go out to play' as a peculiarity of the more formal organization found in reception classes.

In the present study some interviewees thought that playtime for the younger children should be abolished. A special playtime is not necessary if children have free access to their own outdoor play area. Others in the study disagreed, saying that some children appreciate the opportunity to play with older friends and siblings. It was suggested that break or snack times present valuable opportunities for small groups of children to interact with adults. 'Milk' or 'drinks' time could occur on a rolling basis. For example, a milk bar or café could be set up where individuals could go when they wanted to rather than having to suspend the activity of the whole group at once.

In practice the schools that were visited were making attempts to introduce children to playtime gradually. By adopting a flexible approach, particularly in the first few weeks, teachers and headteachers felt that potentially stressful times for children had been averted. A number of arrangements had evolved reflecting the physical constraints of school playgrounds and staffing available. It was interesting that by the summer term almost all the children were expected 'to go out to play'. The most common concessions to providing appropriately for four year olds at school playtimes were to provide a separate playtime from the rest of the school or to provide a separate playground.

Other examples and variations of these themes were as follows:

✿ No fixed playtime in the morning. By working as a team (three teachers and a nursery nurse for 70 children) an indoor/outdoor free play session was provided for the first hour of the morning. This was considered to take into account the 'bursts of energy' characteristic of this age group.

✿ No special playtime at the beginning of the year. Teachers arranged their own playtime at any time they felt like taking it. There were opportunities for indoor/outdoor play so that children were able to choose when they wanted to go outside or be energetic. When the children felt confident they were gradually introduced to playtimes in their own playground, which was shared with the second years. These slightly older children also had a choice of playgrounds.

✿ A separate playtime for the reception children in the nursery playground. While the nursery children were busy with indoor activities the reception class children used the large play equipment. On Friday afternoons, towards the end of the summer term, the children visited the 'big playground'. The aim was to 'help the youngest children get used to the more boisterous playtime sessions with older children'.

✿ All the reception children had a choice of going out to play or staying in the classroom. The ancillary spent the time in the classroom and read or played quietly with the children.

✿ A staggered playtime. In small schools reception teachers went outside with their class at convenient times. In larger schools with limited outdoor space the first and second years had playtime together and the third and fourth years went out to play at a later time. There was a staff rota system, which meant that teachers had to do their 'duty' more frequently. They did not mind this because they considered that 'playtime is now much less hassle'.

✿ Playtime evolved over a year. At the beginning children did not have playtime, small groups then joined in when they were 'ready' and eventually they all went out but to a playground separate from the rest of the school.

Even where schools tried to be flexible about their arrangements, they found that the children were very happy to go out to play because they enjoyed being with older siblings and friends. Staff commented that they too needed playtime! This was not just because they felt they needed a break from the children but because it was one of the few opportunities they had to talk to colleagues, especially those working with other age groups.

Other paradoxes came to light in our observations in schools. For example, new entrants visiting schools, perhaps for the first time, were often expected to join the class in the playground at playtime. In one school the outdoor play space is often used for activities, such as playing with water, sand and wheeled toys for the youngest children during the summer term. Equipment is put away at playtime so that the whole school can go out to play. The youngest children return to an area that had earlier been a hive of activity and is now a barren piece of tarmac.

Observations in different schools revealed that attempts have been made to provide a more interesting environment with areas designated for 'quiet reading' or 'running around' and brightly coloured number games marked out on the asphalt. However, the most common observations were that playgrounds were not particularly exciting places to be for the youngest children. For example:

The youngest children have up till now played in a separate play-ground. Today, however, the weather is very warm and the youngest children are allowed to play on a small grassed area because it is cooler and the tarmac is unbearable in the heat. This grassed area has mature trees, tree stumps to sit on and large tyres to play with. It is shared with the rest of the school. In the tarmac play-ground there is nothing for the children to do except some fading number games marked on the ground. It seems no wonder that when it was time to 'go out to play' one boy sat on a chair and another hid under the table before eventually being persuaded to join the other children in the playground.

Headteachers were aware that the insensitive use of 'playtime and dinner time can destroy all that has been built up' in offering children a gradual and flexible induction to school. One parent commented about her son's experiences: 'They go out to play in reception – that's a new experience, going out to play with the others. He came home full of it, he loves it.'

## Becoming a Pupil

A gradual introduction to school and sensitive treatment by adults is essential for younger children admitted to reception classes in infant or primary schools. They have not only to make sense of their physical world but also to learn the implicit and explicit messages transmitted by the adults working with them. By gaining an understanding of the language, rules and rituals of the classroom and school and by unravelling the often concealed expectations of the teacher, children learn to become pupils. Our classroom observations highlighted the following aspects of becoming a pupil:

✿ getting to know the unfamiliar language;
✿ learning rituals and ground rules;
✿ interpreting adults' expectations;
✿ becoming part of a class.

### Unfamiliar Language

As Cleave *et al.* (1982) pointed out, bewilderment at unfamiliar words and questions, uncertainty about toilet arrangements and not knowing what to do next pose problems for children's smooth transition from their pre-school provision to primary and infant classrooms. The difference in language used in the home and in school has been the focus of attention over the past few years. Studies have shown that children can have rich language experiences at home, in contrast to the often limited opportunities provided in many classrooms (Tizard and Hughes, 1984; Wells, 1985). In the present study there were many examples of words being used that could lead children to be confused or uncertain about what was expected of them. It has already been noted that asking a child to stop playing to 'go out to play' must cause difficulty in understanding for some children in their first days in school. Other examples observed include the following.

- ✿ References to the 'hall'. The school hall is a totally different concept to the 'hall' most children experience at home.
- ✿ 'Line up at the door and we'll go outside'. This probably makes little sense to children who are accustomed to free movement between indoors and out or to those that do not know what a 'line' is anyway.
- ✿ 'First the apples go swimming, then the acorns ...' or 'ladybirds, go and get your lunch boxes'. Such labels are used by teachers to organize the movement of groups of children. Although children quickly learn which applies to them, for new entrants to an existing group or children for whom English is not their first language, such instructions can cause great difficulty.

## Learning Rituals and Ground Rules

In some classrooms movement of children at lunch and playtimes avoided 'lining up' and was organized by selecting individuals or small groups in different ways. For example, children were allowed to go to lunch if they had a specific colour, identified by their teacher, on their clothing, if they had a particular type of shoe, if they had a baby brother or a sister, if they had a specific letter of the alphabet in their name and so on.

Most children already have their own perceptions of and expectations about 'big school' and observation of them 'playing school' can be a salutary experience for any teacher. Classroom routines are encountered early and regularly in school careers. Children respond to them rapidly and accept them quickly. In the present study remarks such as 'are you sitting still and quietly', 'sitting up straight and tall', 'sitting beautifully' or making a 'smart queue' were used as a form of organizational control. Children were often rewarded when they were 'sitting nicely' by being allowed to choose a book to read or to do a special job for the teacher.

There were many rituals, often peculiar to each school, but usually related to large group time. One such example was reported in the researcher's notes:

At the beginning of the morning and afternoon sessions there is a register 'ritual'. The children gather on the carpet for a group discussion about all the exciting things that have happened to them. This is called 'listening time' (does this mean they do not have to listen at other times?). At the end of the discussion a 'helper' is chosen. This child then chooses someone to be their helper and the pair of them count the number of children, the number of ticks in the register, the number of bottles of milk needed and so on. The two 'helpers' are responsible for distributing milk and keeping the books tidy later in the morning or afternoon.

## Interpreting Adults' Expectations

Children very quickly make sense of their world and learn what is expected of them by adults, but they also rely on each other to reinforce their interpretation of the teachers' expectations or instructions. For example, a group conversation, while undertaking a teacher-initiated activity, shows children's uncertainty but willingness to please.

> Do you have to write? ...
> Which way up does it go? ...
> I'm going to have it this way ...
> What colour hair did she have? ...

As children became more confident they were observed initiating younger children who had not yet managed to work out the system, into the expected conforming behaviour they had already learned. There were instances of 'you're not allowed to do that, they're not playtime toys', or 'you can only do that when ...' or 'you're not allowed to have ...'.

Often it was not just classroom 'rules' that had been learned, but school rules too. For example, at the end of one playtime the youngest child ran up to her teacher to give her a cuddle. The teacher greeted her with 'you didn't run did you Clare?' The little girl shook her head. She was beginning to learn that 'children do not run in school'.

Children have clear ideas about what is happening in their classrooms. For example, their comments about what was 'work' and what was 'play' were illuminating. 'Drawing is work' we were told by one four year old, although other children explained the difference as 'You all get turns but sometimes teacher says', 'It's a game because you can go in the house and play house games' or 'When you can choose, that is playing – it is not playing when the teacher said I had to do this'. For a more detailed example see Chapter 5, p. 65.

Teachers' expectations are often misinterpreted by children. If children are given the freedom and independence to follow their own inclination in a teacher-suggested activity, the end product is often not that anticipated by the teacher. For example, one teacher explained: 'I was really surprised. They had been asked to draw a treasure map. I thought they would draw an island with sea and trees and so on but they didn't. They drew a trail, like the snail trails we did the other week ...'.

Sestini (1987) and Drummond (1988) remind us that children may be introduced to an inappropriate environment without complaining or resisting. They continue to do their utmost to survive and satisfy the demands adults make of them. Teachers strive to establish a cooperative class, which is a group of children who do what the teacher expects of them. In Willes's (1983) illuminating study of the process of children learning to become pupils, adult approval is one of the key factors in the successful initiation into becoming a pupil. 'It can be argued that finding out what the teacher wants and doing it, constitutes the primary duty of a pupil' (ibid., p. 138).

When adults have such an important part to play in enabling children to become pupils, it is essential that attention be given to the values and attitudes that are transmitted. In most classrooms there are large group times where children discuss their news, ideas and views with adults. They learn to speak one at a time, take turns, value each other's contribution and so on, but they also learn what is acceptable to the teacher and the value given to their ideas. An extract from the researcher's notes helps to explain:

> The children told the teacher and the rest of the class about their news and showed them various things they had brought in. The list included new hair-slides, plans for tomorrow, swimming achievements, birth of a baby sister, visits to Kew Gardens and to the seaside, a dream, new books, a card, a tooth coming out and buying a new fish for the aquarium. The teacher tended to encourage anything that could be educationally valuable: for example, a map of Kew Gardens, reading the card, looking at the books. Things like the hair-bands or slides and bracelets were gently acknowledged but not elaborated upon.

## Becoming Part of a Class

When teachers operate with large groups there is a tendency for them to address children as 'all', 'class 8', 'everybody'. Some children have great difficulty in realizing that this includes them. As one teacher commented: 'Adam why is it that you never think it means you when we talk to everyone?' This reminds us that:

> Homogeneity is an illusion ... we [teachers] have ways of treating young children as if they were members of a homogeneous group, classroom rules and regulations are designed to create homogeneity from diversity and difference ... the notion of the unique individual sometimes seems grotesquely at odds with the context in which we invite four year olds to exercise their uniqueness. (Drummond, 1988, pp. 2–3)

Although schools exist as social microcosms and the youngest children are expected to be part of the whole school, it is difficult to achieve a balance between the needs of four year olds and the demands made by school organization. It is particularly difficult with large classes and overcrowded classrooms. The lack of adults to help the reception teacher increases the pressure to urge children into conformity and to become pupils. In our study children were initiated into school routines over a period of time. As one mother commented, 'becoming a pupil takes half a term' and a nursery nurse observed that when four year olds are admitted annually 'the gelling of the class takes a good term'. For children in other schools the process takes longer. Observations at the end of the summer term, when the youngest children had been attending school part-time for two terms and full-time for over half a term, revealed that some were still finding it difficult to fulfil the pupil role expected of them. At this stage of the year the reception teachers often felt that the children were 'really blossoming now and it would be a shame to lose them'. Most children had learned what the teachers expected and valued. During a sunny afternoon towards the end of the summer term, for example, in one school:

> a group of children used blocks to mark out the plan of a house. A different group of children established a similar 'base' around the corner but within sight of the other group. Long bricks and plastic construction sets were converted to guns and a 'shoot-out' followed. As the teacher approached with 'they're not guns are they?', the children immediately changed the angle of the offending 'weapons' and claimed to be 'hoovering up'! As the teacher withdrew the mock battle continued. Another teacher walked towards the group and before anything could be said the children volunteered the information, 'we're cutting the grass now'!

It has been suggested that by the age of six children 'closely mirror their teachers' opinions of their own and their peers' academic worth. By this age they have also learned to use the criteria that the teacher uses and can list them' (Crocker, 1988, p. 51). However, as one child confidently informed a newcomer who was spending an afternoon in school with his parents, 'You'll get used to the new things that we do. I didn't know what to do to start with'.

## Conclusion

To help new entrants become confident pupils there should be a gradual, gentle start to school. This can be encouraged through good
home–school liaison, through staggered entry procedures, part-time
attendance and flexible starting and leaving times. Awareness of
potentially difficult times like registration, assembly, lunch and playtime should lead to sensitive arrangements being made so that young
children are able to feel secure and can meet new challenges with confidence.

# 4 The Activities

Once the children are in school, careful thought has to be given to the activities that the children do. At the age of four development is proceeding rapidly in all aspects – physical, intellectual, social and emotional – and an appropriate curriculum must recognize and encourage this development. The activities are very much bound up with the curriculum. They are in a sense the vehicle through which much of the curriculum is transmitted.

This chapter explores the curriculum with regard to breadth and balance and continuity with the National Curriculum. It considers how the various subjects can be integrated, how different activity areas can be defined or linked and how use can be made of the wider environment. Attention is then turned to the quality of the activities, whether they: offer challenge and extension, meet the needs of individual children and offer opportunities for talking as well as doing.

## A Broad and Balanced Curriculum

The interviewees stressed that **activities should be of sufficient range and variety to allow children to experience a broad and balanced curriculum**.

In recent years there have been attempts on both sides of the Atlantic to define what constitutes a broad and balanced curriculum in the early years. These definitions are usually rooted in a child-centred, rather than subject-centred, philosophy in which the focus is the development of the individual as a whole person. Thus, a balanced curriculum is one which 'considers the whole child and all aspects of development' (Dowling, 1988). In the USA, the 'whole child' view is upheld in a position statement issued by the NAEYC on developmentally appropriate practice for four- and five-year-old children (Bredekamp, 1986). The statement recommends that experiences are provided that stimulate learning in all developmental areas – physical, social, emotional and intellectual.

The present study of LEA guidelines revealed that while there is general agreement with the whole-child view, there is less consensus about what an appropriate curriculum should contain. Half of the guidelines took as their framework the nine areas of learning and experience defined by HMI in *The Curriculum from 5 to 16* (GB.DES, 1985b), which are: aesthetic and creative, human and social, linguistic and literary, mathematical, moral, physical, scientific, spiritual and technological. Others omitted the social, moral and spiritual aspects and emphasized the importance of language and first-hand experiences in developing concepts and skills.

Since the guidelines were written, HMI have published their document *The Education of Children Under Five* (GB.DES, 1989b), which may help to clarify matters. They say that a broad and balanced curriculum for the under-fives 'places emphasis upon the major aspects of children's physical, emotional, social and cognitive development'. They recommend the nine *areas* of learning and experience listed above as a helpful framework for curriculum planning, within and across which the *elements* of learning – knowledge, understanding, skills and attitudes – may be developed concurrently. The Rumbold Report (GB.DES, 1990b) endorses this view.

The activities and experiences to be included in the curriculum are often arrived at by describing the skills that children should acquire. These skills may be grouped in various ways. For example, in *The Curriculum from 5 to 16* (GB.DES, 1985b) skills are grouped under eight headings: communication, observation, study, problem-solving, physical and practical, creative and imaginative, numerical, personal and social skills. However, those headings were intended for children from five years of age. Curtis (1986), in a detailed discussion of curricula for three and four year olds, draws up a similar list but also emphasizes motor and perceptual skills and cultural awareness.

The most detailed guidelines went a stage further and related skills to specific activities and experiences which afforded opportunities to develop them. For example, creative activities offered opportunities to develop and practice motor skills such as cutting, painting and pouring and social skills such as sharing and clearing up. Rather than prescribe specific activities, some of them posed questions as a means of suggesting to teachers what they should consider.

The majority of early years activities are multi-purpose and can offer a variety of learning opportunities. Thus, within an appropriate framework, decisions about the actual detail of an activity will depend on the intentions and professional expertise of the teacher.


## Continuity with the National Curriculum

During the first year of the present study (1988), educationists were already looking ahead to the National Curriculum, which children aged five to seven were scheduled to begin in September 1989. At that time, our interviewees could see no reason why an appropriate early years curriculum should not fit well with the proposed programmes of study, although they stressed that breadth should not be sacrificed in a narrowing-down to the core subject areas.

A statement from the National Curriculum Council (NCC, 1989) acknowledged that many of the activities already undertaken by children under five correspond to Level 1 attainment targets in English, maths and science, and called for 'a broad and balanced curriculum which includes elements of the core and other foundation subjects of the National Curriculum' (para. 4.14).

However, by the second year of the study, teachers were expressing reservations about the effect of the National Curriculum on children's activities. They felt that the National Curriculum:

❂ could impose limitations by focusing on a narrower range of experiences than they already provided;

❂ contained serious omissions: for example, early years teachers were concerned to promote good language and social skills that were not given emphasis in the National Curriculum but which were imperative for later stages of education;

❂ could present difficulties for children for whom English is not their first language because their 'starting-point' is different from that of English-speaking pupils;

❂ could be difficult to implement in mixed-age classes because the younger children's activities involve freedom of movement and can be noisy.

Fears were also expressed that National Assessment at seven would put pressure on teachers to concentrate on the 'intellectual' aspects and in particular to emphasize skills associated with literacy and numeracy. This could exacerbate the situation reported by HMI (GB.DES, 1989c) that: 'for the majority of four year olds the curriculum is insufficiently broad and balanced. In many classes there is an over-emphasis on some aspects of the basic skills of literacy and numeracy' (para. 4). In elaborating on this 'over-emphasis', the report continues: 'Too much work focused too soon upon the formal aspects of reading and writing when the four year olds undertaking it needed richer experiences for developing speaking and listening' (ibid., para. 27).

Time has shown that the anticipated pressure from National Testing is indeed having an effect on teachers of five to seven year olds. A pilot study of teacher time in Key Stage 1, commissioned by the Assistant Masters and Mistresses Association (AMMA), and carried out two terms into the start of the National Curriculum, found that teachers were concentrating on the core subjects of English, maths and science 'at the expense of a broad and balanced curriculum' (Campbell and Neill, 1990). The report continues: 'This pressure has been intensified perhaps by the decision taken recently by the Secretary of State, to remove the non-core subjects from statutory external assessment at the end of Key Stage 1' (p. 31). It is to be hoped that the pressure will not 'wash down' on to teachers of four year olds, although it is difficult to see how it can be avoided where four year olds are taught in classes with older children.

By the time fieldwork was in progress (the school year 1988–9) preparations for the National Curriculum were already under way in the schools and most of the schools in our study were reappraising or revising their curricula. Their plans took account of the under-fives in the school, including the nursery where there was one. Although adjustments rather than sweeping changes were being made, teachers felt that planning for the entire age range of the school enabled them to identify any gaps and thus improve on previous practice.

In the reception class, teachers were considering how the activities they provided for four year olds fitted with the Level 1 attainment targets. Most of them came to the conclusion that they were already 'on the right lines' and that very few changes would be required. Indeed some felt that the activities they already provided went 'well beyond the requirements of the National Curriculum'.

Teachers commented on the relative merits of the programmes of study and attainment targets for science, maths and English. By and large the science document was considered the best of the three because 'it does not assume that children have already acquired some knowledge to start with'. The English document in particular was declared to 'assume too much' and to break down the earlier stages into insufficient detail. This has led some schools to interpose a 'Level 0' in their planned curricula. As one coordinator pointed out, 'In the beginning we need to spend an awful lot of time on speaking and listening, as well as mark-making and early reading activities which precede Level 1.'

The **need to ensure continuity between the activities of under-fives and the National Curriculum** has been of widespread concern among professionals in early years education. This concern is shared by HMI who conclude their report on the education of children under five (GB.DES, 1989b) by saying:

> The best work with under-fives has always taken account of the need for continuity with the teaching and learning which takes place in the next stage of their education. The new legislation adds considerable importance to ensuring that full account is taken of the need to promote curricular continuity and progression. (para. 73)

Increasing concern as to how the attainment targets would relate to the early years curriculum in general and the experiences of four year olds in particular has prompted groups of early years professionals across the country to try to clarify this issue. A document published by one such group (Early Years Curriculum Group, 1989) uses a series of subject and topic 'webs' to explain how the various attainment targets are covered by appropriate provision in the early years classroom. For example, one subject web shows how Maths Attainment Target 1, Level 1, is covered by activities in the following categories: 'outdoors', 'the home corner', 'the creative area', 'books', 'blocks and construction', 'games and puzzles' and 'malleable and natural materials' (ibid., p. 6).

As the Early Years Curriculum Group points out: 'the education of the under-fives is not something separate and apart, but is the beginning of the continuum of learning'.

## Integrating Subject Areas

Although the National Curriculum is divided into subjects, it is not appropriate to teach young children in this way. The professionals interviewed stressed that **the early years curriculum should be an integrated one** because children of this age do not perceive separate subject areas. This view constitutes one of the ten principles of early childhood education drawn out by Bruce (1987) from the work of the early pioneers and more recent theorists and researchers. The principle states that 'learning is not compartmentalized – everything links'.

The interviewees emphasized that it is through a multidisciplinary range of activities that the young child develops the skills that will eventually be required for literacy, numeracy, science and so on. While the range of activities should be multidisciplinary (embracing a number of subject disciplines), individual activities appropriate for young children are themselves likely to encompass several subject disciplines. Subjects such as language, maths, art, science and technology are often indistinguishable from each other. For example, in one classroom:

> the children had designed working models using Lego. They organized races and discussed the 'fastest' and 'slowest' vehicles. The teacher introduced the use of a sand-timer to see how far the vehicles could go in a set time. The distances were then measured in hand spans. Slopes and ramps were constructed to see what would happen. Finally, the whole activity sequence was recorded in words and pictures.

Although the children are not conscious of the subjects being covered in the activities, it is important that the adults are aware of what is going on. For example, if the 'nine areas of learning and experience' are applied to the Lego sequence described above, it can be seen that at least seven of those areas are involved:

✿  physical (using manipulative and motor skills);

✿ technological (designing and constructing models, slopes and ramps);

✿ mathematical (timing the vehicles and measuring the distances covered);

✿ scientific (seeing what happened when slopes and ramps were introduced);

✿ linguistic and literary (discussing and recording the activity);

✿ creative (illustrating the activity);

✿ social (collaborating with others).

## Balancing Different Kinds of Activity

The professionals interviewed recommended that **the range of activities appropriate for four year olds should comprise a balance between different kinds of activity**: group and individual; movement and calm; noise and quiet; and the novel and the familiar. (Equipment and materials to facilitate these kinds of activity are discussed in Chapter 6.)

### Group and Individual Activities

Teachers in the study tried to provide a balance between activities that allowed children to participate as a whole class, in groups and pairs and as individuals. (For a detailed discussion of grouping see Chapter 9.) A typical morning or afternoon session included opportunities for the following.

✿ Whole-class activity, such as registration, discussion, listening to stories, singing songs, chanting rhymes.

✿ Teacher-led group activity, such as planning, collaborating, learning new techniques and skills, making and decorating things, collecting, observing, talking and recording.

✿ Spontaneous groups/pairs, such as constructing and model-making, building and dismantling, playing board games, engaging in imaginative/fantasy/pretend play.

✿ Individual activity, such as listening to tapes, looking at books, painting at an easel, writing and recording, drawing and colouring, matching and sorting, experimenting, using sand and water and other malleable substances, using wheeled toys.

Of course these categories are not exclusive: many of the group activities are performed individually and vice versa.

## Movement and Calm

Because young children's energy tends to occur in bursts, they need not only the freedom to move about and develop large muscle movement but also opportunities for rest and calm. A balance of activities of both types may be achieved through the adults' careful attention to both the choice available and the pattern of the session or day (see Chapter 5).

Young pupils need to be able to move around both when carrying out the activity and when going from one activity to another. Opportunities for calm may be a natural requirement of certain activities and may also occur as 'interludes' when the group is gathered and seated. Children, like everyone else, need to be physically inactive sometimes.

Here are some examples of both types of activity noted during the study. (There are of course many more.)

✿ Encouraging *movement*: for example, large muscle activity with climbing equipment, wheeled toys and large blocks; dramatic play, dressing-up, using puppets; action rhymes, dancing, musical games; going for a walk, searching for mini-beasts, exploring the park, visiting the shops; taking photographs, gardening, washing the dolls, treasure-hunting; clearing up.

✿ Encouraging *calm*: for example, sitting (or standing) at table activities such as matching, sorting and puzzles; creative activities such as writing, colouring, cutting-out and sticking; concentrating on computer games; listening to stories, reading or looking at books, watching a television programme.

## Noise and Quiet

Young children need opportunities to make a noise without repression. They sometimes need to be rumbustious and let off steam; in addition, noise is often natural to their activities. They also need occasions when they can be quiet in order to concentrate on an activity, become aware of others, listen to different sounds or experience quiet. A balance may be achieved by planning for both types of activity to occur during a session. Here is a selection from those noted in the study.

✿ Encouraging *noise*: such as woodwork, especially using hammer and nails; exploring blustery weather by, for example, flying scarves in the wind; musical activities and the exploration of sound; reciting poems and rhymes and joining in stories and choruses.

✿ Encouraging *quiet*: such as activities requiring intense concentration; looking at books, watching television and listening to others;

stalking mini-beasts; examining things closely, especially using a magnifying glass or microscope.

## Novel and Familiar

While young children need a certain amount of stimulus from new and interesting activities, they also need the security of a familiar environment with certain predictable events and routines. To this end, the classrooms in our study typically contained a number of activities or activity areas that were 'permanent features' while other activities were changed or modified from time to time. The more or less permanent features of these classrooms, in terms of the type of activities regularly available, were: home/house; large and small construction; creative, especially painting; sand and water; language and literacy; maths; and books/story. The details of the actual activities might be left unaltered for a period to ensure that every child had a chance to try them. They might then be changed for a time and re-introduced to allow consolidation to take place. Changes in the activities might occur as a result of the daily pattern; a fresh stimulus or idea; or the introduction of a new piece of equipment or different materials.

The afternoon activities were broadly similar to those of the morning, especially where children attended half-days only. When children were full-time, some of the morning activities were modified or replaced with other activities. (Patterns of the day are discussed in detail in Chapter 5.)

Novelty was often introduced into familiar activities through a new piece of equipment or different materials. These might be supplied by the children or adults. For example: introducing a meal table to the home corner to encourage skills in sorting and laying cutlery and choosing a menu; adding a real steering wheel to large block activities to stimulate pretend play; exchanging writing booklets for postcards or paper and envelopes to encourage different uses of literacy skills such as letter-writing; replacing powder paints with fluorescent paint to encourage creativity and imagination.

A change of direction or new impetus might be brought about by objects or events that captured the children's interest. These were introduced by children as well as adults. For example: a broken keyboard encouraged the use of investigative and fine motor skills in its 'repair' and reconstruction; a talk by a parent stimulated the creation of a garden; changing the quiet area into a 'jungle' renewed interest in words and books.

## Linking Activity Areas

The interviewees recommended that **activity areas should be clearly defined**. In the classrooms, different types of activity were usually assigned to clearly differentiated areas (see Chapter 5). Broad differentiations were made mainly for practical reasons and, where space allowed, were often assigned as 'messy', 'quiet' and 'noisy' areas. Activity areas were usually delineated by low furniture, curtains and screens, or simply different types of flooring. Within these broad delineations, the typical classroom for four year olds included areas for house play, dressing-up, small construction, large construction, reading, listening, writing, maths, painting, modelling, sand and water activities.

However, the interviewees also advocated that **activities should be carefully sited so that children could make natural linkages between them**. For example, the construction area could be next to the home area so that activities could extend each other; the mark-making or writing activity could be next to the book area so that children could make connections between reading and writing and between printed and hand-written symbols. On the other hand, it was important that activities of very different kinds did not interrupt each other. For example, books and construction sets were not regarded as compatible neighbours.

Many instances of children making links between different activities were noted in our study. Examples are given in Chapter 5 of links between house play and colouring; house play, large blocks, painting and writing; and sand, water and small-world play.

Other spontaneous linkages made by the children included: house and maths activities for a 'shopping expedition'; reading and writing activities for a 'visit to the library'; science (batteries and bulbs), small construction and junk-modelling to make 'a lighthouse'; outdoor storage shed, climbing area and wheeled toys for group fantasy play. It may actually be more difficult for children to make spontaneous links between activities in large units where areas are separated by walls, than in self-contained classrooms where space is more limited. The possibilities of links are almost endless. Careful planning is required to ensure that links can occur and to allow children time to explore these possibilities fully during their play.

## Offering Challenge and Extension

Professionals agreed that **situations should be created in the classroom in which the activities are challenging and can be developed and extended by children or adults**. They suggested, for example, that an activity area might be set up as a vet's surgery or a hairdressers' or a travel agents' shop, and this would not only stimulate new experiences but could be extended and developed by the children.

In the schools studied, teachers of four year olds set up a number of imaginative and challenging situations to stimulate and extend children's activities. These were primarily intended either to stimulate a specific area of activity or to span several areas. For example:

✿ A jungle (formerly the book corner) with animal mobiles and models, real plants, green tissue leaves and creepers, and appropriate books, puzzles and table games to promote language skills.

✿ The same book corner later became a haunted house in which a cupboard door opened to reveal a ghost (made from a sheet draped over a balloon), a large chest with a masked dummy climbing out, net curtain cobwebs, a collection of bones and, suspended from the ceiling, a variety of birds, bats, snakes and spiders.

✿ An underwater cave including a submarine and loading bay. The loading bay was stocked with large blocks and boxes, and with labels, charts and tick lists for recording arrivals and despatches. Instrument panels comprising a variety of clocks and dials were made and used by the children. There were books on ships, fishing, marine life, shells and rock formations, and a collection of goggles, telescopes, periscopes and binoculars to try out. Experiments were conducted with air tanks, pipes and snorkels, and materials were explored for properties of floating, sinking and absorbency.

The HMI report (GB.DES, 1989b) gives a similar example (p. 13). The home area had been turned into a 'hospital' and provided a stimulus for literacy and social skills. 'Patients' checked in at the reception desk where their details were written down by the 'receptionist'. A telephone was used to contact their 'relatives', and at various intervals 'ancillary staff' provided meals and snacks for staff and patients.

## Using the Environment

The environment, both within and beyond the school, is an essential ingredient in children's education. Interviewees recommended that the **activities should make use of the environment beyond the classroom, both within the school and in the neighbourhood**. In the schools studied, activities beyond the classroom occurred during indoor/outdoor play, in and around the school premises and outside the school.

**Indoor/Outdoor Play**

Opportunities for children to move freely between indoor and outdoor activities form a basic part of nursery education and should also be an essential component of provision for young children in infant classes (see Chapter 5). However, schools frequently suffer from insufficiencies of staff, space and equipment to provide adequately in this respect. Only two of the infant/primary schools in our study provided for substantial periods of indoor/outdoor activity in the nursery tradition. Opportunities were provided outdoors for games and gross motor activity, gardening, sand, water, woodwork, construction and painting. (For a detailed description of the use of outdoor space see Chapter 5.)

**Activities Around the School**

Apart from regular visits to places like the hall, dining-room and school library, activities for four year olds sometimes take place in parts of the school other than their usual teaching area. Observed examples included: making a flower bed in the paved courtyard outside the classroom as part of a project; searching the school garden for mini-beasts to study; following a treasure trail across the playground; mapping routes from the classroom to other parts of the school.

**Activities Outside the School**

Examples of activities extending into the environment beyond the school occurred during the study. Visits were made into the neighbourhood and to places or special events further afield. Excursions were made to the shops, fire station, rail station, library, allotments, park, theatre and zoo.

One class took a walk around the school catchment area and the children mapped their routes from home to school. This developed into an interest in maps and scale, and culminated in a visit to a model village where the children were able to experience being 'giants'. The HMI document (GB.DES, 1989b, p. 32) gives another example of good practice in the use of the local environment, where four year olds watched the building of a new supermarket opposite the school. This led to a discussion about different types of buildings, with particular emphasis on the children's homes, and the construction of a 'house' in the outside play area.

# Meeting the Needs of Individual Children

The professionals interviewed stressed that **activities must be appropriate to the needs of the individual child**. Activities that are **flexible enough to take account of individual diversity** are widely considered to be very important because children of this age span a wide range of experience and ability. They come into school from a diversity of communities and home backgrounds, and with different pre-school experiences in nurseries, playgroups and so on. A variety of learning situations should therefore be provided that acknowledge this diversity and respond appropriately to it.

Curtis (1986) comments on the different environments in which children live and suggests that the learning experience provided for children from high-rise flats, for example, should place emphasis on 'developing gross motor skills and unrestricted movement within both the outdoor and indoor play areas' (p. 127).

Children starting school are also likely to be at different stages of development with a diversity of skills and interests. The Early Years Curriculum Group (1989) note that: 'a six months' age difference between children at this stage is developmentally much more significant than a similar age difference in a group of older children. The younger the children the more important it is that their individual learning needs are identified and planned for...' (p. 1).

In the USA the NAEYC (1986), in their position statement on developmentally appropriate practice for four and five year olds, adopt a similar stance and recommend that different levels of ability, development and learning styles are expected, accepted and used to design appropriate activities. In considering whether an activity is developmentally appropriate, they suggest that two questions should be asked: Is the activity suitable for a child of this age? Is the activity right for this individual child?

Pitching the activity at the right level for the individual child can be difficult. As Curtis (1986) observes: 'Too great a move forward can produce a "boomerang effect" resulting in negative responses, but equally too small a progression can lead to boredom and indifference' (p. 128). To meet individual needs, interviewees recommend that the activities should: have relevance and meaning for the child; provide opportunities for individual progression and extension.

## Relevance and Meaning

**The experiences offered through the activities must be relevant and meaningful for the individual child.** Otherwise, as one LEA adviser said, school for some children can be 'an objectionable, alien experience'. During the study, teachers tried to make activities relevant and meaningful for the children by, for example:

❁ using the sound of children's own names to teach awareness of different rhythms in a music activity;

❁ providing real items for children to use, such as a cash till in the 'shop', and saucepans, mirrors, curtains, cutlery and crockery in the home corner (for further suggestions see Chapter 8);

❁ building on recent school events; for example, a visit from the school doctor stimulated the setting-up of a 'hospital corner';

❁ setting-up a data base on the computer of items gathered by the children; for example, after a walk in the park the children sorted out their collection of stones, feathers, cones, chestnuts, acorns and crab-apples. These were programmed into the data base so that children could run off bar charts and pie charts showing the relative quantities of items gathered. As the youngest August-born four year old explained, pointing to the graph on her print-out, 'Crab-apples is the biggest [set] because there are 18 and stones is the littlest because there is only one.'

### Individual Progression and Extension

Many activities were noted that allowed children opportunities to progress at their own level and pace. Here is a selection:

❁ writing activities that could be performed at the child's own level, whether in emergent scribble or well-constructed sentences;

❁ children's own stories put on the computer disk so that extracts could be selected and illustrated by individuals; these were incorporated into children's own 'story books', which were later displayed on the bookshelf for others to read;

❁ creative activities where children had total freedom within the constraints of the materials provided; for example, developing any pattern, picture or model of their choice with the materials set out on the table.

Providing activities which meet the needs of every child in the class is not easy: to make it work, good teacher–child ratios are essential. Careful planning is also necessary (see Chapter 5).

## Offering Opportunities for Talking while Doing

Interviewees were adamant that **opportunities must be provided for children to talk about what they are doing while they are**

**doing it**. Indeed, the combined development of practical activity and language was declared by some to be 'the very basis of learning'.

Educationists maintain that this combination of doing and talking allows children to develop their knowledge, understanding and skills and share experiences.

## Developing Knowledge, Understanding and Skills

Opportunities to talk about their activities helps children to develop not only intellectually but also socially. As HMI explain in their report,

> With young children, many productive ideas are generated through play and practical activity. The quality of discussion and the adults' questioning at the time, and later, are important in enabling child-ren to consolidate and increase their knowledge and understanding of important early mathematical, aesthetic, linguistic and scientific concepts. In these activities the children also acquire considerable social skills: interacting within a group, and learning about sharing and fairness in taking turns. (GB.DES, 1989b, para. 23)

Educationists have pointed out the importance of talk in relation to specific aspects of development in the early years. For example, Cur-tis (1986) sees early practice in talking and listening as fundamental to the development of reading and writing skills later on. Bruce (1987) notes the relevance of doing and talking for the development of crea-tivity and imagination because it allows children to rearrange ideas, words and experiences. Metz (1987) describes the essential relation-ship between talking and early practical mathematics. Language is needed to discuss and explain what is happening: the teacher should listen to children's interpretations and then explore all the possibilities with them.

Matthews (1987) explains the crucial nature of talk in children's early representation and drawing, which are the beginnings of sym-bolization. Children's work often reveals 'breathtaking sequences of the growth and proliferation of symbol systems' (ibid.), yet it is vital that teachers understand what is going on so that they can provide the necessary interaction to support this development. (Examples of teacher–child interaction during activities observed in the present study are given in Chapter 5.)

## Sharing and Exploring Experiences

The sharing of experiences, both at the time they happen and after-wards, can promote greater understanding of the experience, develop language and, through exploring the experiences of others, enhance social skills. However, it is essential that there are sufficient adults present to allow this to happen. Many learning opportunities occur spontaneously and unexpectedly and bring with them the urgent need to communicate. An example of this was observed in the study.

> Jon, who had been busy at the water tray, went to the classroom sink to wash the bubbles out of a funnel. The tap was stiff and as he turned it full on the water suddenly gushed into the funnel, causing a fountain to shoot up into the air. Surprised and excited by this miracle, Jon shouted to the teacher, 'Mrs B., Mrs B., come and have a look at this!' Unfortunately, the teacher was busy with a group at the other end of the room and could give no more than a cursory glance to Jon's discovery.

Experiences like this occur without warning and it is important that there is an adult at hand if the child wants to share it. Otherwise who knows what learning opportunities may be lost?

On a more positive note, many instances were observed when adults were involved with children, in both teacher-led and child-initiated activities. As HMI explain:

> Through listening and talking in groups children are enabled to explore other people's experiences and to modify and extend their own... All pupils need to be given ample opportunity for discussion of a wide range of experiences encountered inside and outside school. (GB.DES, 1985b, para. 48)

## Learning from Others

One of the ways in which children learn is by interacting with others who are more experienced than they are. Bennett (1989), referring to the work of Bruner and Vygotsky, explains that it is through interactions with 'more knowledgeable others' that a child's learning potential is often realized. These 'others' may be adults or children.

Curtis (1986) notes that there is evidence to show that children often make effective teachers because there are occasions when they can explain quite complicated issues to their peers more satisfactorily than an adult can. Instances of this were seen in the present study, and while we would not recommend that four year olds be put in mixed-age classes, we have to say that it was in classes with more than one year-group that these instances were particularly noticeable. For example:

❧ In a small rural school with a class of four to seven year olds, the older children helped the youngest ones by 'showing them the ropes', servicing their activities and making sure they observed the ground rules of the classroom.

❧ In a class of four and five year olds, the second-years shepherded the first-years around the school, accompanied them to distant toilets and helped them with their classroom activities.

Curtis (1986) cites evidence to show that the most sustained and productive conversations occur when children work together in pairs, and that exchanges last longer in child–child dialogue than in conversations between adults and children. In the present study, teachers reported that young children for whom English was not their first language often talked with each other in their own tongue during activities, but tended to fall silent when an adult approached. To encourage conversation the staff deliberately created opportunities when the children could play together without adult intervention.

Almost all the activities available in the classes observed were potential sources of child–child talk. For example, in large group discussions children were encouraged to tell the others about their experiences and the things they had made or brought into school. In small group activities children were heard discussing the colours they were going to choose, the size of the paper they needed, which way up it should go, why the water in the water tray was bubbly, how they should control the water that was overflowing, whether more water was needed in the wet sand tray... The list is endless.

Sylva *et al.* (1980) noted that some of the richest dialogue occurred in home corners or dens where an enclosed space had been created. However, young children do not talk *all* the time. Pollard (1989) was surprised to find that the four year olds in her study were silent for half of the observed time, interacting with neither peers nor adults.

## The Adult's Role

Educationists suggest that the adult's role in the simultaneous development of language and activity should include the following.

### Providing a suitable environment
Opportunities to talk and listen to others in groups promotes what HMI (GB.DES, 1985b) call 'a context of shared experience' between adults and children. A crucial factor in this context is the atmosphere of the classroom. Curtis (1986) explains that children are more likely to converse freely when the emphasis is on shared experiences with an adult, rather than an instructive approach that conveys the idea of the 'all-knowing' adult.

*Giving children something to talk about*
Simply to provide interesting material in a relaxed environment is not enough. For young children, talk needs to be an accompaniment to real experiences within and beyond the classroom.

*Helping children to express themselves in words*
Adults should provide children with good models in the use of language. Adults should also help children to articulate their discoveries and phrase questions.

*Listening to what children are saying*
Listening carefully to what children are saying helps adults to be aware of the way in which the child's thinking is proceeding. This in turn enables adults to evaluate the activity and their own aims for the child. It also enables them to pick up on any misunderstandings that could lead to persistent errors in later learning. In mathematics, for example, Metz (1987) explains that fundamental mistakes can occur through misunderstandings that have a linguistic origin.

*Knowing when to support and extend*
Research (Sylva et al., 1980) indicates that children are more likely to stay at an activity and develop it when there is an adult nearby who supports what the child is doing. If, in addition, adults understand what children are trying to do, they are more likely to offer opportunities to consolidate and extend their learning.

Adults in the present study used all kinds of activities to promote dialogue and discussion with the children. A selection of the many instances we noted give a flavour of the possibilities: planning activities with the sand and water; following up a theatre visit by making a photo album about it; discussing a dandelion seed brought by a child; exploring ideas for making masks. Other examples may be found throughout Chapter 5. A particularly detailed one is given on pp. 92–3. Of course, not all examples of adult–child dialogue in activities are initiated by adults. An example of child-initiated discussion is given on p. 96.


## Conclusion

To encourage the all-round development of the child, the curriculum for four year olds should be broad and balanced. Within this breadth and balance there should be links with the main elements of the National Curriculum to promote continuity and progression. Subject areas should be integrated, offering a multi-disciplinary range of activities. A balance should be provided between noise and quiet, movement and calm, novelty and familiarity and group or individual activity.

Activities should be carefully sited to allow children to make links between them, thus expanding their learning opportunities. Situations should be created that offer a challenge and can be extended by the children; use should be made of the environment beyond the classroom. The activities must have relevance and meaning for the child and be flexible enough to meet individual needs.

The combined development of language and activity is essential to learning and children must have opportunities to talk about what they are doing. It is especially important that sufficient trained adults are on hand to capitalize on the learning that can occur when children are engaged in this way.

# 5  Teaching Approach

Because four year olds are naturally curious and enthusiastic and deal in concrete experiences rather than abstractions, they learn best through an active 'play' approach that allows them to explore, investigate and make sense of the world.

This chapter considers the role of play in learning and the need for careful planning if such an approach is to be effective. Attention is paid to organizational aspects of timetabling and grouping that facilitate this approach. The discussion then focuses on the use of children's first-hand experiences as a medium for learning and teaching, in which the adult starts with what the child can do and intervenes where appropriate to take the child further.

At this age, children are beginning to take responsibility for themselves and they need opportunities for autonomy in their learning. The discussion turns to the balance between adult and child in initiating, choosing and controlling activities, and the chapter concludes by considering how this approach links with the requirements of the National Curriculum.


## Play

Professionals interviewed in the study stressed the importance of play in the education of four year olds. In this they are well supported by the work of 20th century psychologists such as Isaacs, Piaget, Bruner and Smilansky who, amongst others, agreed that play is the starting point for cognitive development in the young child.

The interviewees saw **play as an approach to teaching and learning**. Play was described as 'an experiential activity-based approach through which the child makes sense of the world'. It is 'the basis of all other activities': the whole range of curriculum activities can be subsumed by and embedded in play. LEA guidelines adopted a similar stance. Play was regarded as the natural way for young children to learn and was commonly described as 'the vehicle that provides access to the curriculum'.


### The Role of Play in Learning

Participants shared the view that play is perfectly compatible with the needs and characteristics of four year olds. It offers a multidisciplinary approach that stimulates exploration and discovery, and permits children to take risks and make 'mistakes'. It allows the children to be involved in organization and decision-making and provides opportunities for them to choose and discriminate, practise and consolidate, concentrate and persevere. Play facilitates the development of a range of skills and concepts, including oral language and early reading and number skills. It can help children to develop socially; it also allows them to express their feelings.

Other studies support and extend this list. For example, from their research on play and problem-solving with three to five year olds Sylva *et al.* (1976) concluded that play helps problem-solving, reduces the stress of anticipating success and failure and helps shift the emphasis of the task from product to process.

Furthermore, Royall (1989) suggests that play offers a multi-sensory approach that promotes a greater awareness and understanding of the environment and the people in it, and is therefore a particularly useful approach to learning for children with special needs, especially those with multiple handicaps.

What children do when they are playing is summarized by the Early Years Curriculum Group (1989) thus:

> Through play children practise and consolidate learning, play with ideas and develop what they know. In their play children also dare to take risks, negotiate, solve problems, initiate, anticipate, rearrange, restate, reflect and integrate, and consolidate their knowledge and understanding. (p. 2)

Some of the interviewees saw play as also having a compensatory role for some children because it offered them a freedom and contact with resources they may not have at home. Children are in some ways more restricted nowadays in the use of their environment because of threats to their safety. There may be very limited opportunities to play in the neighbourhood, the garden or even the home.

## Teaching Children How to Play

Teachers in the study said that some new entrants are so inhibited that they have to 'be taught how to play'. Children needing most encouragement to play were either 'clingy' children who lacked confidence or children from homes where the play materials traditionally associated with young children were not evident when staff visited them. Unconfident children were said to respond more positively when they had seen others enjoying the activities and had been coaxed into trying them out for themselves. Teachers reported that at the beginning of the year some children preferred the 'quieter' activities and avoided imaginative play, construction toys and the messier activities like finger-painting and dough. They needed to be shown how to use the materials and encouraged to be more venturesome.

Some children had been accustomed to playing alone and needed to be carefully drawn into play with others. For example,

> a father expected his four year old daughter to do 'homework' each morning before going to school. This consisted of reading, writing and doing sums on lined paper. Her teacher said that the child had to be 'weaned away' from concentrating solely on pencil and paper activities in school and deliberately encouraged to paint, make models and play with the sand and water.

## Work and Play

Despite the widely acknowledged importance of play in children's learning, its use in the classroom does not appear to be practised as much as it is preached. Much of the problem seems to lie in the fact that it is often attributed too narrow a definition: 'play' is defined as the opposite to 'work'.

Professionals interviewed in the study said that some teachers hold play in low esteem and expect children to complete their 'work' first. Research supports this view. For example, Cleave et al. (1982) noted that, while the emphasis in nurseries was on play, primary schools made an explicit distinction between play and work: children were allowed to play in the classroom as a reward for finishing their 'work' – the more formal tasks of literacy and numeracy. In the schools visited by Bennett and Kell (1989) play was observed to be 'very limited and very limiting', often acting merely as a 'time-filler'. This was attributed in part to teachers' low expectations of play and their role in it.

A serious problem here is that young children often seem to accept and even like the notion of work, and can appear to be settling down to formal tasks without too much difficulty. Sestini (1987) warns that, although her study showed that four year olds in school adjusted readily to the expectations made of them, it does not follow that these expectations were appropriate. She calls on teachers to examine their own assumptions about play and to question their role in developing children's skills and concepts.

In the present study, staff in schools trying to provide appropriately for four year olds defined play as an all-pervasive approach to learning. They said that children 'need to play'; 'it's the way they learn'; 'a style of learning'; 'I've never thought of it in terms of play versus work'; 'The children enjoy what they are doing without realizing they are learning. Play *is* their work'. In a few schools the word 'play' was applied only to playtime in the playground. All classroom activities were referred to as 'work' in order to give them equal status. For example, children were said to be 'working with the bricks', 'working in the sand' and so on.

However, conscious attempts on the part of adults to avoid the work/play dichotomy do not necessarily prevent the children from making such a distinction. Children in the study had various ideas about what constitutes work and play. Sometimes these were associated with age or with the opportunity to choose activities. For example, a four year old in an early years unit volunteered the following: 'This is the playing class. The other classes are working classes. When you go in there you can choose in the afternoon and not have to do any work. If you have your work done in the morning you can choose all the afternoon.' Other children associated work with producing something or with sitting still. For example, one four year old said 'Work is busy work – when you make something.' Using a kit with hammer and nails he had made a picture of a hang-glider. He regarded this as working because he had 'made something'. A girl making a picture said she too was working, but the children dressing-up and walking about were playing 'because they're walking about. I can't walk about so I'm not playing'.

In another school, the following conversation took place between a group of children and the researcher. (The researcher's questions are in brackets.)

We've made a fire engine with Lego and now we're going to make a flying car.
[Have you been doing this all the morning?]
No, we did our work first.
[What was that?]
Well, we had to do our writing and finish our books and get ready for our mums coming.
[Are you working at the moment?]
No, we're playing Lego.
[What do you have to do to play rather than work?]
Well you need toys to play, like sand, that's play. And the cars are play and things like that.
[Do your teachers come and play?]
No, teachers don't play, they just watch and help you with what you're doing with work.

It is interesting to consider how children acquire these notions of work and play. Do they learn them from older children, from their parents, from the staff at school or from the world at large?

## The Status of Play

Adults who consciously try to avoid distinguishing work and play may nevertheless give signals that they regard some activities as having higher status than others. They may give praise or material rewards like gold stars, smiley faces and 'Well done' stickers for certain achievements. The value they set on an activity may also be signalled through non-verbal clues such as where they direct their attention, spend most of their time or get most involved.

Observational studies of four year olds in infant classes (Sestini, 1987; Stevenson, 1987; Sharp, 1988) showed that teachers tended to concentrate their attention on reading, writing and mathematical activities and spend relatively little time with other activities such as sand, water and imaginative play. When a range of activities are in progress some teachers, especially those without ancillary help, use the time to hear children read and check writing and number work. To make the play approach successful, it is essential that there are sufficient adult helpers for teachers to be able to involve themselves in all aspects of the play.

Teachers themselves told us that a problem with play is that it often has no tangible end-product and this makes it difficult to demonstrate children's progress. They may therefore unconsciously set more value on activities such as reading and writing and be more dismissive of activities in the home corner or sand tray.

In the best examples of more appropriate practice, teachers made deliberate attempts to accord all types of activity equal status. They used various strategies, for example:

✿  in one reception unit teachers made a point of spending time in areas like the 'theme' corner (in this case a 'space station') because they felt that this 'gave value to the activity, especially in the early stages';

✿  in another school, both the teacher and the nursery nurse involved themselves in all types of activity. The nursery nurse took responsibility for two or three activities per session and spent most of her time with these. The teacher, however, spent a short while at each activity and at the same time maintained a general overview of all the activities in progress.

Even with the best of intentions, behaviour does not always match up to expressed beliefs. Also, children and adults are likely to have different perceptions about what is going on. The discrepancies between what people say, what they do and what others make of it all are illustrated in the following example:

The reception unit team expressed the belief that it was important to 'attach value to all the activities, including sand and water play, so that children realize that other activities are as important as language and number'.

The teacher said that she tried to give value to all the activities and would never say 'You can play when you've finished your work'. She thought children acquired their ideas of work and play from their parents.

Parents told the researcher that they liked the approach used in this class. They felt that 'work happens alongside play'. The children 'start learning and reading much earlier and it's much more fun'.

On the days of observation in the reception unit, the teacher spent most of her time with language and number, and the nursery nurse with art and craft activities.

A four year old in the unit explained that what he was doing was definitely not playing because 'Miss H. told me to do this'. He added 'When you choose, that's playing'.

## Play Throughout the School

Many professionals held the view that play should not be the prerogative of the youngest pupils but should be 'a continuous process' throughout the school. They pointed out that some schools already have a play coordinator on the staff and recommended that every infant school or department should have one.

The success of play as an all-school approach especially demands the cooperation of the staff and the support of the parents and governors. This is by no means easy to achieve. Even the most enlightened schools clearly had a long way to go in this respect. For example:

a chair of governors said that play should be used throughout the school because 'it is an important part of the child's world'. However, he went on to explain that it is 'important to do the basics first' because a whole day away from home can be long and tiring for young children. This means that if they play in the afternoon and fall asleep 'they're not missing anything academically'.

The adoption of play as an approach throughout the school requires that its value must be communicated to all concerned; it must also be fully understood and accepted by everyone involved.

## Communicating the Value of Play

Atkin (1981) argues that the dilemma facing teachers is that because they are expensive, salaried and trained people, they feel that they must show themselves to be doing more than merely playing with the children. She suggests that play will always be less than it could or should be because it takes place in buildings called 'schools', which are staffed by 'teachers' whose ultimate aim is to prepare children for 'work'.

Professionals interviewed in the study pointed out that a problem for teachers is that the play approach can look chaotic to the uninitiated onlooker. Teachers may worry about appearances and find it difficult to explain or justify this approach to critics. Furthermore, schools tend to be oriented towards a more sedentary day, especially for older children, and this creates difficulties for teachers who are conscious that the noisy activity of their younger pupils is disturbing other classes. Ultimately, teachers need to have confidence in what they are doing so that they can explain to others what is going on.

The schools used various strategies to explain appropriate practice to parents, governors, colleagues and visitors. These included written explanations in the form of booklets and posters around the classroom explaining the various activities; 'open evenings' with talks, videos, photographs, demonstrations and opportunities for parents to try out activities provided for four year olds; and arrangements for parents to spend time in the classroom either informally or at specific times.

Some of the interviewees suggested that because of its associations with leisure and trivial pursuits the word 'play' should be replaced by a phrase such as 'activity-based learning' or 'contextualized learning'. Others contended that 'play' was important in the philosophy of early years education and that its true meaning should be communicated and explained.

## Types of Play

In describing play, the professionals interviewed distinguished various types of play in different ways. Some defined play in terms of activities such as 'imaginative', 'constructional' and 'domestic' play. Others described play according to whether an activity was undertaken alone or with other children, referring to 'solitary', 'parallel', 'associative' and 'cooperative' play. A few called for a balance between 'structured' and 'unstructured' play.

Manning and Sharp (1977) argue that 'if play in the infant school is to promote children's learning, it must be structured'. They explain that by structure they do not mean a rigid set of rules and conditions, but that play can only be 'a successful learning situation when the teacher builds on the child's spontaneous play and takes her cues from the children'. This requires careful observation and sensitive adult involvement. These ideas were explored by Sylva *et al.* (1980) who found that the more structured activities were associated with play that was 'challenging'. By studying children aged 3½ to 5½, they also found that the younger ones were more likely to engage in challenging play when interacting in pairs, whereas the older ones engaged more in challenging play when interacting with adults.

Sestini (1987) corroborated these findings but warned that while pre-structured activities may facilitate concentration and be cognitively complex, 'they may also inhibit some of the characteristics of learning we aim to encourage, e.g. creativity, divergent thinking and imagination'. It is therefore important that there is a balance between children's spontaneity and adult guidance so that learning opportunities are maximized.

One primary school openly adopted what was called a 'structured play' philosophy throughout the school. The headteacher explained that they were 'creating an environment in which children can respond at a variety of levels and within which teachers are able to target learning opportunities. To make it work, this approach requires professional people who know what they are doing. Planning is vital'.

## Purposeful Play

Whatever the terms used to describe play, the professionals interviewed agreed that play should be purposeful. The LEA guidelines gathered express a similar view and stress that if play is to become more than just an occupational activity, the teachers's role is crucial. This means that although the child may be playing freely and spontaneously, the teacher must be aware of the potential of the activities and have clear aims and intentions for the children's learning. Play requires very careful planning.

# Planning

### Aims and Intentions

**An appropriate teaching approach requires that the adult has clear aims and intentions, both for the activity and for the child.** It is particularly important to be clear about aims for young children in school because, as shown in the preceding section, it is all too easy for 'play' to be misconstrued as trivial and purposeless.

## The Need for Better Planning

On the basis of their recent visits to schools, HMI stressed the need for better planning for four year olds in school. HM Senior Chief Inspector in his annual report (GB.DES, 1990d) noted the contrast between 'the purposeful activities carried out in the effective nursery classes' and the 'narrower, less demanding provision made for four year olds in some primary schools'. More specifically, the HMI survey (GB,DES, 1989c) found that:

> in the majority of primary classes with four year olds there was little evidence of teachers' systematic planning for the introduction and development of knowledge, concepts and skills through investigation, imaginative play, the use of natural materials or construction. The activities available frequently lacked an identifiable aim or purpose. (para. 23)

A very real difficulty is that what teachers intend to teach is not necessarily the same as what children 'learn'. One reason for this is that the teachers' intentions are not always made clear to the child. Bennett (1989) found that although the teachers in his study generally knew what they wanted to do and planned accordingly, activities were often inappropriately presented or explained and teachers thus failed to communicate their intentions to the children. For example, in an activity designed to encourage shape recognition children were asked if they would like to colour in some circles. From observations and talks with the children, Bennett concluded that no recognition of shapes had taken place or was deemed to be necessary because the task had been defined as 'colouring-in'.

## Levels of Planning

Planning for the younger pupils may occur at school and class level and involve aims and intentions for the activities and for the children. Adults' aims and intentions need to be clear at all stages and should link with each other. However, staff tend to represent their plans on paper in highly individualized ways making grids, tables, flow-charts, lists and descriptions of varying complexity to suit their own requirements. Because of the idiosyncratic nature of these plans, the examples given below are intended to aid description rather than represent models of good practice.

### At school level
Schools planned the curriculum in terms of both subject areas and cross-curricular themes. Sometimes these were subsumed by an over-

arching aim, such as language development, in which case planning at all levels was designed to maximize opportunities for children to develop their language ability. For example:

An urban infant school in which very few children spoke English as their first language. Seven home languages and a number of dialects were spoken, and many of the children also began learning Arabic at the mosque from the age of five. While the school favoured a multicultural approach and a respect for each other's family background and customs, there was an emphasis on developing fluency in English throughout the curriculum. The interior of the school was rich in colour, stimulus and imaginative ideas. Activities revolved around themes. In the reception class, which had admitted 32 four year olds from all seven language groups, each theme formed the basis for a vocabulary of English words, which were used on labels around the room, on mobiles hanging from the ceiling and on packs of materials made by the team. Every opportunity was taken to make use of this vocabulary so that the children became well acquainted with it. Some activities were designed to stimulate the need to record in writing. The teacher stressed that it was paramount that children had a reason to write so that their writing was purposeful. By the summer term, some of these children were writing English in sentences.

Sometimes themes or topics were planned throughout the school with each class developing the details according to its own interests and abilities. For example:

In one school the current theme was 'Shapes' and each year group worked on this theme at an appropriate level. In the reception class a 'Shapes Corner' was set up in which items of various shapes were collected. Wall friezes and table displays took up the theme, and the team made activity cards and games that involved the recognition and use of shapes. At the same time, the class was also developing the theme of 'Transport – Things that Go' and the two themes were linked: the tractor had 'round' wheels, the hot-air balloon was a 'sphere', the space rocket was a 'cylinder' and so on.

School themes were usually initiated by the headteacher or collaboratively by the head, staff and children. Work on the theme was often displayed in shared areas such as halls, foyers and corridors, and was believed to 'help integrate children of all ages and give them an understanding of what they each contribute' (see Chapter 11).

Some themes were designed with an emphasis on specific curricular areas. For example, teachers used themes like 'Our Village' to focus on the human and social area, 'Movement' on technological aspects and 'Our Senses' on scientific learning and experience. All of these could of course be developed into cross-curricular themes.

Because children of this age do not perceive separate subject areas, cross-curricular themes were used by some teachers to encompass all or most areas of the curriculum. For example, in one class a school theme on 'Houses and Homes' provided almost limitless scope for all kinds of activity: a tour of the neighbourhood to study the variety of houses and gardens stimulated oral discussion and writing (language and literacy), map-making (mathematical), model-making (aesthetic, creative and technical), deciding how to illuminate the models (scientific) and so on.

### At class level

Teachers in the study planned the work of their class to fit in with the overall school plan. As one teacher explained, 'I plan each day within a weekly plan which fits into my plan for the term and the whole-school plan'. In one school, the reception class theme 'Moving' was a sub-theme of a whole-school craft, design and technology (CDT) project. This theme permeated classroom displays and children's activities, and both the teacher and the children were involved in its planning and development:

> On the walls there were captioned pictures of body movements such as jumping, hopping and skipping, and a cut-away chart of a child's body muscles. A table display invited children to investigate the movement of various objects such as a gyroscope, a yo-yo and the bubble in a spirit level. Painting activities explored ways of making paint move across paper, for example by blowing it with a straw, floating it as oil paint on water and pressing paper on it to take prints.

In another school the teacher planned the key features or 'trigger points' of the theme 'Our Environment'. The trigger points took the form of visits to places like the local church, a farm and a zoo. She drew up a plan linking the theme with various curriculum areas such as maths, language, science and religious education. Details would be worked out with ancillary helpers and children as the theme and interests developed. Alternatively, themes were sometimes initiated by children.

Although the development of a theme is often a series of spontaneous responses to events and stimuli as they occur, it does not have to be haphazard and unplanned. Teachers planned thematic work carefully and at the same time flexibly. Some themes lasted only a few days; others were developed over several weeks or terms. Some teachers changed their themes regularly, such as every term or half-term; others allowed the theme to continue for as long as the children were interested.

The most detailed planning was seen in one school where a reception class teacher devised a half-termly flow-chart based on a theme agreed with the rest of her team. The members of the team (a nursery nurse, a support teacher and a 'floating' teacher) then made packs of materials to fit in with the theme. The flow-chart took account of various aspects of children's development such as linguistic, mathematical and motor development. Each week the class teacher wrote a forecast of activities covering all curriculum areas and made notes on each child's progress. Forecasts were quite common and if adhered to or amended where necessary, could act as both a plan and a record of content covered.

### At activity level

All adults working in the classroom need to be clear about the purpose of the activities with which they are involved.

The adult's intentions for the activity may be general or specific. One reception teacher said that the main purpose of the activities was enjoyment: she wanted children to 'enjoy the activities so that they got the most out of them'. With regard to reading, for example, she wanted children to 'enjoy and appreciate books as real books'.

A nursery nurse explained how she planned each of her activities in consultation with the teacher. She kept a 'planning book' of the topics, ideas and activities she hoped to cover each week. These were flexible because she 'tried to work in response to the children rather than impose a curriculum on them'.

### At child level

To maximize learning opportunities the purposes of an activity should be related to the needs of the child who is carrying it out. However, the HMI survey (GB.DES, 1989c) found that, where children are admitted early to school, this is not usually the case and the curriculum is not as well matched to their educational needs as it should be.

Planning tasks to match each child's needs is particularly difficult to achieve in mixed-age classes. In another survey (GB.DES, 1989b) HMI found that tasks were often least appropriate for the youngest children.

In the present study, teachers with mixed-age classes made a conscious effort to provide activities that could be used in different ways by different children. For example, in a class which spanned the entire infant age-range from four to seven, a similar writing task served to develop one child's understanding of language and another child's letter-forming skills.

Because of the considerable range in young children's abilities and development, differentiated tasks are still necessary in classes of a single year-group or less. For example, in one class of four year olds a sewing activity was used by one child to make a simple collage and by another to work an intricate design with a variety of stitches. Not only can the same activity serve a different purpose, but different activity areas can be used to serve a similar purpose. For example,

> in a class of four and five year olds, the teacher wanted the younger children to practise sorting things into relative sizes of 'big', 'middle-sized' and 'little'. She had found that although they could easily distinguish 'large' from 'small' or 'big' from 'little', they found it difficult to say that something was 'bigger than this but smaller than that'. After a short discussion with the teacher, the children were asked to choose an activity and begin it by sorting the available materials according to size. They could then go on and develop the activity in their own way. Several children went to the home area and set up the story of 'The Three Bears', sorting the beds, porridge bowls, spoons and chairs into the appropriate sets. Others selected model animals of various sizes and matched them to their 'footprints'. Tom, one of the youngest children, went to the construction area and chose some coloured bricks. He built walls and a roof. Then he carefully balanced some of the bricks on top saying, 'These are chimneys. This is little, this is middle-sized...'.

Mismatching the task to the individual can have serious consequences for the child, not least because a task that is unsuitable can result in the child being labelled a 'failure'. As Stevenson (1987) reports: 'Sometimes the match between child and activity went wrong, the challenge set was inappropriate and, as a consequence, I found children of four and a half...being pointed out as "slow" or "not very good"'. In order to match activities to individual needs, HMI note that: 'in the best circumstances, the teaching is informed by a careful assessment of the overall programme and the response of each child to the learning activities which are provided' (GB.DES, 1989b, para. 18).

## Who Does the Planning?

HMI (GB.DES, 1989b) recommend that, wherever possible, teachers should involve other adults who work in the classroom (nursery nurses, ancillary helpers and parents) in planning the activities. They explain that 'interdependence of the different adult roles favours joint planning' (para. 18).

In the present study, teachers who had the help of other adults in the classroom involved them to various degrees in the planning (also see Chapter 11). In the best examples the teacher, nursery nurse and regular helpers met as a team to plan and discuss activities and their responsibilities for them. In small schools, it was possible for all the staff, including the headteacher, to be involved in planning and discussing the younger children's activities. This sharing of expertise and ideas not only benefits the children but can also promote staff development.

Children are sometimes involved in planning their own activities. Some schools, especially those adopting the High Scope approach advocate that children should 'plan, do and review' their activities from an early age. The High Scope approach was developed in the USA (Schweinhart *et al.*, 1986) and in recent years has found a following in the UK. Based on Piaget's theory of child development, it identifies some 50 'key experiences' grouped under headings such as active learning, planning and evaluating, using language, representing experiences and ideas, classification, seriation, number concepts and spatial and temporal relationships. The daily schedule revolves around a 'plan-do-review' sequence and is broken down into routines including planning time (children plan with adults), work time (children carry out plans in activity areas) and group time (group discussion of work time).

Three of the schools studied adopted aspects of this approach, especially planning. During planning time, children discussed what they wanted to do and then recorded their plans in various ways. For example, in one class of four year olds the plan developed as follows. At first, the children took their name tag and hung it on a peg beside the picture that denoted the activity of their choice. Later in the year, they had a weekly planning sheet on which they linked the day of the week with a coloured line to the appropriate picture on the sheet (see Figure 5.1). Later still, some children were able to record their plans by writing a sentence about each activity (see Figure 5.2).

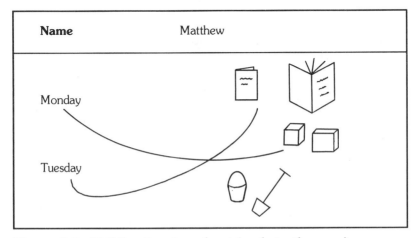

**Figure 5.1: Child's planning sheet (early in the year).**

| Name | Matthew |
|------|---------|

Monday    I plan to go to the construction area

Tuesday   I plan to go to the reading area

**Figure 5.2: Child's planning sheet (later in the year).**

## Organizing the Time

The organization of time should be sensitive to the needs of both the children and the adults working with them. Children need time to pursue activities at their own pace and to get involved in, develop and even complete an activity. **Time should be organized with the minimum interruption to children's activities. There should, however, be some overall pattern to the day** to help children feel secure and to give them a sense of time.

### Flexible Timetabling

Flexible timetabling was advocated both by professionals interviewed and in the LEA guidelines collected. Timetabled 'fixtures' like assembly, play, lunch and hall times should be avoided as they present difficulties for young children by interrupting their activities and overwhelming them with noise and large crowds (see Chapter 3). Segmenting the day into small, rigid compartments for specific activities and events is not regarded as appropriate for young children. The interviewees were adamant that four year olds should be in classes organized so that they were not constantly being interrupted either by timetable fixtures or by adult-directed activities.

Early years educationists (J. Joseph, P. Cooksey and M. Roberts (GB.DES, 1985c); Bennett, 1987; Weir, 1988; McCail, 1989) are united in their plea for young children to have time to follow their chosen activity at an individual pace. Research (Barrett, 1986) supports this view and recommends that children should have time to think, reflect, consolidate and master what they are learning so that they can apply concepts and ideas within their own interests.

Stevenson (1988) found that if children were allowed to spend long periods at a time on an activity, they did so. She pointed out that 'we know that at four it is "now" and "self" that are the most crucial factors in a child's development, and yet we interrupt their thoughts and problem-solving to divert them to another activity'. It was noted that, given the opportunity, some children were able to sustain interest in a self-chosen activity for an entire block, or even several blocks, of time. Here is an example of one of the youngest children in the class developing an activity throughout a day. The example is taken from the observer's notes.

It is July and Ben has been at school for nearly a year. He is not yet five years old.

During the morning Ben was busy with a set of plastic prehistoric animals. First he was by himself, matching the animals to their 'footprints' on a set of cards. When he had finished, he was joined by another boy who had been building with wooden bricks nearby. Together the two boys constructed a 'zoo' on the floor into which they put the animals. The teacher joined in the activity, and the discussion focused on how the animals might move about – walking, flying and so on. Eventually the discussion turned to an animal with flippers and the teacher asked if they knew of any other creatures with flippers. The boys found this difficult and the discussion was curtailed because it was time to get ready for lunch.

The 'zoo' was left on the floor and Ben returned to it at the start of the afternoon session. The teacher brought him some books in which he could search for pictures of animals with flippers. Eventually Ben found some seals and decided to make a book of his own. He fetched some paper (which had already been folded in half and left in a drawer for the children to use) and 'copied' some of the pictures into the book he had made. He also tried to copy from the model animals, pointing to an ichthyosaurus and saying 'It's got flippers'. Even though he found the models quite hard to draw, he persisted until he had filled his book with pictures and 'writing'. By the time he had finished, it was time to pack up for the end of the afternoon session.

Of course not all children of this age are able to maintain interest in an activity for such long periods, and consideration must be given as to whether the blocks of time allocated may be too long for some children, especially early in the school year. In one mixed-age class, for example, some of the four year olds who had been at school for almost a term were still showing signs of flagging towards the end of the morning session and resorted to sucking their fingers. While this

raises issues about the needs of the individual child and adult intervention (pp. 90–95), it also prompts questions about the overall pattern
of the day and the balance of the different types of activity within it.
These are discussed below (see pp. 78–80).

Flexible timetabling can be beneficial not only to the children but
also to the adults working with them. Adults need time to become involved with individuals and small groups and to observe and listen to
children's needs. The interviewees suggested that organizing periods
when children can maintain activities for themselves allows the adult
more time to become involved with individuals and small groups. It
also allows the adults time to observe children doing the activities so
that a cycle of planning, review and evaluation can be implemented
more effectively.

Thomas (1987) suggested that teachers of this age group need to
take time in which to listen to children. Flexible school timetabling,
with freedom from interruptions, can help the teacher who would
otherwise find it impossible, with so many children, to observe and
listen in order to ascertain needs and evaluate progress.

## Dividing up the Day

Professionals advocated that the day or session should be punctuated
with certain predictable routines. Children of this age quickly become
accustomed to the fact that at some stage there is a change of activity
or a narrowing of choice and that washing hands, for example, sig-
nifies the approach of lunchtime.

Organizing time into some kind of coherent pattern that has relevance for the child requires sensitive planning. In the schools studied,
the morning and afternoon sessions were broadly similar in pattern
and content. Time was organized into two blocks per session, each
session being divided by some kind of 'break'. The break took the
form of playtime or, where formal playtimes were avoided, a sub-
stitute for playtime such as time spent outdoors (or, if raining, in the
hall). The afternoon session was usually shorter than the morning session and some schools dispensed with the afternoon break.

In practice, the actual operation of the daily routine varied from
school to school and appeared to be influenced by the weekly timetable for the school hall, how often activities were tidied up and
packed away and how often the class was gathered together as a
whole.

### Hall times
Apart from corporate events like assembly, the weekly timetable
usually allowed the youngest classes to have additional regular use of
the school hall, or similar venue, for specific activities such as music, a

television programme, PE and so on. Sometimes these events took place in the company of other young classes, such as music with the nursery or television with the other reception classes.

### Tidying up and packing away

How often children were expected to tidy or pack away activities varied according to individual teachers' organizational preferences and the constraints imposed upon them. For example, some teachers had a packing-up time at the end of each session (all activities put away) and a tidying time in between (activities tidied on to tables or into areas ready for further use later); whereas others had a packing-up time during the afternoon, with a tidying time before lunch. In the former case, activities could be carried on into the second half of the morning; in the latter they could be carried over into the afternoon as well. In practice, some activities remained unchanged so that children could develop them, while new ones were introduced to provide stimulus and variety.

The need to pack away activities was sometimes dictated by events beyond the teacher's control. For example, in one school meals were served in the classrooms and all morning activities had to be cleared away so that tables could be laid for lunch. Children were usually warned when packing-up time was imminent, with the teacher announcing, for example: 'You have five minutes to packing-up time'.

### Whole-class times

Teachers differed in terms of how often they brought the children together as a whole class. Punctuating the day with regular whole-class events provided a change between periods of noisy activity and calm, and enabled the teacher to achieve a balance between individual or small group and large group activities.

Whole-class gatherings occurred regularly in all the classes and were used for activities such as registration, sharing news, planning and discussing, listening to stories, making music and so on. They occurred mostly at the beginning and end of sessions and sometimes before or after the break.

In several schools arrival time was staggered: the activities were set out in advance, children came into the classroom on arrival and chose an activity straightaway. However, the practice of completing the session in a similar way was not encountered, presumably because children were required to help clear up their activities before going home. The final packing-away time was invariably followed by a whole-class activity such as story-time, during which parents arrived to collect their children.

One infant school was trying out an innovation at the start of the afternoon session. The first ten minutes were given over to 'silent reading' throughout the school. The youngest children chose a book from the shelves and 'read' it quietly. All those present in the school, including all staff and visitors, were asked to respect this time and participate in it. This was considered to foster a positive attitude to reading. The quiet time provided a period of calm after the hurly-burly of the lunch-time play and encouraged a gentle start to the afternoon session.

## Grouping

In early years classrooms, groups tend to be of three main types:

✿   adult-led groups for story, discussion and similar activities;
✿   organized activity groups;
✿   spontaneous groups and pairs that occur naturally in the course of children's play.

Research in infant schools (Cleave *et al.*, 1982) found that most infant classes were also organized into groups for management purposes: children were grouped by ability, sex, age, friendship or simply allocated to a number of parallel groups. However, management groups were absent from all but one of the classes studied.

### Discussion Groups

The professionals interviewed agreed that whole-class times should be kept to a minimum. They advocated that **children should be brought together from time to time for stories and discussions**, but that **groups at this age should be small rather than consist of the whole class**. Such groups were perceived to have social, emotional and intellectual benefits for the children since they afford opportunities for talking and listening to others, getting to know each other, and expressing themselves with confidence.

Group discussion was seen to be used extensively as a means of extending children's learning in a variety of ways. Discussion times were used, for example, to share experiences, explore ideas and develop themes. They were also used to help children plan what they were going to do and review what children had done. They provided opportunities to develop oral language, extend vocabulary and stimulate imagination and role play.

In the following example, four year olds are sharing experiences and trying to solve a problem:

The class pet gerbil, Bubbles, had fallen ill. It was taken home by the teacher but failed to respond to treatment and died. The teacher explained this to the class, drawing on the children's experience of the death of another pet in the classroom. She explained that the gerbil had had a happy life and had lived to a great age for a gerbil. The problem now was that the surviving gerbil, Squeak, would be lonely and something needed to be done about it. After much discussion, the children suggested that the teacher should take Squeak home and introduce him to one of her own pet gerbils. The two gerbils could then be put in together and watched closely to see that they did not fight. If they got on well, both gerbils could be brought into school. The children would then provide them with new boxes and fresh straw.

## Organized Activity Groups

In most sessions there was at least one small group activity which was set up and led by an adult and in which all the children in the class were expected to participate at some time. Such groups were flexible with children coming and going as they completed the activity in question. At the start, the group might consist of children who had made that activity their first choice. Later, they were replaced by others who either joined the group from choice or were called to it by the adult. Depending on the activity, such groups might continue for a session, a day or even several days until every child had taken part.

Activities carried out in these organized, adult-led groups spanned all areas of the curriculum. Many examples occurred during the study, such as the following:

> The class teacher, who was the only adult present, worked with a group of three or four children while at the same time keeping an eye on the rest of the class who were engaged in free choice of activities. Each child selected a pebble and decorated it by choosing colours from the range of paints set out on the table. The teacher discussed with them which size brush would be suitable and how they might mix the colours to produce new ones. When they had finished, the children put their pebbles to dry and chose another activity. Other children asked to join the group or were called by the teacher.

## Spontaneous Groups and Pairs

The interviewees agreed that **frequent opportunities should be provided for children to collaborate in spontaneous groups and pairs**. Whether groups are organized or spontaneous, there is no doubt that they can provide a social context, which is all-important in children's learning (Vygotsky, 1978; Clark *et al.*, 1986; Bruce, 1987; GB.DES, 1989b). Small groups in particular can provide opportunities for children to develop a sense of self and self-esteem, to cooperate and share with others, to negotiate shared meanings and to move beyond their own level of competence.

There is ample research evidence, especially from the USA, to demonstrate the potential of cooperative group activity for enhancing young children's learning. Tudge and Caruso (1988), for example, explain that 'co-operation involves children in the active exchange of ideas rather than passive learning'.

In their study of classes with four year olds, Bennett and Kell (1989) found that although 60 per cent of activities were carried out in the context of small groups, the activities themselves were 'almost wholly individually based' and rarely called for any real co-operative group effort. Citing the work of Galton and Tizard, the authors concluded that although collaborative endeavour is known to be beneficial 'there is virtually no real co-operative groupwork happening in British classrooms'.

However, there are signs that the situation may not be as pessimistic as it sounds and may be improving. One outcome of the in-service initiatives followed up in the present study was that teachers had made conscious efforts to provide more small group activities in their classes. Furthermore, observations in the schools selected for study showed that frequent opportunities occurred for collaboration in spontaneous groups and pairs. Where children were accustomed to collaborative activity there were obvious additional benefits for class teachers, especially those working unaided, because it enabled them to use their time and energies more effectively.

Almost all the activity areas can provide opportunities for collaboration. In the present study spontaneous collaboration was especially noticeable when children were using large apparatus, sand, water, home and other theme corners, or were engaged in making models or in exploring novel materials.

It was also noticed that real collaboration between children seemed to occur most often in groups of two and three. This accords with Sylva *et al.* (1980) who observed that initially three and four year olds found it difficult to play in groups of more than two when involved in imaginative play unless there was adult support. On the other hand, we observed that when children had been at school for nearly a year instances of group play involving eight or ten children sometimes occurred (though availability of space would also be a factor here).

The following examples give an idea of the kind of collaborative activity seen during the study.

### Example 1

In the first example, the youngest four year old in the class (Paul) works on a model with a five year old (Mark).

*Mark* (offering Paul the Lego helicopter he has made): Do you want to play with this?
*Paul*: Yes. (Studies the model) Where does the man sit?
*Mark*: No man sits in it.
*Paul*: Why?
*Mark*: Because it's got controls.

Paul examines the helicopter and tries out the rotor blades. Together the two boys continue working on the model to extend it. An hour and a half later they are still busy and the helicopter, which has become much more complicated, has acquired soldiers with parachutes and swords. Paul explains the model to an onlooker: this man is poised on the edge of the helicopter in a backward position ready to jump; two more men have parachutes on their backs. Paul also points out the two large rotor blades (which he calls propellers) and the smaller one at the back that guides the helicopter.

*Example 2*
In this example, the children are in their third term at school and a group of eight collaborate in developing an elaborate sequence of imaginary play.

Using the large blocks, the home area and the shoe-shop corner, they play together, discussing where they have been and where they are going. Two children prepare tea, two more tidy up the 'dining room' and the rest do the dusting. They eat a hurried meal and return to the shoe-shop to change their shoes. Throughout this activity there appear to be well-established 'rules' so that each member of the group knows what is expected of them. Organizing and developing the activity involves them in constant talking during which they use various mathematical concepts: 'bigger than mine', 'smaller than yours', 'this pair', 'which lid fits', 'how many have you got', 'have I got enough' and so on.

All the activities described in the two examples above were initiated, organized and directed by the children involved. An essential constituent of this kind of collaboration is that children must have sufficient time to allow for planning, negotiating, developing and extending the activity, creating rules and solving the problems they encounter.

## Individual Activities

It is quite common during activities time in nursery and infant classes to see some children interacting in groups and pairs while others operate independently. Most of the activities offer children opportunities to work individually if they wish to do so, either in solitary (alone at the activity) or in parallel (alongside others but not interacting with them) play.

The areas in which four year olds were particularly noticed to pursue independent activities were: writing, drawing and colouring, painting, and some other art and craft activities; number and language games (especially those requiring matching and sorting), and table top activities such as puzzles and picture or pattern-making sets; activities with sand, water, clay, plasticine and other malleable substances; and wheeled toys.

Many of these also offered opportunities for paired and group activity, but children of this age clearly welcome the flexibility afforded by the activities to work together or alone as they wish.

## First-hand Experiences

The professionals interviewed stressed that because children of this age deal in the concrete rather than the abstract, **an appropriate teaching approach is one that places an emphasis on active first-hand experiences**. Four year olds need lots of opportunities to explore the materials, experiment, investigate and try things out for themselves. They also need opportunities to practise, consolidate and extend their understanding through what Weir (1988) calls 'opportunities to play back, play through, re-enact, create and re-create these experiences'.

The emphasis on first-hand experiences is based on the knowledge that young children are naturally curious and questioning. However, as Curtis (1986) reminds us, individuals vary and there may be considerable differences in their exploratory behaviour and their reaction to new stimuli. Some children need encouragement to be more open to novelty and it is important that the classroom environment is as relaxed as possible so that curiosity is not inhibited.

Here is an example of two four year olds exploring the properties of sand, and building on their discoveries:

> Sophie and Natalie were playing with the dry sand in the sand tray. They soon decided that they needed wet sand in order to make a model of a story they had been read. They carried water from the sink in a dish and added it to the sand, creating 'ponds' and 'rivers'. They fetched small-world figures of people and animals and carefully placed them in the model. They then used the scene to describe the story to the other children who had come to watch.
>
> When the two girls were observed a week later, they re-created a similar situation in the sand-tray by again adding water from the sink. This time, however, they discovered that they could make waves with the water and they made up their own story, explaining

to onlookers that 'this is the beach and the sea comes up and makes it all wet'.

## Making Mistakes

Making mistakes is part of the learning process and children should have the freedom to make errors. Professionals were adamant that **children should have opportunities for trial-and-error**. Schools are places where children can very quickly learn to succeed or fail, and studies (such as Cleave *et al.*, 1982) have shown how easy it is for new entrants to learn failure. In many instances of problem-solving there is no right or wrong answer, and it is important that the child feels confident to 'have a go'.

Many opportunities for trial-and-error were observed during children's activities. For example, tall edifices were constructed out of bricks balanced one on another until they toppled over; magnets were tried out on the various materials around the room, clinging to some things and not to others; ramps and bridges were constructed which collapsed under the weight of toy vehicles and had to be rebuilt. In the following example, a child's 'mistake' at the water tray led to a more positive learning experience:

> The water was bubbly and coloured red. Children could select their own utensils from the collection nearby. Jamal, one of the youngest children, took a jug and drank some of the water. He soon discovered he didn't like the taste. He went to the sink and drank some water from the tap. He then tried to persuade his companions to taste the water in the tray. They didn't like it either, but after some spluttering they realized they could also blow bubbles with the water. They fetched some more utensils – funnels, pipes and tubing – and discovered that the larger tubes made the biggest bubbles.

## Using Observation and Written Language

Interviewees advocated that **four year olds should be encouraged to look and observe**. School and class displays on walls and tables are particularly useful in this respect because they can stimulate children's powers of observation. At the same time such displays can include words and phrases to familiarize children with written language and give them occasion to make use of it.

In the following example, an exercise in experimenting and investigating led to a display that encouraged the children to examine and read about the results.

The children had conducted an experiment to see which sticking agents were most suitable for junk-modelling. They had constructed junk models, which were held together by different agents: blue glue, white glue, lumpy glue, masking tape, connecting straws, Sellotape and so on. The agents were then assessed for their strength and durability. After considerable discussion, the models were displayed on a table. Children's statements about their findings were written on cards by the teacher and incorporated into the display. For example: 'Gareth: we tested the boxes to see which stuck best'; 'Andrew: the white glue sticks best'.

Children can also be encouraged to use their powers of observation in the everyday world around them. For example:

A class working on the theme 'Our Homes' went for a walk around the neighbourhood to look at the variety of houses. General features were observed such as whether houses were old or new, terraced or detached, single or multi-storey. Details were studied such as variations in type and colour of building materials, and the shapes of windows and doors, roofs and chimney pots. Using the teacher's camera mounted on a tripod, children were able to take photographs of their own houses.

Given the opportunity, four year olds demonstrate that they are capable of keen observation of detail. For example:

Some children collected caterpillars in the school garden and put them in a home-made vivarium in the classroom. The caterpillars were fed on nettles. After several days of observation and discussion, the vivarium was set out on a table with magnifying glasses, plain paper and black felt-tip pens. Children could study the caterpillars and draw them if they wished. Some of their drawings showed very fine attention to detail. Nettles, for instance, were drawn with veined serrated leaves and fine hairs on the stalk.

These activities were preceded by much group discussion with the teacher and opportunities to study the subject over a period of several days. Also, the drawing materials were deliberately limited (although varied over time) so that children were free to concentrate on their observations rather than on the selection of colours and media. The teacher explained that 'we do a lot of observational work, in fact observation is encouraged right through the school'.

A particular emphasis on the combined development of observation and the use of the written word was noted in schools where children were believed to be entering the reception class with 'impoverished' language skills, or where there was a high proportion of children for whom English was not their first language (for an example see p. 71).

## Process Rather than Product

The professionals interviewed pointed out that an approach based on first-hand experiences focuses on 'doing' rather than 'producing' things. They recommended that **the emphasis should be on the processes rather than the products of learning.**

An important feature of children's learning at this age is that they need a variety of opportunities to acquire and practise similar skills and concepts. As one teacher explained, 'You have to look for lots of different ways of doing the same thing. The computer games are very popular. At the moment they are doing a matching activity. Some of these children wouldn't sit down at a table to do an activity with matching cards (although plenty of these are available), but the technology appeals to them. It's another way of teaching the same thing.'

Teachers often provided activities in which more importance was attached to the processes involved than to the finished products. For example, in a construction activity the emphasis was on the process of building rather than on what was being made: 'Does this brick fit here?', 'How can I make this slope?', 'Which barrel rolls down the slope fastest?'

Of course, placing an emphasis on process rather than product does not mean that children should always be discouraged from completing things or that they should be denied the satisfaction of producing a finished article. In the following example, both process *and* product are emphasized:

> The children were making cards to take home for Mothering Sunday. The focus was on using scissors, selecting from a variety of materials, sticking them on the card and talking about what they were doing and why they were doing it. The children were offered a wide choice of materials and were free to explore them to see what would happen. It was of less importance that some of the cards were so overloaded that it was impossible to make them stand up!

Parents are usually pleased to receive the products of what their children have been doing at school. Those interviewed expressed general satisfaction with 'the way they do things' at school and referred to the things their child had brought home: models, cooking, pictures, writing and books to read together. Most of the parents said their child talked a lot about what they had done at school, although inevitably there were one or two whose children rarely mentioned school.

**Avoiding Commercial Schemes**

The interviewees recommended that **commercial schemes of work should not be used with four year olds**, although some pointed out that if individual children were ready to move on to 'more formal skills' they should be allowed to do so.

The teachers observed were broadly in agreement that commercial schemes were inappropriate for young children. As one teacher explained, 'You've got to be able to draw the curriculum out of children's activities and experiences. It's the way children think. It's got to link with their real life. Our schemes are all home-made. This means that we must know exactly what we are doing. It's all planned and we can support and argue for what we are doing.'

Fears were expressed that some reception teachers would turn to commercial schemes to assist with the National Curriculum, especially in science, which was an area in which some infant teachers told us they had less confidence. The use of commercial schemes may also have effects that are inappropriate in early years classrooms. An evaluation study carried out by one LEA (Pollard, 1989) found that where there was an emphasis on commercially produced work schemes, teachers tended to spend a lot of time on 'task-related organization' like giving out books, marking and explaining to children what they had to do because the children were unable to read or understand the instructions for themselves.

Some schools adopted commercial schemes with the older children but avoided their use with the youngest classes, at least for the first term or two. Many instances were seen of hand-made materials being used instead of commercial equivalents (see also Chapter 8). It was clear that these teachers and their teams were prepared to devote a great deal of their own time in an attempt to ensure that their young pupils were more appropriately and adequately provided for.

# Starting from where the Child Is

The professionals interviewed agreed that **an appropriate approach with four year olds is one that 'starts from where the child is'**. This view is well supported in recent literature and constitutes one of the ten common principles for early childhood education listed by Bruce (1987), which states that 'what children can do (rather than what they cannot do) is the starting point in the child's education' (p. 45). Bruce argues that, in acquiring knowledge, each stage depends on what has gone before and that it is 'the logical and hierarchical sequences which form a network which makes up the whole area of knowledge' (p. 65). Knowledge in turn builds confidence and helps children to organize and control their learning. Indeed it is this very growth in confidence and competence, rather than the actual content of the curriculum, which is crucial to a developmental approach to learning (Blenkin and Kelly, 1987).

However, children come into school with different levels of confidence and competence, and teachers have to take account of this range of needs when they plan the curriculum for young children to ensure that the work is suitably differentiated.

## Different Levels of Competence

Many examples were seen where children were able to proceed at their own individual level of competence. For example:

✿ choosing a range of library books to take home to look at with parents and siblings;

✿ using number games boards with different sets of cards to suit a range of ability, from simple counting to add and subtract and so on;

✿ plain paper made available for children to write freely, whether in 'emergent' scrawl or complete sentences. Examples of children's efforts at all stages of development were included in wall and table displays.

To work successfully, this approach requires that the teacher actually *knows* where the child 'is' and what the child can do. This in turn requires professional expertise, careful observation and record-keeping, and a knowledge of the child's pre-school experience so that these can be built on (see also Chapter 3 and Chapter 6). This is not easy, especially for teachers with large classes and no trained help. Furthermore, teachers need not only to *know* children's levels of competence but also to be adept at switching quickly from one child's level to another. For example, a reception teacher was working with four year olds at a number-and-shapes activity and addressed each child differently. Notice the more complex questions to the second child:

*Teacher* (to first child): What shape is it?
*Child*: Triangle
*Teacher*: Yes. And how many triangles are there?
*Child* (counting): Nine
*Teacher*: Which is the biggest set of triangles?
(Child points.)
*Teacher*: Good boy.
(The teacher notes this on the child's record and turns her attention to another child in the group who is working at a more advanced level.)

*Teacher*: (to second child): How many more cubes has this set than that set?
*Child*: (after a pause): One
*Teacher*: And how many more circles has this set than that set?
*Child*: Three.
*Teacher*: Well done.

### Different Levels of Confidence

Professionals working with this age group emphasized that activities should be sufficiently stimulating to take the child further without causing stress. This requires that the teacher is sensitive not only to the children's individual experiences but also to their levels of confidence. They therefore need to know the children well. For example:

a group of children was enacting the story of *The Three Bears*. The teacher wanted to encourage the less assertive members of the group to overcome their shyness and participate. However, one or two of the children did not have the confidence to do this. The teacher, sensing their discomfort, saved their faces by smiling and saying 'Never mind, perhaps you will have a turn another day'.

## Intervening in Children's Activities

Concentrating on what children *can* do does not mean emphasizing only that which they can do unaided. The professionals interviewed stressed that **a suitable teaching approach allows for sensitive intervention in the child's activities** in order to develop skills and concepts as and when appropriate. They support the view of Bruce (1987) who argues that matching, supporting and then extending children's activities is 'the key' to good teaching.

How far intervention of this kind actually happens is another matter. A recent study by Bennett and Kell (1989) found that the amount and quality of adult intervention was 'poor' and vital opportunities were missed to extend children's knowledge and extend their thinking. A survey by HMI (GB.DES, 1989c), concludes that 'in the most successful work with four year olds, teachers and other adults closely monitored the children's activities and intervened purposefully' (para. 32).

## Knowing When to Intervene

The interviewees pointed out that **sensitive intervention requires the adult to take time to observe the child so as to know when and how to intervene**. Individuals learn in different ways; observation can be used to plan, monitor and evaluate their progress.

## In Which Activities do Adults Intervene?

Observations in classes with four year olds showed teachers intervening in all types of available activities. Particularly apparent was the way in which teachers 'kept tabs' on what children were doing around the classroom. Whether other adult helpers were present or not, it was typical of these teachers that they kept a general eye on what was going on, and this inevitably resulted in many exchanges of a mainly supervisory or checking nature. They also involved themselves for longer periods in specific activities while still maintaining this overall watch. Lengthier interventions were noted in all types of activity, ranging from sand, water, construction and imaginative play to mathematics, literacy and scientific inquiry.

It was noticeable, however, that a teacher with no adult helpers present usually intervened only for short periods in any one activity and was therefore unable to pursue a particular line of inquiry in any depth. This accords with the findings of Bennett and Kell (1989) who attributed the paucity of intervention in their sample partly to a lack of ancillary support.

This inability to get involved for longer periods in children's activities necessarily influences both the teaching style and the purposes such interventions can fulfil.

## Styles of Intervention

Among the teachers participating in the study there were obvious differences in their usual style of intervention. The following examples illustrate the extremes observed.

*Example 1*
The first example is a teacher with no ancillary help. She is working with a class of 26 children spanning a two-year age range. This brief intervention is typical of her style:

> Tom, one of the youngest four year olds, is engaged in a sorting activity using a number of small parcels wrapped in paper of different patterns. First, he sorts them quickly according to their wrappers,

muttering 'I'm getting on well'. The teacher, who is passing close by, notices what Tom has done.

*Teacher*: Good. Can you find ones of the same size now, ones which are just right?

This is more difficult because the parcels are fairly similar in size. Tom sets them out on the table and sorts them again, matching them carefully in pairs. There are several parcels left over. The teacher remains at hand with an eye on the rest of the class.

*Tom*: Mrs B., I can't find no more to match.

*Teacher* (looking at what he had done): No, there aren't any more are there? What would you like to do next?

*Example 2*
The second example is of a teacher in a two-teacher reception unit for 57 children with regular assistance from one or more ancillaries. The example is typical of this teacher's style. On this particular occasion, however, there are three helpers (two parents and a pensioner) present besides the other class teacher, and this enables her to become involved at some length in a specific activity.

The teacher is working with a small group of four year olds. On the table are magnifying glasses, soft paint brushes, rulers and some books and cards about caterpillars and butterflies. The children have been using the magnifying glasses to examine the caterpillars, which they found in the school garden.

*Teacher*: Let's see how long the caterpillars are. How long is this one?
(A small black caterpillar is put on the table and a child holds a ruler to it.)
*Child*: One on the ruler (i.e. one centimetre).
*Teacher*: We'll have to measure them every day. Let's measure another. How long is that one?
*Children*: One.
*Teacher*: Are they both the same size?
*Children*: Yes
*Teacher*: Where's the big one?
(They search the plant for the larger green caterpillar. Eventually they find it and use a paintbrush to coax it gently on to a sheet of paper.)
*Child*: He's curled up in a ball! Now he's dropped into the mud!
(The teacher retrieves the caterpillar and puts it on the paper.)

*Teacher*: How are we going to measure it do you think? Where do you start on the ruler?
*Child*: The beginning.
*Teacher*: Can you see its head? What number does it go up to on the ruler?
*Child*: The end of the two.
*Teacher*: Get your magnifying glass and see if you can see its head. Does it look different from the others?
(The children look with their magnifying glasses. The caterpillar crawls off the paper.)
*Teacher*: I wonder if we could see a caterpillar trail like we saw a snail trail.
*Child*: You could on a black piece (of paper).
*Teacher*: Can you find a black piece? Quick, he's crawling off again!
*Child*: It's going to put its tentacles out.
*Teacher*: Has it got tentacles?
*Children* (looking through magnifying glasses): No.
*Child*: Butterflies have tentacles.
*Teacher*: Yes. Perhaps we'll read that story 'The Very Hungry Caterpillar'. Can you see something moving at the front of his head?
*Children* (looking intently): Its mouth.
(Teacher puts the caterpillar on the black paper.)
*Teacher*: Let's see if it leaves a trail. Does it?
*Children*: No.
*Teacher*: So it must be moving in a different way from a snail. How is it moving?
(Children look through their magnifying glasses. At this point the teacher is called away to another group. The children continue the discussion.)
*Child*: He hasn't got any legs.
*Another child*: Yes, he has!

This example demonstrates what can be done when there is sufficient adult help and underlines yet again the need for good adult–child ratios for this age group.

## Purposes of Intervention

Adults intervene in children's activities for a variety of reasons, and the purpose of the intervention may call for a particular style. For example, many interventions are expressly to check children's understanding and may involve fairly closed questioning – questions that encourage only brief or monosyllabic answers. Pollard (1989) found that this type of questioning was the most popular strategy used by teachers in her study, and she suggests that if more investigative work had been seen there might have been more opportunities for open-ended questioning techniques, which help children review what they have done, arrive at hypotheses and work out solutions to problems.

Instances of both closed and open-ended questioning techniques were noted in the present study, sometimes being combined in the same intervention sequence (see the 'Caterpillar' example above).

Examples of intervention that appeared to fulfil different purposes were also noted. Apart from interruptions to children's activities for supervisory or managerial reasons (for example, to attend another activity or control a particular behaviour), instances were observed where adults working with four year olds intervened ostensibly in the following ways.

✿ To help children with difficult tasks: for example, completing a puzzle, threading a needle, untangling knots.

✿ To check and extend understanding: for example, a boy is working at a weighing activity. The teacher sits down beside him and adds a brick to tip the balance.

*Teacher*: Watch. Is it the same now? Does it balance?
*Child*: No.
*Teacher*: Well, see if you can make it balance, make it the same.
(Child puts more bricks into the pan.)
*Teacher*: Does it balance now?
(Child nods.)
*Teacher*: Are you sure?
*Child*: Yes.
*Teacher*: Now, watch this. I'm going to put in one, two, three, four bricks. Can you make it balance?
(Child puts beads and toy cars into the other pan. Eventually the balance tips.)
*Teacher*: Does it balance now?
*Child*: No.
*Teacher*: Which side is the lightest?
*Child* (pointing): That.
*Teacher*: Good boy...

✿ To stimulate imagination and encourage the development of particular skills (in this case language):

Some children made a dustcart with large building blocks. The teacher asked them what they were going to do with the dustcart. The children said they were going to put 'the rubbish' in it but did not know what to use for rubbish. After some discussion with the teacher, they decided to collect the contents of all the classroom waste-bins in the school. The teacher discussed with them what they might collect the rubbish in. Eventually, they arrived at the idea of asking the caretaker for a plastic sack. The rubbish was collected, the sack deposited nearby in the 'dustcart' and a large group discussion about rubbish began.

✿ To stimulate reasoning, hypothesizing and problem-solving:

A group of children are building a space-ship with large plastic blocks of various shapes and sizes. This construction gradually changes into a boat and imaginative play develops. Then one boy decides to change the boat into a tractor. He moves the construction around until it resembles the shape of a tractor, but the blocks collapse. The nursery nurse asks the children why the tractor fell to pieces. They suggest that 'there were too many people on it'. The nursery nurse encourages them to think about the roundness of the cylinder blocks and the flatness of the cubes. The children experiment by moving the blocks around, and then decide that it is easier to balance blocks on the flat surfaces than on the round ones.

Clearly, some intervention can serve several purposes, some of which may not have been foreseen by the adult. The 'Caterpillar' example described earlier particularly demonstrates how, given time, an intervention can encourage the development of language, observation skills, mathematical concepts, decision-making, reasoning, hypothesizing, problem-solving, personal and social skills and a gentle approach to living things.

Even activities like clearing-up can provide opportunities to extend children's learning. In one example, a nursery nurse helps children to tidy away shoes that have been used for sorting into pairs. She discusses with them who might wear each type of shoe: high heels, trainers, boots and so on.

## Knowing When Not to Intervene

Although sensitive intervention is important to young children's learning, **adults need also to know when *not* to intervene**. Intervention in a child's activity is not always appropriate and can sometimes even be counter-productive. Teachers and nursery nurses stressed the need for children to have opportunities to play freely without the presence of an adult. It is also necessary for the adult to take time, both to stand back and observe the child and to allow the child to develop the activity.

## Initiation, Choice and Control

An essential part of the teaching approach concerns the balance of control between adult and child over the child's learning.

The professionals interviewed agreed that **an appropriate teaching approach is one that recognizes children's interests and builds upon them**. This has implications not only for adults' intervention in children's activities (see previous section) but also for the initiation, choice and control of the activities.

### Initiating Activities

Professionals advocated that **there should be a balance between activities initiated by the adult and activities initiated by the children**. In either case, themes or topics might develop that could be pursued for as long as the children are interested in them.

Adults were found to be more likely to initiate activities to do with language, number, art and craft and the more organized small group activities like cooking. They were also likely to initiate group activities such as singing, story and discussion, although these occasions were frequently used to pick up on and develop children's interests.

Frequent examples were seen where teachers picked up and expanded on ideas or activities originated by an individual child or group of children. Often these were discussed with the rest of the class, thus generating further interest and activity. Here is an example of activities originating from an object that a child brought to school:

> A child brought in a bird's nest containing four blue eggs. It had been found abandoned in her grandmother's garden. The nest was shown around and discussed at large group time. It was then put on display for children to look at and handle gently. Later in the week the nest was set out on an activity table. Children who chose to do so were encouraged to observe the nest closely and make drawings and models. A discussion about birds followed. The next day another child brought in a decoy duck. This was compared with a stuffed wild duck and both ducks were made available for the children to observe and handle. These activities gradually expanded and developed into a project on the outdoor environment, which lasted several weeks.

In the next example, children's ideas form the basis of further activity:

> In a school with a particular emphasis on children's oral language development, the teacher writes down children's ideas, the stories they make up and some of the verbal descriptions and explanations

they give at group times about what they have made. This encourages children to appreciate the value of the spoken word and its relationship to written language. The children obviously enjoy having their ideas and comments noted, and their stories are often put on tape and made available for other children to listen to in the story-corner.

Child-initiated activity also occurs within certain limits prescribed by the activity or the equipment and materials provided. In some classes it was the adult's preferred style to initiate one or two small group activities and let children pursue the other available activities as they wished. The ideas children initiate and develop in this way can be rich and varied. For example:

> On this particular occasion the teacher initiated a painting and a colouring activity. However, the children were free to pursue their own activities with sand, water, large and small construction, junk materials and so on. One child made a junk space rocket. He spent most of the time working out how to make it fly with the aid of a rubber band and how to prevent the people from falling out on take-off. In the same area, three children worked together to make a model village with an assortment of different houses. The focus of their activity was on painting and decorating the outside of the buildings, which involved them in much discussion.

## Choice

**An appropriate teaching approach with four year olds is one that provides opportunities for children to make choices**. This entails that the teacher has a sufficiently flexible framework for children to have some control over their activity and to operate as 'independent learners'. Choices can be made both in terms of selecting an activity and in making decisions about how to carry it out.

*Choice of activities*
Some of the interviewees made the point that children should have a balance between self-chosen and compulsory activities. Compulsory activities would include teacher-led sessions such as story-time, discussion and music. But even here, one or two argued that children aged four should be free to decide whether or not to join in such activities.

Research (Cleave *et al.*, 1982) has shown that the greatest difference between activities in infant and nursery classes is the degree of choice that children have. Children in nursery schools or classes are likely to have three or four times as much free choice of activity than children in infant classes who may spend as much as two-thirds of their time in no-choice situations. This is clearly inappropriate for nursery-aged children in infant classes. Indeed, the recent HMI survey (GB.DES, 1989c) reports that 'the best work with four year olds in primary classes reflects a suitable balance between directed and self-chosen activities' (para. 8). Allowing children opportunities to choose and develop their own activities frees the teacher to 'interact effectively with individual and small groups of children. Where possible they involve other adults, parents or ancillary staff in classroom activities. This facilitates better organization of the work, more suitable teaching approaches, increased adult–child interaction and a broader, better-balanced curriculum' (ibid.).

Even when the teacher is the sole adult in the classroom, providing opportunities for free choice allows a more efficient use of teacher time. For example, it helps create much-needed time for observation and evaluation. As one teacher explained:

> I have no ancillary help in the afternoons so I let the children choose which activity areas they want to work in. While they are busy I try to observe two children and write comments about their progress. I also try to introduce a new activity with a small group. It's lovely because the children are used to working in this way and can look after themselves quite well.

During observations in schools we noted what the youngest fours chose when they had complete freedom of choice from a wide range of activities. Fifteen children with July and August birth dates were observed in five different schools during the spring and summer terms. These observations showed that their main preferences changed very little from their second to third terms in the infant class. Given the opportunity, their favourite first choices of activity were the house area for imaginative play, large blocks for imaginative play, small construction for model-making, the water and wet sand trays and painting.

Teachers sometimes felt that children needed to be encouraged away from the activities they chose when they first came into the class, so that they experienced a more varied curricular diet. For example, one child in the study was often absent and when he came to school he invariably chose to play with the bricks. He found holding a pencil difficult, so the teacher was now encouraging him to paint or draw as well.

In the best practice there is nothing haphazard about allowing children a choice of activities. The teacher is always aware of what children are choosing and may guide their choices so that they select activities most suited to their needs. Sometimes a delicate balance has to be struck between allowing children complete freedom and encouraging them to choose specific things. This is especially true where a child persistently avoids a certain activity or spends too much time in the same area.

*Choice within activities*

The interviewees pointed out that young children should not only choose activities but should also be involved in the organization and decision-making required to carry them out. HMI support this view. In their survey (GB.DES, 1989c) they noted that much art and craft work for four year olds was 'heavily prescribed' and that opportunities to learn from imaginative play were 'limited'. They therefore suggest ways in which children can be more constructively involved in these activities. For example, 'children could design material for the curtains in the house area. They could be involved in decisions about colour and shape, and solve the problems of how to mix paint to the right consistency' (para. 28). Whether an activity is chosen by the child or prescribed by an adult, there can still be opportunities within the activity for making choices. These may include choices about where to carry out the activity, who to carry it out with, which materials to use and how to use them, which methods to adopt and so on.

Many such opportunities occurred in the classes in the present study. Here is a selection from our observations to give the reader an idea of the kind of choices that children were given:

❁ choosing whether to paint indoors or outdoors;
❁ deciding whether to work alone with the Lego or jointly with others;
❁ selecting a colouring medium and fixative to use for junk-modelling;
❁ electing either to use a sentence-maker, copy the teacher's writing or write freely;
❁ developing a game with wheeled toys and making up the rules.

Making choices like these entails that once an activity has been chosen, the teacher must be able to hand over to the child a certain amount of responsibility for carrying it out. This can be difficult for some teachers who may worry about relinquishing control over the child's learning. However, as Dowling (1988) points out, 'if the accent is to be on developing personal, rational autonomy the teacher must positively encourage independent thinkers, those who question authoritative statements and sometimes choose to tackle things differently' (p. 59).

The extent to which young children can take responsibility is not always fully appreciated. As one headteacher commented, 'Four year olds are the most under-estimated age group in the school'. (The organization of space and materials to promote children's autonomy is discussed in Chapters 7 and 8.)

*Controlling activities*

Giving the child some autonomy in learning does not mean that the adult abdicates responsibility and leaves the child to get on unaided. The teacher has to judge how far it is necessary to exercise control over what the child is doing if the aims and intentions of the activity for the child are to be met. Professionals recommend that **an appropriate teaching approach is one in which control over the activity is negotiated with the children rather than being imposed upon them**.

In the schools visited in the study, instances where an activity was very closely controlled and directed by the adult were only rarely seen. Most of the teachers in the study adopted a flexible style when working closely with children on an activity. This example is typical of the way in which opportunities for individual choice and expression were allowed to develop even within the confines of a prescribed set of tasks.

> As a follow-up to a pirate story on the child-initiated theme of 'buried treasure', the teacher organized a group activity to make treasure maps. The first step was to give the maps an ancient appearance by soaking the paper in tea. The teacher then expected that the children would draw an island with the sea around it. Instead, they chose to draw a route to the treasure based on a 'map' they had previously made of a snail's trail. The teacher modified her plans in response to the children, and the treasure trail they had devised on paper led to the laying of a real treasure trail in the playground. Some children made maps for the others to follow. One child, whose father was a cartographer, put a key on his map. This led to a discussion on the purpose of the key and the introduction of specific symbols and colours.

> In another activity on the same theme, the teacher arranged for the children to receive a 'letter' from the pirate in the story. The activity was primarily intended to stimulate children's early literacy skills and imagination: reading the letter, writing a reply and making pirate pictures. However, some of the younger fours were still drawing people without a body, so in order to develop their observation and symbolizing skills the teacher asked them to think about the shirt the pirate was wearing. Another child who always used the same colour was encouraged to distinguish different ones by the colours of the pirates' clothes.

In these ways the teacher ensured the development of activities, both with groups and with individuals according to the learning needs of the children.

# Teaching Approach and the National Curriculum

Looking ahead to the National Curriculum, staff in the schools studied believed that the activity/play-based approach they espoused was, in principle, quite compatible with the proposals for the National Curriculum. They considered that this approach particularly encouraged children to be independent in their learning, to plan and review their own activities and to work co-operatively with other children, all of which were advocated in the National Curriculum. Some conceded that the National Curriculum might even be beneficial because it provided a framework that might help some schools to improve their practice. It might also help teachers to 'firm up on their approach' by focusing their aims more clearly, and encourage them to think more deeply about what they were doing and why they were doing it.

However, staff were by no means complacent about the National Curriculum and its possible effects on their approach. They warned that teachers must not allow their priorities for and expectations of the children to be adversely affected by pressure on 'what had to be taught and when'; aiming too rigorously at attainment targets could restrict children's opportunities to develop their own ideas and ways of working. Efforts to ensure that all subject areas are covered might destroy teachers' spontaneity in responding to children's interests and, as one teacher said, could curtail 'some of the best teaching – the bit the children remember'.

The Early Years Curriculum Group (1989) acknowledges these concerns and asserts that

> It is important that the principles of early years education, particularly those which relate to the ways in which young children learn, form the basis for considering how the National Curriculum can be implemented. In interpreting the National Curriculum we must ensure that these learning processes are acknowledged and strengthened. (p. 4)

# Conclusion

Play is an appropriate approach in the education of four year olds and its value should be acknowledged and explained to all concerned. However, play is not the prerogative of the youngest pupils but can be a continuous process throughout the infant school and beyond. To be effective the play approach requires careful planning. Adults must be clear about their aims both for the activity and for the child, and all members of the team should be involved in planning how to achieve these aims.

Timetabling must be flexible with minimal interruption to activities. Children need time to develop an activity or idea and adults need time to observe, listen and, if appropriate, become involved. Although children should be brought together for stories and discussion, groups at this age should be small and whole-class activities should be kept to a minimum. Children should have frequent opportunities to collaborate in spontaneous groups and pairs.

Four year olds should also be given every opportunity to explore, experiment and investigate and to make 'mistakes'. They should be encouraged to look and observe and make use of written language displayed around the school and classroom. The emphasis should be on the process rather than the products of learning, and the use of formal commercial schemes should as far as possible be avoided.

An appropriate teaching approach starts from 'where the child is', taking account of individual levels of confidence and competence. Children should be allowed to proceed at their own level and pace, and adults should judge when and how to intervene and extend learning. Adults should also recognize children's interests and build upon them, negotiating a fine balance in the initiation and control of activities. Children should be given opportunities to make choices, both in the selection of activities and in how to carry them out.

# 6 Monitoring and Recording Progress

With a growing emphasis on school effectiveness and the beginning of the National Curriculum and assessment at seven, the monitoring and recording of children's progress from the beginning of their school careers has assumed major importance. At the time of the study, many schools and LEAs were reappraising their procedures and planning better ways of recording information.

This chapter considers what it is appropriate to monitor in four year olds, what procedures are used, whether account is taken of pre-school experiences, when monitoring is done and who does it, how progress is recorded, how records are used, and what are the implications of National Testing for children starting school.

## What to Monitor

Early years educationists stress the importance of **taking account of the all-round development of the young child**. It is not enough simply to look at cognitive attainment levels; it is also necessary to consider physical, social and emotional aspects of development because all of these interact to help or hinder the ways in which the young child learns. This view is supported by the Early Years Curriculum Group (1989) who explain that:

> knowledge of attainment levels alone does not give the teacher the information necessary to plan for young children's future progress: it is also of critical importance to understand children's development in the areas of physical health, perceptual ability, emotional stability, social competence, eagerness to learn, willingness to persevere, and other characteristics relevant to school progress. (p. 19)

The LEA guidelines provided varied considerably in the amount of space devoted to monitoring and record-keeping. While a small minority omitted it altogether, those at the other extreme went into great detail, offering suggestions and examples of record sheets. The general message was that information should be gathered that would help the teacher understand 'the whole child' and plan for the next stage of their development. To this end they emphasized that monitoring should focus on each child's stage of development, each child's progress and curriculum evaluation. They stressed, however, that the processes of assessing, recording and evaluating should be regarded as an *aid* to teaching and not as a directive to teach towards.

## Monitoring Procedures

The interviewees were in agreement that

✿ LEAs should assist schools to develop monitoring procedures;
✿ all schools should have procedures for monitoring children's progress from the start of their school careers;
✿ procedures must take account of young children's diversity and previous experiences.

### LEA Assistance

The study of LEA guidelines indicated that even where some written guidance was given on monitoring and recording progress, it was often up to individual schools to devise their own procedures.

Our work in schools in the year 1988–89 revealed that LEA monitoring procedures were in a state of flux. Most of the authorities involved in the study already had a system of county pupil record forms in maths and English for children from the age of five, and these were in the process of being changed to fit in with the National Curriculum. At least one LEA was known to be designing a similar pupil record for science.

One of the LEAs regularly screened all pupils at seven plus, mainly for 'diagnostic purposes'; this was expected to cease with the advent of National Assessment at seven. Another LEA screened all pupils at five: teachers completed a record form for each child on which various aspects of emotional, social, physical and cognitive development could be rated as giving 'cause for concern'. (The possibility of widespread screening on entry is discussed below.)

Two more LEAs had set up working parties to consider profiling, which would provide fuller information on individual children's progress. One of these LEAs was already piloting an early years profile for use throughout the nursery and infant stages. The profile was intended to be a 'developmental extension' of the existing pupil record, which began at the end of the first infant year. The profile provided for comments on the social, communicative, conceptual, physical and aesthetic areas of development and was accompanied by detailed guidance on its completion.

Several of the LEAs arranged in-service support for early years teachers, which included some attention to monitoring, assessment and record-keeping for children under five (see Chapter 11 for a detailed discussion of INSET support). A survey of under-fives record-keeping in Great Britain (Moore and Sylva, 1984) revealed that fewer than half of authorities had any kind of standard record for use with children under five. Most records took the form of checklists of structured comments under a series of headings. The researchers concluded that more guidance was needed and that this should be offered not just to teachers but to all staff concerned with the under-fives.

There does not seem to have been much improvement in this situation. HM Senior Chief Inspector, in his Annual Report for 1988–89 (GB.DES, 1990d), states that in the primary sector existing arrangements for assessing, recording and reporting on children's performance are for the most part 'inadequate and inconsistent', and that this is an area where improvement 'is needed and is long overdue'.

A survey carried out by the Inspectorate late in 1989 on how primary schools were implementing the National Curriculum (GB.DES, 1989d) found that most schools had not received much help from their LEAs on assessment and some were pressing ahead to improve their own procedures. At the time of the present study some early years educators welcomed this opportunity for improvement. They referred to a long tradition in nursery education of monitoring progress and saw the introduction of the National Curriculum as a chance to 'sharpen up' on their procedures and help raise the status of early years education generally.

**School Procedures**

During the present study, a similar state of flux was found in the schools. Whether LEA guidance was available or not, most schools were going ahead and reviewing their procedures.

The professionals interviewed supported the view that **monitoring and recording procedures should start at the beginning of the child's school career.** Furthermore, records that run throughout the school should share a common language so that misinterpretations are kept to a minimum. The importance of consistent school procedures was spelt out by HMI (GB.DES, 1989c) who found that 'more effective practice usually occurs where ... from the earliest stage the children's work is carefully assessed and recorded to ensure continuity and progression in their learning' (para. 9).

Continuity in monitoring and record-keeping was an aspect of which all the schools in our study were aware, not only from the nursery but into the junior or middle schools and beyond. Records were designed for use throughout the school and began in the nursery class if there was one. In some schools, the various components were kept in a folder for each child. Several schools liaised with others in their area (primary and secondary) in order to design a common record system.

## Taking Account of Children's Previous Experiences

The interviewees recommended that **records should take account of the diversity of young children's experiences before they arrive in school.** This includes any attendance at nursery or pre-school provision outside the home and also the variety of interests, abilities and attachments the child brings from home and community.

*Nursery and pre-school attendance*
Classes receiving new entrants, unlike classes farther up the school, are rarely composed of children who have a shared educational experience. One child may start school straight from home, while another may have attended a variety of pre-school provision from babyhood. Even where there is a nursery class it is unlikely that every child will have had a place in it. Where there is no nursery class (as is more often the case) children may have attended a playgroup, day nursery or nursery class elsewhere, or several or none of these.

Earlier research showed that the passing-on of records from agencies like these tended to be haphazard and piecemeal, and in any case was not always regarded by either side as especially beneficial (Cleave *et al.*, 1982). In our study, there was little evidence of any systematic improvement in continuity with playgroup or nursery records from outside the school. However, some schools had made a special effort in this direction, for example:

> Admission to the school's nursery class was often based on priority of need, with referrals from health visitors and the Social Services taking priority. If children were unable to have a nursery place, there were three playgroups in the area. Two of these had excellent liaison with the school, with staff on both sides visiting regularly.

Several schools in the study, however, were in areas where there was little or no alternative pre-school provision. In these schools there were no previous records to be passed on and any information came mainly from the parents.

*Information from parents*
Most of the schools in the study liaised with parents and children before entry (see Chapter 3). On admission, a form was usually com-

pleted with details of name, address, emergency contact, major illnesses and so on, and sometimes any attendance at a playgroup or nursery was also noted. In addition, several schools devised their own procedures for gathering relevant information. For example, one school with a nursery class asked parents for details about the child's interests and abilities before admission to nursery. Parents were asked 'Does your child: Like looking at books? Enjoy drawing? Speak confidently? Attempt to write?' and so on. This information then formed the starting point of the child's school record.

It is important that schools are aware of the influences and experiences in the child's pre-school life so that these can be understood and built on in school. As Lally (1989) explains, if schools do not make use of parents' detailed knowledge about their own child, 'they run the risk of underestimating children's cognitive and linguistic ability and of offering a curriculum which is less rich than the experiences the child is having at home' (p. 1).

# When to Monitor

LEA curriculum guidelines and the professionals interviewed made it very clear that **the monitoring of children's progress should be a continuous process, carried out by observation in the course of normal classroom activities.**

## Monitoring During Normal Classroom Activities

Monitoring children as they go about their activities enables the *context* of what they are doing to be taken into account. Depending on their purpose, observations can focus on an individual or a group of children or on an activity.

It is important to be clear about *why* these observations are being made. Reflecting on the first term of the National Curriculum, Tann (1990) notes that the major function in focusing observations was to clarify why the teacher wanted any particular information, for this determined 'what evidence they needed to collect, how to collect it and how that information would be used to inform their teaching'. Lally (1989) is helpful here. She points out that regular observation provides the main tool for gathering information about children because it enables the adult 'to build up a picture of what each child can do, or would be able to do, with sensitive support'.

**Time to Monitor**

The interviewees stressed that **adults must have *time* to observe and assess children and their activities as part of the ongoing development of the curriculum.** To allow time to do this, it is essential that there are appropriate adult–child ratios (see Chapter 9) and that the classroom is organized so that young children can service and maintain their own requirements (see Chapter 8) and take some responsibility for their own learning (see Chapter 5).

That infant teachers are finding it difficult to make enough time for monitoring Key Stage 1 of the National Curriculum has already been well documented. Studies by HMI (GB.DES, 1989d) and Tann (1990) found that the most pressing change for teachers appeared to be that of making time for monitoring, and even those who were good class managers found it hard to create enough time for observation and assessment. HMI (GB.DES, 1989b) noted that it was even more difficult to do this successfully in mixed-age classes.

Traditionally, observation has always been an integral part of good nursery practice and, although our study preceded the start of the National Curriculum, some reception teachers already observed children regularly to monitor their progress and evaluate the curriculum. As one teacher explained: 'I observe the children while they are getting on with their daily lives. I use my observations to monitor their likes and dislikes, to note what they choose to do and to see how the activities might be extended. I look for their individual interests and note any lack of confidence. I then try to encourage them to fill in any gaps.' The same teacher commented that it was particularly important to observe children closely at this stage because 'it is a period of rapid changes'.

Perhaps one of the difficulties of finding time for observation is the notion that one has to 'stand back' to observe. This is sometimes understood as 'standing and doing nothing', which goes against the grain in a classroom full of active young children. Also, teachers feel that they should be seen to be 'teaching' and not standing around apparently doing nothing (see Chapter 5). One argument against this is that observation need not take *extra* time or indeed entail standing back and doing nothing, as the example described above shows. However, most of the teachers set aside specific times for observation. Here are three examples from the range of strategies used:

- ✿ The teacher, with the support of a team, was 'timetabled' to observe children on Friday afternoons.
- ✿ The teacher tried to carry out observations during the afternoons when children had free choice of activities. Each afternoon, while they were busy, she tried to observe two children and write notes

about their progress (no adult support was available at these times).

✿ The teacher tried to observe children whenever she could (part-time ancillary help was available). She said, 'There's a knack to observing children at an activity; you have to know what you are looking for.' For example, she might set up a play situation specifically intended to help language development; she would then observe the children in that situation to see, for instance, whether and how conversation developed. She also observed individual children at certain activities. This was related to the record-keeping system: children kept their own weekly records of the activities they had chosen and the teacher encouraged them to complete any gaps. One child, for example, had to be persuaded towards messier activities such as painting and sand play. The teacher made a point of watching what the child did with these activities and made notes of her observations.

## Implications for Training

The interviewees pointed out that some teachers of four year olds in infant classes would benefit from training in observation skills and the evaluation of activities. Our work in schools and other recent studies (GB.DES, 1989d; Tann, 1990) support this view. Our study also suggests that teachers would appreciate guidance in methods of recording children's progress and in understanding the purpose of such records. Both initial training and in-service courses in early years education need to give attention to the whole question of observation, evaluation and assessment, especially now that Key Stage 1 of the National Curriculum is underway.

A study of a selection of in-service initiatives suggested that there is a growing awareness of this need and some course providers were already making it a component of the course. For example:

On one such course, videos of individual children provided a useful basis for trying out observation skills. Members were then encouraged to carry out observations in their own and other classes and to discuss these with follow-up support.

In another initiative, early years staff regularly met in 'support groups' to consider observations of specific activities. Ideas were exchanged, tried out in the classroom and discussed at the next meeting. The whole exercise culminated in the production of a useful series of booklets generated from observations of children at these activities.

(For further details on initial and in-service training, see Chapter 11.)

## Who Does the Monitoring?

Interviewees recommended that **monitoring should be team-based, involving the teacher, the nursery nurse and ancillary helpers, the parents and the child.** They pointed out that some schools were already keeping records of progress in the form of diaries shared by staff, parents and child.

Most of the teachers involved nursery nurses and ancillary helpers to some extent in the monitoring process. Involvement ranged from having discussions about individual children to entering comments and pieces of work in children's record files. In one class all the regular helpers, including parents and other members of the local community, contributed to reading records whenever they listened to children reading. Parents also contributed in this way when their child took a book home to read with them.

In one school deliberate attempts were made to involve parents, staff and child in a three-way consultation about progress:

> Towards the end of the first year parents received a brief 'profile' with comments on their child's progress in the various curricular areas. The following week, parents were invited into school during the day to 'share the children's work with them'. Parents went into the classroom and sat down with their child to look through a selection of their early and later work. The head and ancillary staff were on hand to answer questions and look after the rest of the class. When children had finished discussing their work, they took their parents to the relative peace and quiet of the staffroom to meet the teacher. A discussion then took place between child, parents and teacher.
>
> The researcher noted the minute detail with which children explained their work to their parents. The parents said how much they appreciated the opportunity of seeing their child in the classroom environment and discussing what they had seen with the staff. As one parent commented, 'I think it's a very good idea because it means you can talk with your child about what they've been doing. I was amazed how much my daughter could remember, even though she had done some of the things months ago'.

(Opportunities for parents to visit the school are discussed in Chapter 3.)

## How Is Information Recorded?

Professionals stressed that **if monitoring progress is to be effective, it is essential to keep good records.**

It is important to remember that there are two aspects to be considered here: the evaluation of the curriculum and the assessment of children's progress. These two aspects are closely related and the former is to some extent recorded in the latter. Curriculum evaluation looks at the experiences provided for the children, and assessment examines the individual child's reactions to these experiences.

## Curriculum Evaluation

Curriculum evaluation is closely linked to curriculum planning, and records often function as both. LEA guidelines addressing these issues often treated them together through a discussion of termly themes, weekly planning sheets and records of the curriculum areas covered.

A great deal of curriculum evaluation may go undetected by the observer because it happens in the teacher's mind and is not necessarily written down. Good teachers are continually making a mental note of whether their intentions for individual children are being met (see Chapters 4 and 5). In this sense, evaluation of the curriculum cannot be separated from the reactions of the children to that curriculum.

Our classroom observations revealed that teachers evaluated the experiences they provided in the following ways:

*By observing individual children*
For example, Debbie was described as another girl's 'shadow'. The teacher, wanting to increase Debbie's confidence, encouraged her to play with two other children in the house corner. A game developed in which the house was burgled. The teacher noted that Debbie was beginning to join in and that eventually she was 'coming up with some good ideas'.

*By asking children questions*
For example, Seb needed practice in distinguishing blue and yellow. The teacher wanted to know whether his difficulty was in 'seeing' or 'naming' these colours. She asked him to pick up all the yellow beads from a tray that had been spilt on the floor. Seb did this accurately with great concentration. When the teacher asked him what he had done he said, 'Picked up some beads'. When she asked him what colour they were he was unable to tell her.

*By listening to children talking*
For example, the class had been on a trip to a lake. The teacher wanted to know what the children had taken from the experience so she asked them to talk about what they had liked best. Karen told them how she had played in the sand by the lake and taken photo-

graphs. She had filled buckets with water to pour into the sand to make channels. Ann, Jon, Rob and Darren had together made boats out of plastic containers. They had floated the boats under the bridge and watched them come out on the other side. They had found they could sink them by making waves. If a boat got too much water in it, it sank. Don talked about the fish and demonstrated with his hands how big they were. He commented that their mouths were 'like circles'.

*By looking at children's products*
For example, the class had taken part in a whole-school project based on Roald Dahl's *The Enormous Crocodile* (see also Chapter 10). By looking at individual children's subsequent work in the classroom, the teacher was able to see how participation in the project had influenced their ideas. The wet sand tray became a model of the story setting with lakes and rivers; the woodwork bench sported a model palm tree; junk materials produced a lighthouse; small construction was used to make a zoo; children's booklets revealed pictures and writing about aquatic animals and birds; and so on.

*By holding staff and team discussions*
For example, at their weekly meeting members of one reception team agreed that the display they had envisaged was too adult-oriented and more attention should be paid to what the children wanted to do.

Information gained in these ways was not necessarily recorded formally but was more likely to be stored in note form and incorporated into further curriculum planning and development or records of individual children's progress.

## Children's Progress

The HMI survey (GB.DES, 1989c) found that with few exceptions records of the progress of four year olds in infant classes were poor. 'Records were limited mainly to social profiles and attainments in reading and mathematics. Occasionally they included samples of the children's work in language and number' (para. 25). The LEA guidelines were in agreement that written profiles, developmental checklists and samples of work should form the main constituents of a child's record. A few LEAs also specified details that should be noted on admission. However, the main message to schools was that record-keeping methods should be quick and easy to use.

Some LEAs already provided detailed guidance on recording progress in specific subject areas, notably maths and English, and, increasingly, science. Manchester's 'Early Literacy Project: A

Framework for Assessment' (1988) is an example, offering nursery and infant schools information on literacy profiles, monitoring and analysis sheets, running records, standardized tests, child interviews and observations, parent comment cards and so on.

It is important to remember that records of curriculum subject attainments alone are not enough, because teachers of young children have to be aware of the development of the whole child as a person. They should therefore describe the child's progress as an effective learner in school, and include reference to physical development, health, social competence, motivation, attitudes and disposition. The interviewees recommended that information should be kept in a folder or file for each child, containing a profile of their development and samples and photographs of their work to show progression. Some professionals were in favour of developmental checklists, but others warned that these could be too limiting on the information they conveyed.

Most of the teachers in the study kept three kinds of records: records completed by the adult(s), records completed by (or with) the children and samples of children's work.

*Records completed by the adult*
Most teachers kept regular records of progress in specific subject areas, most commonly maths, English and science; many of them also kept separate reading records noting titles of books read by the child and dates of completion. Subject records were broken down into skills and concepts, usually arranged in lists but sometimes grouped imaginatively into concentric circles or the petals of 'flowers', which were coloured according to the term in which the skill or concept was acquired. Subject records were often marked on three dimensions according to whether the component had been introduced, partially understood, or completely grasped. However, all these records were very much under review at the time of the study and were in the process of being re-designed.

The most comprehensive records formed part of an all-round profile of the child with comments on personal attributes such as independence, cooperation and confidence, and other relevant notes and observations. Most of the teachers kept a profile on each child, which was updated at regular intervals (such as half-termly) and whenever it was felt necessary in between. The various profiles covered progress in all activity areas and also included aspects of physical, social and emotional development, attitudes, health, special abilities and needs, teaching approaches found to be effective and any other information the teacher considered relevant.

Extracts from typical profiles seen in the study are given in Figures 6.1a and 6.1b.

| | | |
|---|---|---|
| NAME _____ | DATE OF BIRTH _____ | |

Comments:            Date:      Signature:

**Physical Development**

Gross motor

Fine motor

Coordination

**Figure 6.1a: Part of a typical profile used with four year olds.**

**Physical Development**

Gross motor includes:

    Mobility – run, jump, hop, climb...
    Balance – stand on one leg, walk backwards, walk along line, climb steps...
    Agility – checks own movement, dodges objects at speed, uses space appropriately...

Fine motor includes:

    Hand and finger control, use of pencil and scissors, fitting constructional toys and jigsaws, striking, hammering, screwing, folding...

Coordination includes:

    Throwing, catching, steering wheeled toys, pedalling, threading, buttoning...

**Figure 6.1b: Extracts from explanatory notes for completing a profile (not meant to be used as a checklist).**

*Records completed by (or with) the children*

Records completed by children in schools in the study consisted mostly of planning and recording their activity choices. Exceptionally in one school, each child had a large book that accompanied them through the primary stage. During their first week they drew a picture of themselves on the first page and 'wrote' their name. Each term they added to the book and when they left the school they took the book home.

Children's plans of their activity choices also functioned as a partial record of what they had done (see Chapter 5). Simple planning sheets, on which they marked their first choices, were begun in the nursery class and became more sophisticated as children grew older. The sheets were retained by the teacher so that imbalances in the child's classroom experiences could be easily detected. Figure 6.2 is typical. For other examples, see Chapter 5.

It is important to be aware of the status given to the various activity areas in the child's record. For example, cues about the value given by teachers to different activities may also be signalled through the kind of work samples selected to be put in children's folders.

*Samples of children's work*

When recording progress by retaining samples of children's work, it is important to be aware of how the samples are selected. It is relatively easy to collect samples of work done on paper (writing, drawing, painting, collage and so on) but more problematic to store three-dimensional creations, non-expendable materials or abstract ideas. There is therefore a danger that the samples do not provide a balanced record of what the child has actually achieved. There is also a danger that 'paper work' appears to the child to be more highly valued than, say, a block construction, a box model, a musical innovation or an idea contributed to a class story.

Thought must be given to ways of noting and perhaps recording children's progress even when there are no tangible end results. Many instances were seen, for example, where children used construction sets to make quite complex models, sometimes elaborating and developing them with other children throughout a session or day. It is seldom practical to retain these models: space is scarce and others need access to the materials. However, it is important that such activities are valued, and teachers employed various strategies to ensure that the constructions did not simply vanish without trace:

✿ In one class children were encouraged to draw and 'write' about their models. This work was made into booklets that were displayed in the classroom and later either taken home or retained as a record of the child's progress.

| Area | Monday | Tuesday | Wednesday | Thursday | Friday |
|---|---|---|---|---|---|
| wet  | ✓ | ✓ | | ✓ | |
| house  | | ✓ | ✓ | | ✓ |
| block 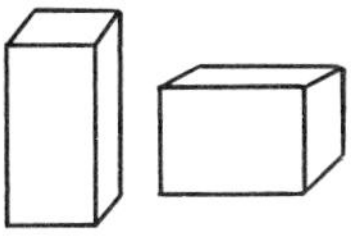 | ✓ | | | ✓ | |
| music 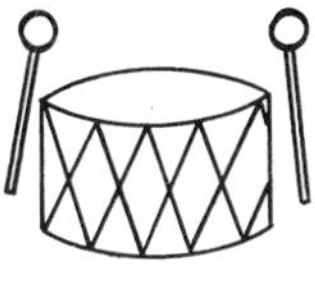 | | | ✓ | | ✓ |
| quiet | | ✓ | ✓ | | ✓ |
| etc. | | | | | |

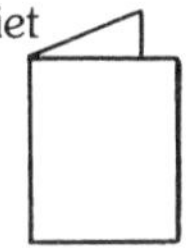

**Figure 6.2: Part of a child's activity sheet in a nursery class.**

✿ In another school, where children's language skills were believed to be under-developed, the emphasis was less on graphic representation and more on oral discussion. Children were encouraged to talk about their model, describing what it was or explaining how it worked to the group or class. Some of these explanations were written down by the teacher.

✿ In some classes, photographs were taken of children's work. These were displayed or put in folders as part of the child's record.

Professionals in the study suggested that more use could be made of photographs, videos, tapes and transcripts to record children's progress across the whole range of classroom activities.

## What Are Records for and How Are They Used?

When making records, **it is important to be clear about their purpose and for whom they are intended**, as this will influence what information is needed and how it is collected and presented.

Ultimately, monitoring and record-keeping have two main functions: curriculum planning and evaluation and the assessment of children's progress. These two strands were often indistinguishable from each other in the uses to which records could be put. Evidence from LEA guidelines, interviews with professionals and observations in schools suggested that in the early years records should be used:

✿ to monitor the effectiveness of curricular provision: observations and staff discussions were useful here and were said to be particularly informative when monitoring the development of themes;

✿ to plan, develop and extend the experiences provided: observations could be used to spot children's preferences, interests and difficulties; development and progression over time could be noted (such as, by the summer term children were working more collaboratively with each other); the activities could be modified or extended as appropriate;

✿ to pinpoint individual children's special interests, strengths and needs: these provide a basis on which to build and develop curricula and can assist in the early diagnosis of learning difficulties;

✿ to ensure a range and balance of experiences for each child: observations and records are useful in recording individual preferences, dislikes and avoidances so that serious gaps can be plugged and confidence boosted;

✿ to enable support and guidance to be given where needed: records provide headteachers and others with information to seek

appropriate support, whether in the form of resources, staff training or remedial help for an individual child;

✿  to provide a basis of information for parents and other early years
professionals: the relationship between parents and other professionals is essential to give a balanced picture; agencies other than
the school (health visitors, GPs, social workers and so on) may
also contribute relevant information; to be effective there has to
be communication, co-operation and collaboration between all
concerned so that appropriate understanding and support can be
offered to the child, the family and the school;

✿  to ensure continuity: monitoring and record-keeping are no less
important in the early years than at any other stage because they
can be used to establish continuity from the start; they can help to
clarify the progression of themes and to promote the continuity of
children's experiences from pre-school to school, from class to
class and from nursery through to the junior or middle school;

✿  to link with the requirements of the National Curriculum.


## National Curriculum Assessment


### Reactions to Proposals for Assessment at Seven

The interviewees were confident that the integrated nature of the early
years curriculum and the practice of observing children in the normal
course of the day in order to monitor their progress and develop activities, could provide an excellent model for monitoring the progress of
older children. Most of the children being observed in the study would
be involved as seven year olds in the first full-scale national assessments of English, maths and science in the summer of 1991. At the
time of the study, however, headteachers were reluctant to commit
themselves to too much crystal ball-gazing. While some were reappraising their procedures to fit in with the proposed changes, others
had decided to wait until the proposals had become realities.

The interviewees expected National Assessment to have both benefits and disadvantages for their work with four year olds. On the *positive* side there were those who believed that National Assessment (as
proposed) would link well with their current practice because:

✿  the assessment would be based on continuous records instead of a
one-off test result;
✿  the teachers already used observations to monitor progress and
plan accordingly;
✿  the pupils were used to working independently and in groups on
different activities;

✿ the proposed SATs (standard assessment tasks) would fit in with the way the children worked and therefore would not present a threat.

On the *negative* side, some interviewees expressed fears that:

✿ assessment at seven would mean that some children could be labelled as failures from an early age;
✿ the assessments might be used to draw unhelpful comparisons between children (and between their teachers and schools);
✿ attainment targets (notably for English) assumed too much at Level 1 and needed to be broken down into smaller components for monitoring purposes; it would not be easy to separate out the speaking, listening, reading and writing components at this stage;
✿ the infant stage of schooling would be 'rushed through' in order to perform well at seven;
✿ children with language difficulties or for whom English was not their first language might by unfairly assessed;
✿ teachers would not have sufficient time to take the proposed requirements and responsibilities on board. This fear has since been supported by the HMI finding (GB.DES, 1989d) that during the first term of the National Curriculum 'lack of time for undertaking work on assessment and recording was a major obstacle' (para. 36).

### Implications for Assessment on Admission

Several interviewees, notably headteachers and curriculum coordinators, expressed concern that if children were to be assessed at seven there should be some kind of 'baseline' from which their progress could be measured. Because children came into school with a wide range of experiences and abilities, there was some support for the view that children should be assessed on admission to school. It was suggested, for example, that a simple checklist might help to establish the child's 'starting-point'.

The use of profiles on entry (such as Hereford and Worcester Education Department's *Pupil Profile Level One* or Wolfendale's (1987) *All About Me*) can provide useful *qualitative* information but cannot offer a baseline for a linear measure of progress. The arguments against linear measurement are strong, not least because *quantitative* tests for this age are considered to be too crude (Desforges, 1989).

Some attention has been paid to this issue in the USA where, in some areas, standardized tests have been used to assess whether young children were 'ready' for kindergarten. As a result of their test scores children could be refused admission, retained in a pre-kindergarten class or assigned to a remedial or special class. None of these strategies had proved advantageous for the child; indeed, they could actually screen out children who might have benefited from early entry into education. Anxiety about the unreliability of such tests and their potentially harmful outcomes for the child prompted the NAEYC to recommend that decisions about young children's education 'should be based on multiple sources of information and should never be based on a single test score' (Bredekamp and Shepard, 1989).

At the time of writing (1990), the debate about baseline assessment in the UK is unresolved.

# Conclusion

Monitoring and recording young children's progress must take account of physical, social and emotional as well as cognitive development because all these aspects interact to help or hinder learning. To promote continuity, all schools admitting under-fives should have procedures for monitoring children's progress from the start. Procedures should take account of the diversity of young children's development and previous experience so that these can be understood and built on.

Monitoring should be a continuous process, carried out principally through observation during the course of normal classroom activities. It is essential that adults have sufficient time to observe individual children. This can be difficult for the hard-pressed teacher working single-handedly with a class of young children. The situation is made much easier when there is ancillary support. Monitoring should be a team effort involving the teacher, nursery nurse, ancillary helper, parents and child.

For monitoring to be effective, good record-keeping is essential to evaluate both the curriculum and the child's response to it. It is important to be clear about the purpose of the records, how they may be used and who will have access to them, since these considerations determine what information is sought and how it is collected and presented.

At the time of the present study, monitoring and record-keeping procedures were being re-appraised to make them compatible with the requirements of the National Curriculum. Practitioners appreciated courses in observation and evaluation skills and guidance in recording and using the information gained. LEAs and training institutions have a continuing role to play in providing support in this respect.

# PART THREE

## Towards Appropriate Provision

If practice in infant classrooms is to satisfy the educational needs of four year olds, the environment must allow and encourage such practice to take place. Attention must, therefore, be given to the use of space, the provision of suitable equipment and materials, and appropriate staffing ratios.

# 7 Space

Four year olds are characteristically physically active and energetic so they need space both indoors and out in which to move freely and be spontaneous. Motor development is at an important stage so they need opportunities to practise motor skills and coordination, and to test themselves physically in a safe environment. Early years educationists are united in their plea for adequate space for these young children. Improvements in the physical environment should be made because young children are active both physically and mentally. They need space and a good quality environment both indoors and out. This is endorsed by the Select Committee: 'Young children need space to move about freely and have direct access to a secure area for outside play' (House of Commons, 1988, para. 5.11).

In some parts of the country the falling pupil roll in primary schools has led to early admission classes being formed. Often children were allocated classrooms as they became available regardless of the suitability of their use for younger children. It is only in the infant and primary schools in the authorities where there is a well-thought-through policy or where the headteacher has made it a priority, that the youngest children have access to the most appropriate space available both indoors and out. 'The setting in which learning takes place is crucial to the quality of provision' (Dowling, 1988, p. 102), and, as one teacher explained to the project team, four year olds need space to feel 'safe, valued and relaxed with areas to move and express themselves'.

## Outdoor Space

The opportunities for children to be active physically and mentally can be extended by teachers if the outdoor area is included in their planning and organization of activities for this age group. Through play involving gross motor activity children are able to use their bodies to experience spatial awareness and develop their confidence.

It is important that they learn to control their bodies. Children's body images change as they grow so they need constant practice to enable them to master gross motor skills and to develop fine motor skills. Physical activity for young children should be provided in enjoyable and purposeful ways and not just limited to timetabled hall sessions. Movement and physical activity is a 'medium of learning that is direct, spontaneous, which provides immediate feedback and which is possible without dependence on words' (Boorman, 1987, p. 245).

In practice the project team found that the teachers in nursery schools were offering far more outdoor experiences for their children than teachers in infant or primary schools. This was the case even where the nursery buildings were old and the outdoor space limited. In one nursery school, for example:

> The children only remain inside if the weather is very severe. The gardens and buildings are built on several levels with steps and ramps between them. As a rule, the buildings and their surrounding gardens are self-contained. Sometimes children go on 'outings' to the other parts of the school. In the gardens there are lots of mature trees and shrubs with little winding paths and narrow alleyways for the children to play. The space is very interestingly divided up. There are places for the children to dig as well as to play in sand or with water, and there is a pond which has been specially made by the teachers and children so that they can go pond-digging. The dismal black brick walls that surround the gardens are painted with brightly coloured murals. There are many flower beds with flowering plants, which have been planted by the staff or children. There are plenty of sheltered areas where the children can play under

cover, and lots of climbing equipment, slides, trolleys and barrels and so on for outdoor activity. There are storage sheds for the large equipment. Some of the equipment is fixed and the rest is selected on a daily basis. Some of the table-top activities are put outside on the verandah.

In contrast only a few of the infant or primary schools in the study provided permanent outdoor activities for their youngest pupils. HMI also report that: 'Four year olds in infant classes rarely had opportunities for outdoor activities due, in part, to the lack of access to suitable play areas and to supervision and resourcing difficulties but also because, in most cases, the value of outdoor play and the contribution it can make were not well understood (GB.DES, 1989c, para. 29).

In the present study there were constraints on the teachers with the youngest children in their classes that prevented them from using the outdoor area as they would have liked. The greatest difficulties were caused by inappropriate positioning of classrooms, no outdoor access from the classroom, inadequate staffing for appropriate supervision or vandals making equipment unsafe to use.

The LEA guidelines and the interviewees considered that **the outside area is an important aspect of appropriate provision for four year olds in infant and primary schools.** This area should be:

✿  safe and secure;
✿  provided with adequate storage facilities;
✿  of different types of surface;
✿  flexibly organized to allow movement between indoor and outdoor activities;
✿  an extension of the learning environment.

## Safety and Security

If the outdoor area was not considered to be safe and secure for the children, understandably the teachers would not allow them to be free to explore. Authorities could help by fencing off outdoor space but headteachers were still concerned about the proximity of busy roads and about the amount of space accessible to children. As one headteacher reported: 'There is so much outdoor space that the sheer volume of it is a constraint because you can't just let the children go out at any time'.

In several schools there was no direct access from the classroom to the outside area. Even though some classrooms had suitable adjacent patio areas the authority could not be persuaded to fund a new doorway to make the area accessible. In some cases the children had to negotiate several corridors before they could reach their destination outside.

Even where there is access to an outdoor area, it can be difficult to supervise its use if it cannot be seen easily from the classroom; there is not always an adult available to accompany the children in their activities. If equipment has been vandalized or the fencing is rough and unsafe, children cannot use the outdoor area. The experiences of one teacher are described in the researcher's notes:

> The teacher felt that there was a need for areas in which the children can have outdoor and indoor activities where they are safe and can be seen by the staff. In the school there is an inner courtyard but it is too remote from the four year olds' classroom and is not visible from their room. This means that children have to be taken to it five at a time by the nursery nurse or class teacher, thus leaving the other adult with the remaining 25 or more children in the classroom. The courtyard area is shared with other classes so there is a timetable specifying when it can be used. Sometimes the noisy activity of children using this area disturbs other classes.

## Adequate Storage Facilities

Often the facilities used for outdoor activities were permanent; for example, climbing frames, gardens, paved paths and patios. A few schools in the study provided equipment such as climbing blocks, tunnels, wheeled toys, gravel, sand, wood and water activities. Equipment used outside regularly requires safe storage to protect it from the weather and vandals. Where there is no storage space available indoors, outdoor protection is a priority. Storage sheds were often provided from PTA funds. Children were encouraged in helping to get the equipment out and return it at the end of the session. This provided opportunities for them to be involved in decision making, to practise their language with an adult and to become independent. Observations in one school show how the storage shed provided extra facilities *and* learning opportunities:

> The shed used to store the outdoor equipment became a hiding place when all the items had been removed. The children linked the shed to their 'game', which was based on the climbing blocks and included the wheeled toys.
>
> At the end of the morning session the equipment was put back with the help of the children, and as the children removed the articles in the water tray they tended to 'have a little play with them'. The teacher watched them and explained that it provided them

with extra opportunities to be aware of what the equipment can do and what activities have been offered to them.

In the same class another group were helping the YTS student rearrange the climbing blocks for the afternoon session and two girls were busy sorting the nails from the screws at the woodwork bench. They were involved in a discussion comparing the length of nails and screws.

## Different Surfaces

The interviewees considered that the outdoor area should provide children with opportunities to use wheeled toys on paved paths or tarmac. The grassed areas provided spaces for running and jumping as well as quieter activities such as looking at books. The gardens provided opportunities to introduce children to early science concepts. A variety of surfaces provided opportunities for adventures and exploration as well as opportunities to retreat and reflect upon experiences.

In one nursery school there were grounds of over an acre for the children to explore and the teachers encouraged them to do so throughout the year. Parents were specifically requested to provide wellingtons so that the children could enjoy splashing in puddles and chasing along footpaths. In the infant and primary schools studied there was a reluctance on behalf of some teachers to use the grassed area in the winter months because of inclement weather making it muddy. Where outdoor activities are provided in a few infant schools, they are usually limited to the areas of tarmac. In one school there are paved and tarmac areas adjoining each other. Even though there are no physical barriers teachers are able to limit the amount of space available, making supervision possible; children are only allowed to use the paved area, which can be seen by the teacher. Where schools had accessible grassed and garden areas, the outdoor provision was much more stimulating for the children. Here is one example from the researcher's notes: 'The whole of the play area is very interesting for the children. It is on a hill and contains slopes and dips for them to explore. There is asphalt for running and jumping as well as grass and a number of trees providing some shade where they can play quietly'.

## Flexible Organization

Some teachers with four year olds in their class provide outdoor activities by being more flexible in their teaching approach and organization. This may involve just a watchful eye on outdoor activities while the teachers are engrossed in indoor activities or the activities may form a planned part of the termly theme.

The opportunities offered to the children varied. Some had designated outdoor times and others had freedom of movement between indoor and outdoor provision. Outdoor activities were available all day for children in some schools and for part of the day in others.

*Outdoor activities available all day*
A few schools have access to an enclosed courtyard area or a paved area adjacent to the classroom. Teachers tended to utilize these areas to increase the amount of space available for children to use. Wet and dry sand, water and wood activities were most frequently found in these areas.

Sometimes other activities more usually provided in the classroom, such as Lego, cars, stickle bricks or junk modelling, were re-located to this area. These were particularly popular in the sunshine. Children were also observed sitting on blankets or cushions and talking about the books they were 'reading'. These activities were not available when the weather was very cold or damp. Most teachers in the study and those cited in Vause's (1988) research do not seem to have considered that if the children were appropriately dressed the outdoor area could be used throughout the year.

An example from the researcher's notes illustrates provision where the children are able to choose indoor or outdoor activities all day as long as the weather is suitable: 'A small paved courtyard enclosed by a fence and the adjoining classroom were available to the children. The door was open and a number of activities had been put outside. The figure [7.1] shows the activities provided and the arrangement of the equipment in the courtyard.'

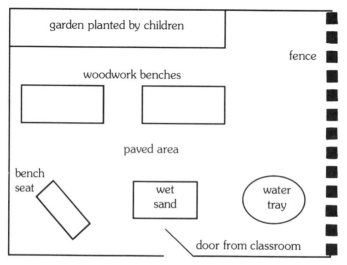

**Figure 7.1: Equipment in the courtyard.**

*Outdoor activities available for part of the day*
Staffing constraints and limited access to outdoor areas reduced the amount of outdoor provision for some children. Teachers found they were only able to provide outdoor activities for part of the day when enough adult help was available to supervise the children. Other teachers found different ways of providing outdoor activities for part of the day.

*Outdoor activities for groups of children*
In some schools outdoor activities are available throughout the day but there are too many children to be given an individual choice of indoor or outdoor activities at some time during the day. For example:

> In one school where there are over 70 children with two teachers and an ancillary helper the children are organized into smaller groups of about 24 children. Each group is given the opportunity to choose between indoor, messy activities like sand, water or art and craft and outdoor activities for some time during the day. The ancillary helper, sometimes with student help, supervises the children who have this choice.

In these circumstances the adults can be involved in the outdoor activities rather than just adopting a supervisory role, but the teachers often still tend to spend their time with the groups of children in the classrooms unless they are making conscious attempts to convey to children that the outdoor activities are as important as those provided inside.

*Timetabled outdoor activities*
Some schools use the outdoor area adjacent to the classroom for activities more normally provided indoors. In one school, for example:

> the table top activities, the water tray, building blocks, Lego and books are taken outside for the afternoon session. There are three classes with three teachers. To give the children a choice of indoor and outdoor activities throughout the afternoon one teacher remains in the classroom with access to the outdoors while the other two teachers spend their time with the children outside. For a part of the afternoon there is an ancillary helper. While the extra adult is available the children are able to use the wheeled toys on the school's asphalt playground.

Other schools timetabled the first hour of the day for the four year olds to be able to use the wheeled toys on the playground. Ancillary help was allocated by the headteacher for this time and the children had the choice of staying inside or going out. This evolved because the staff had recognized that these younger children have bursts of energy and need the opportunities to be physically active as well as to be quiet. They also recognized the potential difficulties that can occur if the youngest children are expected to join in whole-school play-times. The hour of physical activity first thing in the morning makes set playtimes for these younger children unnecessary.

## An Extension of the Learning Environment

'The outside space should be considered an integral part of the learn-ing environment for the children' (Dowling, 1988a, p. 103). In the schools in our study the opportunities for children to choose sponta-neously between indoor or outdoor activities were limited. The tea-chers more frequently used the environment as part of specifically planned activities. There were examples of teachers taking the ma-jority of the class to transfer plants grown in the classroom to a gar-den area. The researcher's observation notes in one school show how the garden area contributed to the termly theme and science activities: 'There was a border of plants that the children had sown as part of their thematic interest in gardens and the outdoor environment. The plants had grown and were now in flower and staked with canes. There was also a 'control' of seeds that had been planted in pots and deliberately not watered...' Other teachers take groups of children to the local shops, park or other areas of the school grounds. Sometimes groups of children go into the playground with their teachers to look at details on the houses opposite as part of the theme 'Homes' or to look at insects, worms, snails and caterpillars as part of science-based projects such as 'mini-beasts'.

These journeys are only possible when there are enough adults available to supervise all the groups. Sometimes these are provided by the headteacher or parents but excursions are more likely to happen when and where there is regular help in the form of a support teacher or a nursery nurse. For example, in one school a support teacher works with a group of eight different children throughout the term. They are taken to the 'wilderness' to collect and observe plants and animals, or they are taken to the 'quad' area to observe, draw and talk about the pets.

Often PE sessions are timetabled for the hall but in suitable weather they are carried out outside. This means that opportunities for physi-cal activity for children are provided in the playground at a time con-venient for their teacher's classroom organization rather than being imposed by external influences such as the school timetable.

There were only a few examples during the time of the project team's observation of teachers or nursery nurses using the children's interest in outdoor activities to develop a teaching point. One teacher, for example, made use of the windy weather. A group of children were watching flimsy scarves float, and the teacher talked to them about the wind and suggested that when they had time they could make a kite to see if they could get that to fly.

## Appropriate Provision

The resources available in infant schools make it difficult for teachers to provide a choice of indoor or outdoor activity for the youngest children. Often choice is only possible when there are enough adults available or when the weather is suitable. Only a few schools had the kind of facilities available to allow children to choose indoor or outdoor activities throughout the day. One such example enjoyed a partially covered area, different surfaces, easy access from the classroom and storage facilities for large equipment. Figure 7.2 shows how it was arranged.

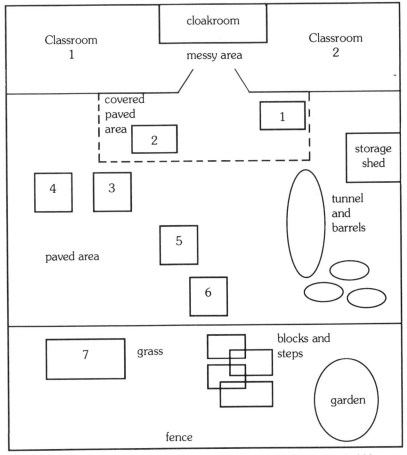

Key: 1, Junk modelling; 2, blanket with Lego and stickle bricks; 3, bubbly water; 4, water; 5, wet sand; 6, dry sand; 7, woodwork bench.
*In good weather the activities were accessible all day. A limited selection was available undercover when it was damp.*

**Figure 7.2: Arrangement for children's outdoor activity throughout the day.**

**Changes Made to Improve Outdoor Provision**

Some headteachers and teachers managed to overcome difficulties because they were committed to providing outdoor activities for their four year olds. Even though there were constraints and they recognized that the provision was not ideal, it was considered to be the best possible given the limited amount of space and adult help available. A few schools overcame difficult circumstances and had provided outdoor activities other than at playtimes by:

✿  moving the four year olds to a classroom with existing outdoor access;

✿  creating access by resiting doors (one school discovered that outdoor access through the classroom was a requirement under the fire regulations);

✿  reorganizing the school timetable to give children some time during the day for outdoor activities or for a choice of indoor or outdoor activities;

✿  organizing staffing so that groups of children have opportunities for outdoor play at different times of the day;

✿  using inner, enclosed courtyard areas, or outdoor areas adjacent to the classroom for sand and water activities when weather permits.

One example where a school was planning changes to make their outside area more interesting and secure is described in the researcher's notes:

The headteacher intended fencing off the outside area. This includes a grassed area and a new paved area so that wheeled toys can be used. The funding for this was provided by the supportive 'Friends of the School'. They had also received £500 from the authority, which had been designated by the headteacher to purchase equipment for the outdoor area. Their choice of equipment had been guided by the nursery class equipment list provided by the authority.

Plans for improvements in outdoor areas in other schools included creating under-cover areas, increasing paved areas, providing wheeled toys for outdoor play, a garden area and increased use of the environment for teaching points.

However it is not enough just to provide the space and activities. It is important that teachers attribute value to the outdoor activities. The following extract from the researcher's notes shows the effect of an adult's presence. 'The classroom door was open all day to give access to the courtyard area, but I saw no children at the activities there until I went outside myself to look at the provision. Then a little girl came out of the classroom and began playing with the sand in the sand tray.'

Other observations showed that where children were given a choice they chose the outdoor activities which involved them physically, mentally and socially. For example, in one school:

where the four year olds were given a free choice of indoor or outdoor activities, only three children decided to stay in the classroom; two of these in the home corner and the other child with the cars on the road map mat. Four children wandered between areas both indoors and out before deciding which activity appealed to them and the rest, about seventeen children, went straight outside and involved themselves on the climbing blocks and wheeled toys.

One of the youngest boys decided to play with Lego, which he did virtually all on his own for most of the morning. Another of the youngest boys in this class chose to play on the climbing blocks and in the shed with the 'gang'. He was very much a part of the gang and involved with what was going on.

A group of approximately eight children grouped and re-grouped throughout the morning. They used the climbing blocks as a base. There was a lot of chasing around the garden and running about. It was a mixed group of girls and boys and they used the whole range of equipment. This included noisy and physical activities on bikes, the wheeled toys, and crawling through tunnels as well as quiet activities like curling up, resting and hiding inside the blocks and the shed.

The use of the outdoor areas enables children to have much more choice and freedom of movement between activities. One child's response to the activities offered in the morning and to those offered in the afternoon demonstrates the importance of a choice of activity and access to more space.

The morning session started and concluded with large group time. There were several activities available for the children to choose from, for example a language activity, painting, a science activity, the home corner and the book corner. The children joined the rest of the school at playtime. The teacher led an outdoor PE session using small apparatus like bean bags and hoops.

During this time one of the youngest children found it difficult to join in the large group time, was unsure what he was supposed to be doing for the science activity and sat at the painting table. He waited for a piece of paper to be provided to paint on although it was easily accessible to him and he could have reached it for himself. At PE time, when the children were required to change their clothes and put plimsolls on, this child needed help with dressing and undressing.

In the afternoon a wide range and variety of activities was available both indoors and out. The provision was much more like a nursery setting with sand, water, climbing blocks and ladders, wheeled toys, construction blocks, books and teacher-directed table top activities. During this session the child who was unsure of himself in the morning was observed organizing his own activities and explaining to adults what he was doing. He spent a considerable amount of time, almost 50 minutes, in the sand pit. He started by taking off his shoes and socks. The nature of his activity changed several times from making roadways to cooking. At the end of this period he put his own shoes and socks back on and went off to climb on the climbing blocks. He found a ladder, which he discovered was long enough to place against the wall, climb up and look into the classroom. The excitement of this discovery was immediately relayed to the teacher.

The difference between this child's passive involvement indoors in the morning and active, enthusiastic participation outdoors in the afternoon was possibly due to the provision in the afternoon being more appropriate for his stage of development.

If the potential opportunities for educational experiences are to be utilized the outdoor environment should be as stimulating as that indoors. It should be far more exciting and interesting than the barren expanse of asphalt commonly provided for playtimes. As Galaghue (1982) suggests: 'The outdoor play area should first of all be designed for children in such a way that it stimulates their interest, imagination and large muscle development' (p. 358). The experiences offered by the outdoors without equipment can be improved dramatically by the permanent addition of sand pits, stepping stones, walls, gardens and tyres for imaginative play. An appropriate use of resources and a carefully planned outdoor environment means that the same skills and concepts can be developed in either the indoor or outdoor space.

# Indoor Space

Just as there are different opportunities in schools for outdoor activities so the buildings provided for indoor activities are varied. Some are new, others old, some are purpose-built, self-contained units, others may have been adapted or the youngest children may be housed in mobile classrooms. There may be only a limited amount of space available and the toilets and outdoor areas may or may not be adjacent to the classrooms. Often older buildings offer opportunities for using space creatively, with small rooms or corners that can be utilized for the younger children as long as there are enough adults available to oversee the activities.

Teachers rarely have any choice about the buildings in which they work but they can choose to arrange the classroom to give it a nursery ethos. The way the building is used 'reflects the beliefs of the adults who work there' (Dowling, 1988, p. 103) and what the teacher does with the space 'can be part of the teaching strategy' (Nash, 1981, p. 154).

The provision of an environment that enables young children to be independent active learners and to be given choices means that a variety of activities needing different amounts of space and floor surfaces should be provided. The environment should be aesthetically pleasing to provide a stimulus for learning, but arranged so that the child is able to act independently.

West *et al.* (1990) noted that the 'physical setting was not ideal' in infant classes. The interviewees and the guidelines in the present study were also concerned about **appropriate indoor space** being available for the youngest children. Appropriate provision would give them:

- ✿ access to the toilets and outside areas;
- ✿ the largest room and the most space;
- ✿ suitable furniture and storage facilities;
- ✿ different types of floor surfaces for different activities;
- ✿ recesses to allow for a balance of different types of activity, for example, areas for movement or for calm; space for individual or group activities.

The HMI survey found a 'considerable variation in the quality of classrooms and other teaching areas occupied by four year olds' (GB.DES, 1989c, para. 39). Even though they found that most classrooms were attractively arranged and maintained, where they were too small to provide a full range of activities there was a 'narrowing effect on the curriculum'.

There was often only a limited amount of classroom space available for the four year olds in the present study. Surprisingly, some of the newer buildings provided conditions that were cramped and had inadequate storage facilities. Many of the older buildings offered generous amounts of space, which could be adapted, but they lacked easy access to toilet facilities.

As Neill (1982) suggests, the design and the use of the space available affects how children and adults work. One of the teachers explained: 'there is not enough space for the age group. This means you can't have some of the equipment out at the same time as other equipment in order to cater for the very wide range of ability and the short concentration span of these children – they need variety'. Another said: 'there is not enough room, particularly not enough suitable floor area where children can have sand and water activities. The lack of space this year was not too bad with only 18 children but there will be difficulties next year with 25 children in the same area'.

## Access to Facilities and the Outdoors

If children are to be encouraged to be independent and to be given a choice of indoor or outdoor activities **they need access to the outdoor area and to cloakroom and toilet facilities.** This chapter has already discussed the limitations with regard to outdoor provision. The schools where children have to walk the entire length of the corridor to fetch their coats and use the toilets before going out to play, and then walk back along the corridor and along another one before they reach the playground, were in the minority in the study. In these schools older children or ancillary helpers accompanied new entrants to the toilet facilities and the playground.

The majority of schools in the study were fortunate enough to have reasonably accessible facilities, which enabled children to administer their own physical needs. However, in old buildings heavy doors often had to be negotiated and these sometimes caused difficulties for the children. In other new purpose-built units proximity was not a problem but the design of the sink units was such that buckets did not always fit underneath the taps. This made it difficult to provide water to fill the water trays. The greatest difficulties were found in schools where the four year olds were in mobile classrooms. Although they had the most space they often had a long way to go to use the toilet facilities and there was no water in the classroom to enable them to wash paint brushes easily, to fill water trays or just to wash their hands. In these circumstances the adults carried buckets of water to and fro.

There were often difficult decisions to be made by the headteacher and teachers in providing the most suitable indoor space for these younger children. Several teachers with four year olds in their classes were provided with: 'toilets and sinks which were accessible to all reception classes and linked the playground with the shared area. Sinks were also available in the shared area. The outdoor area was accessible with a door from each classroom opening onto the playground'.

## The Largest Room and the Most Space

The interviewees stressed that **the youngest children should be allocated the largest room.** This would give them the space to move around and choose their activities. The headteachers and teachers were very aware that this age group needed 'room to move' and 'enough space to make a mess'. Governors also often felt that the space available was not enough. One governor explained how he thought the county architects gave secondary aged pupils more space because they were bigger. In his opinion, this was 'a fallacy because the youngest children need more space'.

It was interesting that most of the professionals at the first stage of the study felt that it was reasonably easy to provide the most appropriate space for the youngest children. This could sometimes be arranged without extra funding but through the headteacher's or early years teachers' commitment to providing extra room for this age group. For example, space was made available for four year olds by:

- ✿ changing classrooms with older children so that the youngest have the largest room, or even two adjoining rooms;
- ✿ team teaching in adjoining rooms (although it was acknowledged that this can sometimes impose irksome organizational constraints);
- ✿ using the existing space more creatively and knocking down some walls if necessary.

### Changing classrooms
In the schools studied, the heads made sure that the youngest children were given more space by allocating them the largest classroom. The changes in one school are described in the researcher's notes:

> Changing classrooms meant that they [the four year olds] now had the use of the quadrangle and outdoor space as well as the largest classroom. The quadrangle was used all the time for all sorts of activities, both cognitive and physical. In the summer they put lino down so that the large construction toys can be used outside. This area tends to be sunny and is therefore used frequently. They are contemplating covering it over so that it can be used even more.

However, changing classrooms to give children the most space is not always ideal. For example, in one school giving the youngest children

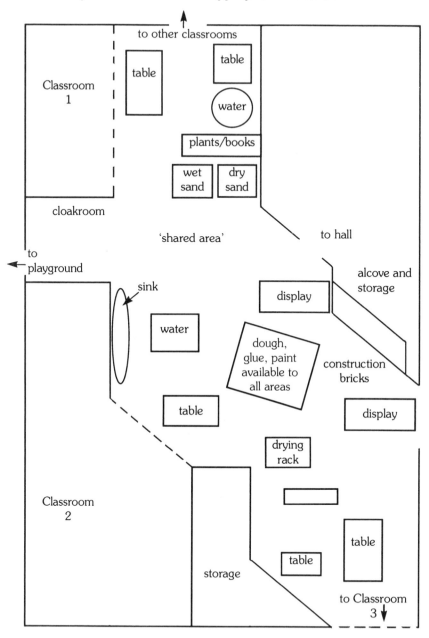

In this school there are three first year classes. Each class has their own area for a base and all three classes use the 'shared area'. The teachers tend to work with small groups of children in the classbase area while the nursery nurse is involved in different activities with individuals or small groups in the shared area. All the activities are provided indoors.

**Figure 7.3: Example 1 of an area shared by more than one class.**

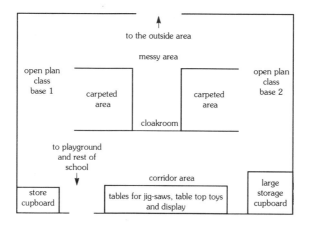

In this school, classrooms and corridor areas are shared. The whole area is used by all the children for activities throughout the day. Each teacher and the nursery nurse tend to remain in a specific area throughout the day. The carpeted areas are used for registration and story time. For some groups of children there are opportunities for access to the outdoor facilities as well as the messy area throughout the day. The nursery nurse supervises these activities.

**Figure 7.4: Example 2 of an area shared by more than one class.**

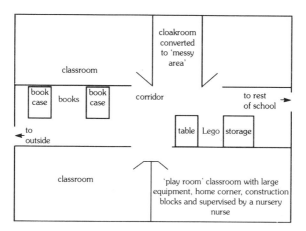

In this school there are two classes of four year olds who are usually based with their teacher in the classrooms. At timetabled times small groups of children from both classes (about six from each class) spend some time in the 'play room' with the nursery nurse. Unfortunately this facility is only available for three half days per week because of the part-time nature of the nursery nurses' contract.

**Figure 7.5: Example 3 of an area shared by more than one class.**

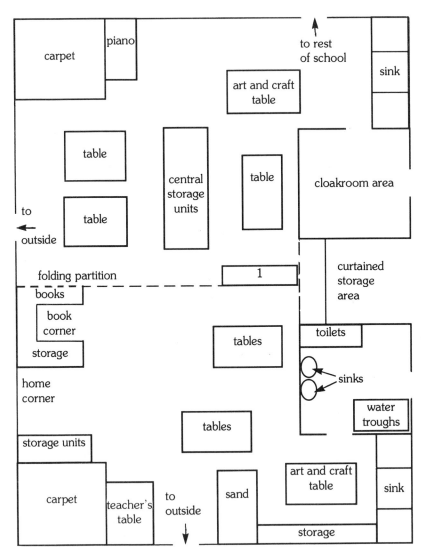

Key: 1, storage unit with aquarium on top.
In an early years unit the teacher worked with older children (five and six year olds) at one end and the nursery nurse worked with the four year olds at the other end, although the children were free to move between areas.

**Figure 7.6: Example 4 of an area shared by more than one class.**

the most space meant that they were a long way from the cloakroom facilities and the playground, and only one of the four classrooms with four year olds in had a sink.

*Adjoining rooms and adjacent areas*
In some schools the youngest children were provided with more space for their indoor activities by teachers using spare classrooms, by sharing adjacent corridor spaces for messy activities or by 'opening up their classrooms'.

Occasionally there were schools with classrooms that did not have a permanent class using them. These were able to be used for large equipment, wheeled toys or construction blocks when and where there were enough adults to supervise the activities. For example in one school the dining room area was used for physical activities when a nursery nurse was available.

*Shared areas*
Often when there was more than one class with four year olds the classrooms were arranged so that the children had a class base and access to another classroom, the corridor area or an adjacent area. These areas were very often used for messy activities like art and craft, natural materials or for construction blocks. If nursery nurses or ancillary helpers were available they often worked with children in this area; if they were not available the teacher had to be in a position to oversee the activities. This was sometimes arranged by another teacher working with some children from all the classes in the shared area rather than in their class base. Figures 7.3–7.6 show four examples of the way schools arranged to share indoor areas between two or more classes.

*Team teaching*
Opening up classrooms and sharing facilities is only possible if teachers are prepared to work together and collaborate about ideas. Team teaching can enable the space to be used more effectively for the younger children. How this evolved in one school is described in the researcher's notes:

> The two early admission class teachers were working together in two separate classrooms. They discovered that they were tackling very much the same things and decided that by sharing the same topic, half of the preparations could be done by each teacher for both classes. This seemed to halve the amount of work. At that stage, approximately three years ago, they were working in separate rooms. They 'opened their doors' and started to swap children, usually for topic work. The set-up that evolved was such that one person provided art and craft activities and the other provided

water activities. The children could move freely between the two. The teachers felt that this was one way of giving children a variety and range of experiences in a confined space. Gradually they changed it so that all the space was available for all the children, with messy activities in one area and more formal activities in the other. The timetabling for the hall and PE were constraints that were imposed on them so they tended to work in this way for certain sessions only. The two classes were treated as one and by working in smaller groups each child had opportunities to do more formal activities or messy activities during the morning or afternoon of each day. It was hoped that they had a chance to do all the activities provided during the course of a week.

In other LEAs early years units had been established. The reception and younger children shared a classroom or adjoining classrooms. See Figure 7.6, which shows how the space was arranged.

### Creative use of the existing indoor areas

There were several ways in which schools had improved the use of the indoor space that was available. These involved not only the use of adjacent areas as previously described but also the modification of buildings, removal of unnecessary furniture and flexible classroom arrangements to encourage greater freedom of movement for the youngest children.

### Modification of buildings

In some schools money had been made available, either through the local authority or PTA funds, to knock down interior walls or resite doors so that the space available could be used more appropriately. Vause (1988) found in her research that benefits had accrued for the youngest children where minor modifications had been carried out to enable imaginative use of the cloakroom area and corridor spaces.

More often the money required for building alterations was limited or not forthcoming and teachers were left with plans of what they would like to do, for example: 'That cupboard space would be more useful if the door opened the other way'; or 'It would be very useful to have access to that alcove area from the classroom'; and 'If that wall was partially removed we would be able to see what was happening and be able to use the shared area even if we did not have another adult to help'. Other plans included using wasted spaces and walkways, and installing peninsular sink units.

In some old school buildings a great deal of changes had been made to accommodate the four year olds. For example, in one infant school:

There was a lot of space in the school that had originally been divided into small classrooms with long wide corridors and cloak-rooms off the corridors. Doors were removed to open up class-rooms and cloakroom areas. Coat pegs were removed from the centre to leave a large area for sand and water activities. Construction kits were used in the wide corridors. Where the corridors were still a thoroughfare displays had been arranged using wooden trel-lises, drapes and tables for working or reading quietly. The other corridors had been adapted by painting them white and providing equipment so that they could be used as a shared area between classrooms.

## Removing furniture

Some schools had increased the amount of indoor space available by cutting down on the number of chairs and tables. Roberts (GB.DES, 1985c) suggests that reception teachers should question assumptions like the need for a chair for each child at all times. This not only cre-ates more space but also invites teachers to consider what objectives their demand for certain activities at certain times fulfils.

In some schools furniture had been removed so that a space was created in the centre of the room and activities were provided around the edge. The teachers who had removed furniture, including the teacher's desk, found that they were able to use the new-found space for other activities. For example: 'We have tried to create more space in the classroom area by moving furniture and investing in a carpet where the children can sit or play'; and 'We moved some of the tables out and created a large carpeted area for number games and made space for the permanent use of water, not just outdoors'. There were also examples of the tables being removed at the beginning of the year, and gradually being introduced as the term progressed when the activities offered to the children required extra tables.

## Flexible classroom arrangements

By having a flexible approach to classroom arrangements, not only could tables be provided as and when they were needed but it was also possible to move the furniture to create play spaces or areas for physi-cal activity instead of only using the timetabled allocation of the hall. The use of folding partitions enabled areas to be screened if groups of children were involved in quieter activities. In one school where the classroom arrangement of furniture was flexible the teacher com-mented: 'the tables that are available vary and the arrangement changes depending on the activity. Sometimes the children move the furniture themselves. Today they have pushed them to one side to give them enough room to build on the carpet with the wooden blocks'. Even where the furniture was child-sized and plentiful, tea-chers were imaginative and improvised extra seating by up-ending trolleys in the home corner. This enabled children to sit alongside each other as if on a settee, or two or three could be used together like seats on a bus or train.

## Suitable Furniture and Storage Facilities

The removal of unnecessary furniture has already been discussed. The items that remain **should be of child height** with low tables and chairs, which makes them accessible to the children who are able to use them without the need for adult assistance. The schools studied provided furniture that was all child-sized and suitable for children to use. In a few schools there were areas with easy chairs which could be used by parents before school or by parent helpers at playtimes.

The existing units were used to store equipment for activities and teachers' and children's personal belongings. There was usually access to shared pencils, scissors, books, puzzles, materials and so on. Professionals suggested that these should be at child level and labelled to enable children to be independent by selecting items for their activity and returning them to their proper place when they had finished.

### Tables and chairs

The interviewees suggested that it was not necessary for children to have their own special place. However, many practitioners felt that it was important that there were enough places for all the children to sit down at the same time. In some schools this enabled activities to take place, in others it catered for lunchtime arrangements. For example: 'The children do not have their own table and chair although there are enough for everyone to sit down at the same time such as lunchtime, which is held in the classroom'. The majority of the schools provided enough chairs for the children to sit on but depending on the activities some children would sit at a table while others sat on the carpet. Researchers' observations revealed that at a table-top activity, where there was a choice of standing up or sitting down to do the activity, some children elected to stand while others sat down. The children commented: 'you can sit where you like, you can sit anywhere, it depends on what you're doing ...'.

### Labelled equipment

Most schools provided children with their own personal drawer or tray to keep their things in. These, along with the other trays or drawers containing pencils, puzzles and other small equipment, were normally labelled with clear writing and pictures not only to enable the children to recognize where things were kept but also to give them opportunities to realize that print conveys meaning.

The children's comments with regard to these drawers were interesting. In one school they said: 'You have your own tray to keep your special things in. I've got my reading book and my drawing in there'. In another school they said: 'This is my drawer. I keep all my things in here. That's his drawer'. When asked how did they know it was his drawer, they replied: 'It's got his name on (child points to name). This is my name.'

A group of children helping themselves to rulers, paper, pencils and so on confidently explained, when they were asked, how they knew where to find things: 'When I need some paper I get some out of that drawer.' (The drawers are labelled with words and pictures.) Four children answered the researcher's question, 'how do you know which drawer to go to', by saying: 'I know where everything is'; 'I can see over the top'; 'I just know'; and 'I looked at the picture'.

## Storage facilities

Storage was not usually a major problem for the schools. Most classrooms had adequate trolleys, bookshelves, trays, boxes and wire racks for displaying books and storing small equipment. The availability of large indoor equipment, for example climbing blocks, was limited. Had it been more generally available, storage would probably have been more difficult.

Nearly all the storage facilities were clearly labelled and sometimes there were silhouettes to enable children to replace the equipment used for their activities in its correct position. This was the case where the storage units were at child height.

Teachers had been innovative and creative in the kinds of storage they found for the equipment for the youngest children. Many had collections of tins or plastic containers, which had been brought from their homes and attractively covered and labelled. One teacher had an interesting arrangement of cardboard boxes, which had been passed on to her by the science coordinator. These were now labelled and located under a work-top. Materials like polystyrene trays, wood, toilet rolls, yoghurt pots and other paraphernalia of the infant classroom were now effectively and tidily stored, but still accessible to the children. The work-top above was used for displaying books and items linked to the theme for the term.

In some classrooms the storage units were arranged centrally, in others they helped to create recesses and separate activity areas.

Sometimes curtains were used to provide areas for storing construction kits or items not in daily use. Some cupboards were too large to be particularly useful for storing things and the lower doors had been removed to enable more space to be available for the children to use the construction blocks. The top cupboards remained as storage for items used only by the adults.

A space saving idea observed in some schools was the wall-mounted teacher's desk. This is composed of wall-mounted drawers with a work-top and a narrow overhead cupboard. This takes up less room than the traditional teacher's table but still gives the teacher an area to keep organizational things, like letters to parents. The floor area underneath can be used to store equipment accessible to the children or to provide extra floor area for the children to extend their activities.

## Floor Surfaces

Different activities require different floor surfaces. Professionals suggested that **there should be carpeted areas and tiled areas to enable a variety of activities to be provided.**

*The carpeted area*
The carpeted area in the schools were found in corners or in the middle of the classroom. It was predominantly used for activities that required children to sit on the floor. In most schools there was an area of carpeting that was large enough for all the children to sit down at once. This was used for registration of large group times, storytime and for small groups of children to use the construction blocks, puzzles, number games, small world activities and any other activities that could conveniently be carried out on the floor.

Where the carpeted area had been extended one teacher commented that: 'the new carpet is much more comfortable for the children to sit on. The increased area allows the children to sit down together for story and other large group activities. The new carpet also forms the floor of the home corner and space for large block play'.

The 'book' or 'language' area was usually carpeted. Sometimes cushions were provided in this area as well. If the area was tiled, carpet squares and cushions provided a more welcoming and relaxing area in which to read or browse through books. In one school this area was so comfortable that a child was observed curled up and fast asleep!

When there was not enough carpeting one teacher described the difficulties she encountered: 'The carpet area is very useful but becomes full up too quickly – it is only used for the large floor blocks of which the class has only half a set – there would not be room for a whole set although the children would love it'.

In most of the classrooms about a third of the floor area was carpeted, sometimes more. Where the majority of the classroom was carpeted the teachers commented that it restricted the provision of sand, water, dough, clay and other messy activities. If there was only a limited amount of space without carpeting these activities could not be provided all at the same time. Where the flooring was inappropriate some schools used large plastic sheets to protect the carpet when providing messy activities. In some older schools there were wooden floors. The caretaker found it difficult to keep the floors clean and attractive if water was spilt or sand ground into the wood. He encouraged the teachers to provide these activities in the corridors, which were tiled. This made it easier to mop up spillages or sweep up sand but not so easy to intervene in or to supervise the children's activity.

*The tiled area*
Access to a tiled area enables teachers to provide the messy activities like sand, dough, water, clay, paint, glue and so on. These areas can be inside or adjacent to the classrooms. Tiles are much easier to keep clean than carpets if paint, sand or dough is accidentally dropped on the floor. It is important for safety reasons that non-slip tiles are used where water is likely to be spilt.

The floor surfaces in most of the schools provide both carpeted areas and tiled areas. For example in one school:

> The flooring was mainly lino tiles although there was a large carpeted area in the toy room and book room. These areas were used as 'registration carpets'. There was also a long, narrow carpet in the corridor area, which was used for construction toys. Throughout the rest of the area there were several mats, carpet sqaures and cushions, which children could sit on to carry out an activity or read quietly.

## Recesses for a Variety of Activities

The interviewees recommended that a range and variety of activities should be provided for these younger children in infant and primary classes. If the provision is to go some way towards presenting a nursery ethos the children need areas in which to play or relax, individually or in small groups. There should be areas where children can be noisy, be quiet or do messy activities. There should be areas for privacy and an open area to encourage movement. Children should be encouraged to do things at different heights: at floor, cupboard and table-top levels. For example, in one class two lots of Lego were provided, one on the table, the other on the floor. The table-top Lego was used with play-people and that on the carpet included wheels so that cars, trucks and so on could be made.

In one nursery visited by the team the indoor space was broken up into several recesses with different activities in them. The classroom was relatively large but had been made cosy by organizing the space into activity areas and corners. The staff had improvised an interesting home area by building it above a storage area and providing a three-step climbing block as stairs to reach it.

One infant school had a generous amount of space available for their children. There were three classroom areas providing a messy room, a quiet room and a noisy room for the children to use. The adjoining corridor and walkways were used as a kitchen area, cooking area and for construction toys. This was unusual and it is far more likely that schools have a limited amount of space. The schools created different activity areas by using:

✿ different floor surfaces;
✿ shared areas;
✿ furnishing, fabrics and displays;
✿ strategically placed storage units.

*Different floor surfaces*
Different flooring enables areas to be created in schools. Earlier discussion in this chapter has already taken into account the variety of activities that can be provided if different floor surfaces are available.

*Shared areas*
Teachers working together, opening up their classrooms and pooling resources, as described earlier in this chapter, were able to share the amount of space available. Access to shared classrooms or other shared areas enables teachers to provide different areas for different activities. This was particularly successful with the help of extra adults.

Sometimes, however, teachers found that having to share activity areas was not always convenient and timetabling the area created its own limitations. This extract from the researcher's notes shows how this was remedied in one school: 'On my first visit there were three tables, one for paint, one for glue and one for dough or clay, but the teachers found that they were always negotiating to use them. They decided to change so that they had one table outside each classroom, which they could choose to use for paint, glue, clay or dough'.

*Furnishing, fabrics and displays*
Furnishing fabrics were often used in the schools to enhance the teaching areas as well as to create areas within the classroom. For example, special 'quiet' areas were sometimes provided by curtaining off an area and providing comfortable seating and cushions. This provided children with a place to relax. Other schools created areas both in the classroom area and in the adjacent corridors by using trellises or bamboo screens. The areas that were created were used for home-corners, reading, Lego and so on. Here is one interesting example: 'The carpet corner has been curtained off by the class teacher with a blackout material and turned into a tree corner containing a huge

model tree, which the children had made from junk. Model spiders and insects hung from the tree and the whole corner was very dark to inspire imaginative play.'

The majority of the schools had interesting and exciting displays throughout the school. These usually included art work by the youngest children. In their classroom the display was usually linked to the theme that was being explored. As well as informative display items there were examples of children's work. In some of the classrooms different materials, like corrugated cardboard, cardboard, cellophane, plastic and tissue paper, were used to create different areas. For example, in one school, in one area there was a cardboard and plastic construction that was a submarine and next to this the children's tissue paper and painted fish were displayed on the walls and suspended from the ceiling to make an 'under the sea' area.

In another school an area was completely separated from floor to ceiling by a paper screen. This had been painted to resemble a door. The corner was entirely secluded for the children but audible to the teacher. The 'specialness' of the area was emphasized by the fact that an adult was only allowed to enter if taken by the hand of a child.

### Strategically placed storage units

Often teachers created areas for different activities and small group work by using storage units and tables to form a low screen. For example, in one school moving the storage unit away from the wall, as shown in Figure 7.7, created two areas, which were then used for building blocks and a painting easel. Another school made a similar change with the water tray, which provided children with access to the two longest sides rather than the two shortest sides for water activities.

The way some schools arranged different areas by using storage equipment and tables is shown in Figure 7.8. Other schools used storage cupboards to create areas, trolleys to delineate the 'edge' of the classroom and tables for language or number activities with a central store for pencils, paper and so on so that the children could service their own needs as shown in Figure 7.9. A central store and areas created by using storage units or book trolleys was used in the shared area. This can be seen if you look back to Figure 7.3.

Changing the use of a room often means that existing arrangements can be adapted to suit the younger children. For example, in some of the schools, dining rooms provided extra areas for physical activity or construction blocks. Another example was the old library area being used by the youngest children. The bays where the books had been kept were repainted and now provided areas for display and quiet areas for small group work.

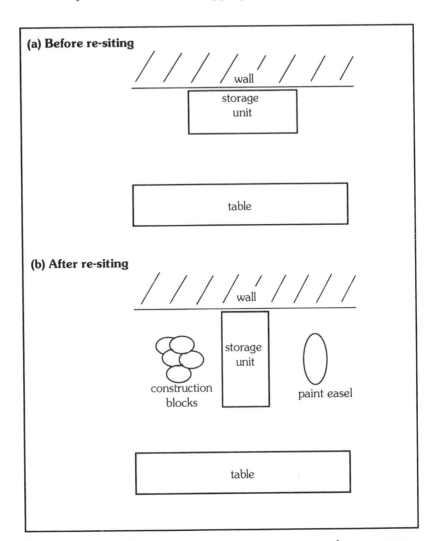

**Figure 7.7: Resiting furniture to create recesses in one area of the classroom.**

Once different areas have been created in the classroom or adjacent areas they are sometimes labelled to remind children where things could be found. They are usually designated for the following activities.

*Tiled areas*
Mainly for messy activities such as those involving paint, glue, water, sand, gravel, leaf mould and other natural materials. Sometimes this area was used for physical activity, small wheeled toys, climbing blocks and large construction sets.

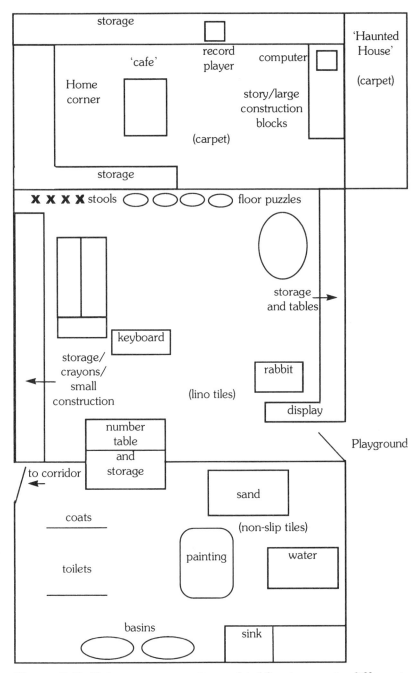

**Figure 7.8: Using storage units and tables to create different areas in the classroom.**

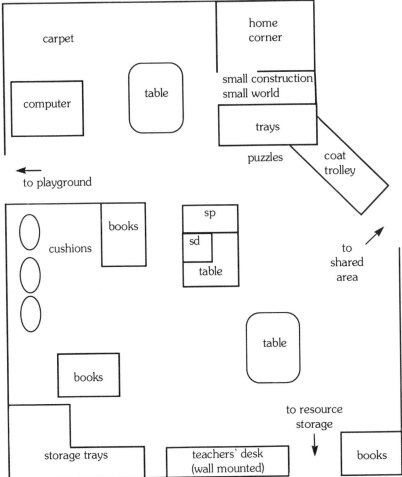

Key: sp, storage and pencils; sd, storage and display.
*Children were able to access equipment from low storage units and central storage space.*

**Figure 7.9: Central storage facilities for independent use.**

*Carpeted areas*
For large group times such as registration or story, and small group activities such as construction blocks and floor toys, or number games, puzzles, small world activities and so on. Activities could be provided at floor level rather than on tables.

*Other areas*
Usually included: groups of tables for language and number activities and teacher-directed small group activities often connected with the class theme; home corners, which were often changed to

fit into different themes, for example, shops, dentists, doctors, veterinary surgery, under the sea and a host of other ideas; book corners with comfortable seating; areas for individual or small group activities like Lego, computers, small world, cooking, music, sewing and so on.

The researcher's notes describe one classroom where activity areas have been clearly defined (see Figure 7.8):

The wet area is located near the sink and has a floor of non-slip tiles to distinguish it from the normal classroom floor, which is of lino tiles. The wet area contains painting easels, sand and water. The home corner is on the carpeted area and is separated from the rest of the room by low storage units and a partition. The book area is separated from the rest of the room by a curtain. Other areas of the main classroom are subdivided by low storage units or tables.

If adjoining areas are equipped with compatible materials children can combine them to extend activities. For example if the home corner is adjacent to the mark-making equipment, felt tips or pencils may be used to write shopping lists; if the Lego is near the water the model boat made from Lego can be sailed on the water; or books can be taken from the book area to read to teddy in the home corner. Here are examples observed in schools:

One of the youngest girls liked to play in the home corner. She explained she was cooking and when asked what she was cooking she said she was making a sandwich. This activity developed into sorting plastic cutlery and paper plates into place settings on the table. Then she went to the adjacent 'colouring table' and drew a picture, which she cut out and coloured to make 'food' to go on the plates.

A group of children observed playing in the home corner first kitted themselves out with shoes from the 'shoe shop'. They made a vehicle from the large construction blocks and went on a journey. It was a hot day so the children used paper provided from the painting and writing tables to make a fan to cool themselves. They returned to the 'vehicle' fanning themselves as they travelled back to the home corner for 'lunch'.

Where the classroom is not very big the close proximity of areas makes it very easy for the children to make links naturally between the activities (see Chapter 5). In one school where different areas had been created the teacher's comment was:

Having the different areas is good because the children know exactly where to go. I can say to them 'go to the language table' and all the children would know where I meant. It is also useful to be able to base all the equipment that the children are likely to need for those activities near that area and their efforts can be displayed there.

## Enabling Changes to Take Place

Many of the changes made in the schools were possible because of the support from the headteacher and enough adults being available to supervise the extra space allocated to the youngest pupils. As one teacher commented, there had been no difficulties in changing the space available for her young charges because 'the headteacher was co-operative and the staff tolerant'.

Changing classrooms, turning rooms into playrooms, moving furniture, providing cushions and so on can be achieved through changing attitudes and commitment to this kind of provision by the teacher. However, other changes, like knocking down walls, resiting doors, paving new areas, covering the patio area, take expert advice and usually a substantial amount of money.

Such changes implemented in schools in the study were usually funded by the local authority. Funding was most often forthcoming when there was support from the adviser. Storage units, carpets and furnishing fabrics, however, were more generally supplied through the school's own capitation allowance.

HMI also found that in some LEAs buildings had been adapted to provide accommodation for younger children. In one LEA 'in addition to the adaptation costs, the LEA had allocated £8000 for refurbishment, which included both furnishings and equipment'. In another authority 'parents had adapted a former cloakroom to create an attractive carpeted activity area and a library' (GB.DES, 1989c, para. 40).

The present study found examples of PTAs and other bodies providing generous support. These funding committees had generally contributed to the purchase of storage sheds, large construction kits and computers rather than structural changes.

Governors, headteachers and teachers were aware and concerned that LMS might make it more difficult to provide appropriate space for the youngest children. As one governor explained: 'We need a bigger hall, a new headteacher's room ... we must put these things on our budget'. On the other hand, some headteachers felt that because they were likely to have more control over their finances they would be able to persuade parents to do some of the painting, fencing and so on more economically and quickly than going through the authority. This may be true in some areas of the country but there are other areas where, for a number of reasons, parents are not able to be as supportive or helpful with either financing or carrying out improvements in the physical environment for their children.

Changes in the organization of space can be made and the new environment thus created can have a dramatic effect on the experiences offered to these young children. Often limited funds prevent major changes from being made, but the removal of unnecessary furniture or the addition of carpets or cushions can influence the activities offered and the teaching approach adopted. Commitment to using the space available as appropriately as possible should come from the whole early years team. For example one headteacher explained: 'We had the money and the resources. It was a collective decision by the staff to change classrooms. Extra funding had been provided through PTA funds for extra resources like the outdoor storage shed and large equipment'.

## Conclusion

The space available for the youngest children should encourage their freedom of movement. There should be access to the outdoors from the classroom. Indoors appropriate furniture and fittings can be used to create recesses for a range and variety of activities. So that children are able to be independent in their use of the equipment and materials available in the classroom there should be suitable storage facilities. There are still schools that are unable to develop the space they have available because of restricted access to additional areas or not enough adults to supervise activities. When appropriate space is provided for younger children in infant and primary schools it is often through the commitment and imagination of the staff.

# 8 Equipment and Materials

The context in which education takes place is crucial and the 'first practical considerations must relate to the creation of an environment within which children will be stimulated to learn ... The room should be planned as a workshop with all the appropriate tackle and gear and designed with distinct areas of curriculum focus' (Blenkin and Kelly, 1987, p. 47).

It is important that the resources in the classroom provide opportunities for the development of the whole child and encourage children to become independent and confident. Through the use of appropriate resources, language and social skills are developed and extended, concepts are formed, imagination stimulated and the environment can be explored. The equipment and materials available to the children provide the chief inspiration for their play. It is important that these are provided as and when they are necessary to enable children's learning to develop and be sustained. Children need opportunities to master the resources and the knowledge they gain informs future learning.

LEA guidelines suggest that a holistic view of learning and the curriculum is supported by the availability of at least the following in a session: tactile materials, mark-making equipment, sticking/collage, construction sets, imaginative and physical activities, books, music, baking, puzzles, computers and/or TV. As Stevenson points out:

> Where children are provided with appropriate materials, they accept the demands made by those materials and use them to further their own experience or to set their own challenge: blocks became fortresses, sand the medium for landscape, monsters were moulded from clay, junk became the vehicle for problem-solving, water was medicine, milk or the ocean and a selection of waistcoats, top hats, handbags, a camera and skirts gave rise to an impromptu wedding' (TES, 23.10.87).

The guidelines provided information about appropriate equipment and materials and details of where they could be obtained for the use of the youngest children in infant or primary schools. The following resource areas were outlined and most of them were observed in the classrooms with four year olds in the schools studied.

✿ Natural materials and equipment to use with them. In the schools studied, these are usually provided on the tiled areas of the classroom and sometimes outside.

✿ Creative materials and equipment to use with them. These are often provided on the tiled area for ease of cleaning.

✿ Construction play equipment and 'small world' toys like play people, cars, zoo or farm animals, which can be used on their own or in conjunction with the large construction kits. These activities often take place on the carpeted areas which are quieter and warmer for the children to sit on.

✿ Domestic play, which includes home corners, dressing up clothes and accessories to encourage the change of use of the home corner. For example, appropriate 'props' could suggest a hairdressers, an opticians, a hospital and so on. Most classes in the study have a 'home corner', which changes with the theme or the children's inclination and interest.

✿ Book corners providing a range of books covering a variety of topics. This area tends to be a quiet area to which children are able to withdraw. There are usually carpets on the floor and cushions or comfortable seating.

✿ Table-top equipment, puzzles and games including language and number games. This often includes teacher-directed activities.

✿ Specific interest equipment and materials that encourage individual or small group activities such as cooking, sewing, using the computer, and theme related activities. This area is often used for children undertaking activities with parents or other adult helpers.

✿ Musical instruments, which should be freely available for young children to explore the world of sound. Although some schools have listening corners with taped stories, musical instruments are not generally available in the schools studied.

✿ Outdoor equipment, which includes large climbing equipment, barrels, tunnels and wheeled toys as well as bats, balls, hoops and bean bags.

This kind of provision does not always seem to be available for four year olds in infant or primary classes. Pollard (1989) found limited areas for children to withdraw to and a lack of areas designated for science or music in primary schools. This was particularly so in small schools and was attributed to less space and money being available. HMI report that:

Few LEAs and schools had recognized fully the resource implications of admitting four year olds to school. Provision for these children was judged to be less than satisfactory both in range and quality in over half the classes. The most common deficiencies were in the provision of equipment for outdoor play, music, early work in science and technology, and materials for craft work (GB.DES, 1989c, para. 41).

The professionals in the study appreciated that there was potentially a vast range of items for teachers to choose from and were reluctant to list resources needed for fear of being definitive or prescriptive. The choice, they said, should be left to individual schools and teachers but the decisions made should offer the children opportunities to experience a range of equipment and a variety of materials. Several of the interviewees said that the equipment and materials should be similar to those provided in good nursery practice while allowing for all areas of the curriculum to be covered and developed.

Professionals were aware that materials that encouraged children to find out how things worked could be used to develop CDT skills; magnifying glasses could develop the observation skills needed for science and art. They also pointed out that teachers should be aware of why they were providing certain materials, such as sand and water. If, for example, the children lived near a sandy beach a novel medium, such as clay, wood or rocks, would provide different experiences for them. Specifically selected items of equipment could be added to the sand to develop early science or maths concepts.

It was clear that the provision in nursery schools or classes seemed to be more generous than in infant or primary classes. Nursery provision was more likely to be equipped with large climbing apparatus, like climbing frames, blocks and slides, tunnels and barrels, rocking horses and see-saws. There also seemed to be more floor cushions, musical instruments and well-equipped home corners than in the infant or primary school classrooms. Often in primary classes such equipment was scarce. One dinner lady commented 'when children have nothing to do they tend to argue and squabble'.

The guidelines collected and the professionals interviewed recommended that the equipment and materials provided should be:

✿   of good quality;
✿   easily accessible to enable children to use them safely and independently;
✿   appropriate to each child's level of experience, which means that there should be a range and a variety of equipment and materials.

## Good Quality

The guidelines and the interviews emphasized that **equipment and materials should be of good quality.** There is nothing more frustrating for a child than attempting to hammer in a nail with equipment that is not appropriate for doing the task demanded or to cut out with a pair of unsuitable scissors. As one child reminded her teacher, 'I don't like these scissors, they are too stiff to open.'

Most teachers felt that they were reasonably well equipped with materials. Stocks of paper and card, paint and adhesive, natural materials and 'junk' materials were usually adequate. This kind of provision was supplemented by using scrap paper and card, off-cuts of wood, or oddments of wool and material provided from the teachers' or parents' personal supplies.

Other resources, such as books, puzzles and games, table-top toys and so on, were considered to be 'good' by the teachers using them. The most dissatisfaction voiced by the teachers was that there was not enough large equipment for indoor or outdoor use, and insufficient construction sets and blocks. In some schools new equipment had been provided and even though it was perhaps limited in quantity it was of good quality. For example the researcher was able to record:

> a group of children were collecting plants, insects and stones. The children were provided with pieces of plastic tubing, magnifying glasses and special plastic containers of different shapes and sizes, some with a magnifying glass built in, to collect specimens and observe them closely and safely. This seemed far removed from yoghurt pots and jam-jars often used for such ventures. It was much safer, more effective and 'looked professional'.

For some professionals, quality was thought to be more important than quantity. For example, it was important to provide good quality tools with which to write and good quality books were generally available in well-presented book-corners, quiet or shared areas. School stocks were often supplemented by books borrowed through the school library service.

## Real Objects

Where appropriate, **the use of real objects rather than toy imitations** can add to the quality of the activity experienced and make it more meaningful for the children. Woodwork activities can make use of real wood, hammers, saws, nails, screws and screw-drivers. Objects used in the home corner included empty household containers, like shampoo or washing-up liquid bottles, shopping bags, irons, mirrors, hairdryers, cameras, brooms, kettles and telephones. For example, in one home corner:

> There are wigs, combs and brushes, slides and clips, scarves, rollers and empty shampoo bottles, and an old hairdryer. A group of children dress up, sort out some money and select a handbag. First they

go shopping (a walk around the classroom), they visit the library (the book corner) and then go to the hairdressers where they 'do' each other's hair before returning to a table to have their lunch. There are full-size plastic plates, dishes and cutlery. The four chairs around the table have cushions that match the table cloth and curtains.

Often the 'finishing touches', like curtains, covers for prams and so on, were made in the teacher's 'directed time' or by parents.

Other examples observed include the use of real plants and gardening tools, real building materials like drain-pipes, bricks, tiles, slates and a workman's helmet, and a real cheque book to copy to make one of their own. Real clothes were often used for dressing up and occasionally used to make collage pictures. Babies, pets, ducks, snails, butterflies, caterpillars and so on were sometimes brought into school so that live examples could be observed, discussed, drawn or painted. Teachers said that children tended to remember these occasions much more vividly than anything that was discussed from books or pictures.

## Sufficient Materials

For some of the interviewees, it was more important to provide a limited amount of quality materials, extending the range and variety over time, than to put out a large quantity of bits and pieces. Others pointed out that **there should be sufficient materials for children to be able to develop and complete the activity and, where appropriate, for several children to be able to use them at the same time.** The importance of this is demonstrated in one classroom:

> there was plenty of cotton wool, material, wool, adhesive and paper for the group of children to finish the masks they were making to wear in their assembly to the rest of the school. On the carpet area adjacent to this activity two boys were involved in a reading game. They became very frustrated when there were not enough words available to complete their sentence. 'I need another "on"' one boy repeated two or three times. They searched through the pile unsuccessfully; eventually they gave up.

Additional equipment and materials may be provided for some of the day or part of the week by pooling equipment or sharing it with another class. However, it is important to organize the activities and teaching approach so that the facilities, equipment and materials are available as much as possible. On the other hand, it was the view of some teachers that limiting access to certain materials and equipment means that children are given a break from them and when they are re-introduced they come out 'fresh and new'.

Even if a limited amount of equipment contributes to children's problem-solving activities it is frustrating for them to use games or do jig-saws when some of the pieces are missing. This means that it is important that care is taken in presenting equipment and materials.

### Clean and Attractive Presentation

Professionals regarded it as **important that materials, particularly natural materials, are clean and attractive when offered to the children.** All the equipment and materials should be presented and displayed so that they provoke interest and appeal to the children and encourage them to investigate them further. For example, dressing-up clothes can be hung up more easily if hooks are supplied, or there is a rail to hang them on, rather than jumbled in a basket.

Towards the end of the summer term a group of children were observed with the nursery nurse washing and cleaning the Lego and stickle bricks in bubbly water in the water tray. During the course of the activity there was a lot of discussion about the things they had built with Lego throughout the year, why they were washing it, what would be happening to them and to the classroom next term and so on.

## Accessibility

It was important, interviewees told us, that the equipment and materials were easily accessible to the children. **The children should know where to find things and should be encouraged to service their own activities and take responsibility for getting things out and putting them away.** Labelling trays, equipment and games, for example, helped children to return things to their rightful place.

The storage arrangements in most of the schools enabled children to select the materials they needed for an activity. In one class, for example,

when the children had completed their colouring, cutting and sticking activity they accessed paper of a colour of their own choice from a storage tray. They used this to mount their picture for display. The teachers usually provided paper and stimulating materials. All the pencils in this classroom were kept in attractive, plastic covered pots. The children were able to choose whether they used felt-tip pens, pencils, crayons or paint from centrally stored resources. They could also help themselves to glue, Sellotape or staples if things needed fixing together.

It was not, however, just the consumable materials that were easily accessible to the children. In many classrooms they could also select table-top activities, small world equipment, construction sets and so on. In the classrooms where children were encouraged to be independent in their use of equipment and materials they had also been shown how to use them safely and properly. For example, children appreciated that scissors should be carried points-down for safety reasons, they were aware that paintings needed hanging on the drying rack to dry properly, they understood that if things were not returned to their rightful place they might not be able to find them next time they were needed. In spite of the children's good intentions teachers were aware that working in this way often looked 'chaotic', but they should take heart from the following observations made in one school:

> The children were very good at getting things out on their own and putting them away. They could do this because everything was clearly labelled and in this school there were silhouettes as well to show where things should be replaced. At the beginning of the art and craft activity they carefully covered the table with newspaper. When they had finished they put the completed articles on a rack to dry and wiped the table-tops. They were able to wash their own paint brushes and glue sticks in the low level sink in the shared area. They helped each other to put their aprons on and take them off. One little girl found a stray top from a felt pen. She picked it up, walked to the area where the pens were kept, noticed by the ink on the lid that it fitted a blue pen and matched it up with a blue felt tip pen without a lid.

In most of the schools almost all the equipment and materials were within easy reach of the children so they could service their own activities. Sometimes, however, teachers felt that they needed some control over what was available on the tables and used the higher storage units to prevent children reaching certain resources.

The tidying-up periods in the classrooms visited by the project team usually involved the children as well as the adults. Sometimes the major part of the process was done by the children. For example, in one school during 'clearing-up time' on Friday afternoon one girl fetched a broom, dustpan and brush and cleaned out the rabbit hutch. A boy fetched another broom and swept up around the sand tray.

In other schools the whole class was responsible for tidying-up. For example, the teacher suggested that 'if everyone picks up a block it will take no time at all to tidy away'. For others clearing-up time became a massive matching and sorting exercise, especially in the home corner:

> The home corner is well equipped with all kinds of kitchen gadgets and 'food' made out of flour and salt which has been baked, painted and varnished. Part of the home corner operates as a restaurant with a table and place settings for four people. There are menus and children can order a specific course, expect to receive it on a plate and then pay for it. At the end of a session all these different commodities have to be put away in the correct place. For example, every potato has to be put back into the potato tin, peas back into the pea tin and so on. The sets of cutlery are in matching colours, with each colour having its own hook to hang on.

Often the tidying up was done very well and only a few of the more difficult jobs were left to the ancillary helper or nursery nurse. By encouraging children to tidy up, other adults in the classroom were able to use this time talking to children and being involved in their activity rather than just 'washing paint pots'.

Quality, quantity and accessibility of equipment and materials is important and can be achieved in offering a range of equipment and materials.

## A Range of Equipment and Materials

**It is important that a suitable range of equipment and materials are provided for four year olds in infant and primary classes.** As HMI (GB.DES, 1989c) noted, the quality of education is reflected in the range of resources available and it is not uncommon to find four year olds using equipment intended for older children.

Professionals suggested that the range of equipment and materials provided should be such that it was able to meet the demands made by children at different levels of ability at any one time. It should also enable progression for individual children over a period of time and provide opportunities for teachers to develop multidisciplinary activities. It was considered important to provide equipment and materials that would foster and reflect a multicultural society valuing equal opportunities. As Manning and Sharp (1977) report:

> children's play in school is dependent to a certain extent on the materials and equipment available; for example, exploratory play is more advanced if both dry and wet sand are provided, if equipment for sieving as well as floating and sinking is at hand. Large constructions leading to imaginative play cannot be made with small building materials. (p. 20)

The schools studied tried to provide appropriate activities for their four year olds by selecting a range of suitable equipment and materials.

## Different Levels of Ability

Through the teacher's selection of equipment and planning of the activities, provision can be made to cater for individual levels of ability. For example, by providing three water trays and a range of pots and pans and scientific pumps the teacher was enabling the children to respond according to their own interests and stage of development. The researcher's notes describe the children's activity:

> There were three water trays outside in the sunshine. Two boys built a complicated system of pots and saucepans and discovered that water came out through the handle of a saucepan. By rotating the saucepan they managed to make the water flow over the side of the tray. They looked for something to catch it in, decided a sieve would not be suitable so used another pot. The accompanying language was both scientific and creative with words like 'overflowing', 'pouring', 'dripping', 'splosh' and 'like a fountain' punctuating their vocabulary.
>
> Later in the morning in the same three water trays three children were busy cooking with the saucepans provided and used extra cups and saucers from the home corner to make a cup of tea.
>
> Towards the end of the morning a group of children spent a lot of time emptying water from one trough to another. They used pots, which they tried to fill using a commercially produced pump. They found this took a long time. As the tray gradually filled with water and because there was no equipment in it, two boys spent several minutes just 'sloshing' around in the water. They seemed to be enjoying the cool feeling and laughed and giggled together as they made gentle splashes.

Sometimes a range of equipment enabled children to draw in the sand trays and then progress to the writing corner where the usual pens, pencils and chalks were available. The language tables in the schools were frequently the focus of the teacher's attention and often provided opportunities for children to operate at the level the teacher had decided they had reached. For example, there were nearly always opportunities to draw a picture about an activity they had been doing or were interested in, and then add some writing, either in the form of emergent writing, which they did freely, or with the correct words using printed word strips to help them.

Teachers often used home-made games, especially for language or number activities, to cater for different levels of ability. For example, in one school:

> The teacher 'found' a box and treasure map buried in her garden. The children decided it belonged to a pirate so they wrote a 'class letter'. The pirate replied telling the children what she looked like. The letter had words and pictures to enable the children to respond at an appropriate level and they were all asked to 'draw me' at the end of the page. Some children produced a picture that was an accurate representation of the details given, like correct jumper colour and so on, others drew people without arms and some just drew the clothes. Similarly the words that went alongside the pictures enabled children to read the letter on their own, read it with someone's help or to make up their own dialogue by referring to the pictures. None of the children appeared to regard this as a reading activity.

In another school the reception teacher made a number of very professional looking board games. They were:

> deliberately constructed to be 'open-ended'. This enabled children to use them at any level including different age groups should the teacher transfer from teaching the youngest children. There were games which involved simple counting from 0 to 5 or 0 to 10 depending on the ability of the child; there were 'chance' cards, which could be used to add, subtract and say 'more' or 'less'. Often the different sets of cards or dice were selected according to the child's ability, but the rules of the game could be changed by the child or the teacher or the children could make up their own rules.

## Individual Progression

The materials and equipment provided should enable children to extend their learning on a daily basis and over a period of time. Manning and Sharp (1977) show how the resources can contribute to structuring children's play and encouraging them to develop their ideas.

The teachers were very aware that the children needed to make progress and to meet the expectations of their next teacher and their parents. Gradually throughout the year the equipment should encourage the development of more complex concepts and refined skills. Just as the range of equipment and materials provided enables groups of children to use it at their own operational level, the range should also provide opportunities to 'take the children on'.

In the schools studied there was concern that the equipment and materials provided should encourage children's individual progress, which should be part of the planned learning environment and should be monitored. The interviewees recommended that this progression should be based on the observation of children. A range of equipment and materials was provided by some of the teachers so that the children were able to develop different skills and concepts throughout the term. For example:

> At the beginning of the term the children planted sunflowers. They monitored their growth and made a booklet about how they grew and the need for sun and rain. They also painted pictures and produced detailed and accurately observed sketches of their plants. The activity was developed by the teacher providing science and maths apparatus like scales and capacity beakers so that children could weigh the soil and measure the water to find out how much was needed. By adding real plants and a cash till a 'garden centre' was created. Equipment for an 'Interflora' section was introduced later in the term and children were then busy making bouquets of paper flowers and writing cards to send messages.

Providing different equipment in the basic resource areas enables individual children to use them at their own level of development as they progress throughout the term. For example, equipping the water tray with bubbles, objects that float or sink, sieves and colanders or boats encourages quite different activities. In one school where the buckets and spades in the sand tray were enhanced by adding sieves and then toy animals, the following observations were made:

> The nursery nurse noticed a child's fascination with sifting the sand and discovering 'treasure' (this consisted of small stones and pieces of paper, which were in the sand accidentally). Later in the day she hid some shells and the excitement provided for the child inspired the nursery nurse to extend the activity later in the week by hiding some toy animal in the sand.

Similarly in another school, children's learning was extended when they were given access to different equipment and materials and time to enable them to develop their ideas. For example:

> Two boys were collaborating in constructing a house from a huge cardboard box. It was so big they were able to get inside. Having done so they decided it was too dark. They enlarged the windows until it was unrealistic to make them any bigger and went on to talk about alternative lighting like rigging up lamps with bulbs and batteries. This they did the next day.

**Multidisciplinary Opportunities**

Examples in this and previous chapters have shown how links can be made between areas of the classroom and between areas of the curriculum. By providing a range of equipment and materials these links can be maintained.

Teachers often used the equipment and materials to stimulate an activity. They usually expected this to be recorded in some way. This was most frequently through drawing or writing, often through model-making and occasionally by children's tape-recording or photographs taken by the teacher. As already shown in Chapter 5 language, maths, art and science were often indistinguishable from each other except in the teacher's mind. The equipment provided by the adult often increased the range of skills demanded in what might have been a straightforward language activity. For example:

> a group of about eight children were reminded about the story *Goldilocks and the Three Bears* by the adult working with them. Three children were asked to organize the chairs, bowls and beds, checking that there were the correct numbers needed. The story proceeded with children adopting different roles, discussing the type of voice needed (language), stretching or curling up to show how big they were (physical) and matching the bowls, seating and beds to the appropriate bear (number). The children were encouraged to remember what came next in the story (sequencing) and there was a discussion about the rights and wrongs of breaking things (moral).

During the course of the study there were many examples of equipment and materials stimulating and enabling children to develop skills and concepts across the curriculum.

**Multicultural Provision and Equal Opportunities**

Provision of a range of equipment and materials enables teachers to respond to and reflect the fact that children come to school from different home backgrounds and different cultures. An awareness of these issues should be inherent in every teacher's philosophy and provision. In the training pack, *Working with Children: Developing a Curriculum for the Early Years* (Drummond *et al.*, 1989), the adults working with this age group are invited to examine their own values and feelings so that appropriate provision can be made for the children.

Multicultural and gender issues are concerned with attitudes (Drummon, 1989a). The resources selected can reflect those attitudes and beliefs. For example, attempts can be made to go some way towards developing appropriate attitudes by providing the home corner with equipment that reflects a range of cultures, using appropriate utensils for making different types of food, like Asian bowls, chopsticks and so on. Dressing-up clothes, dolls and books can be selected to enable different cultures to be represented.

Most of the schools provided equal opportunities for boys and girls to use such a range of equipment and materials, although there was still concern about stereotyping in books. Observations showed that both girls and boys enjoyed activities in most areas. A few schools were aware that 'the boys tend to spend all their time with the construction sets'. To counteract this they decided to discriminate positively towards the girls by timetabling the use of the construction blocks so that 'everyone has a turn'. The observations made in schools showed little difference between the sexes in the activities they engaged in: both girls and boys used the computer, even though it was especially popular with the boys; boys featured in the home/hospital/café corner and were seen hoovering or mopping up; the girls were as adept as the boys at building Lego models and large constructions.

# A Variety of Equipment and Materials

Just as a range of equipment and materials provide children with appropriate activities, so variety in provision enables children to exercise choices and respond individually or in small groups. The variety can be provided by offering different equipment and materials or by changing them over a period of time.

The professionals interviewed suggested that **appropriate provision entails a balance of different kinds of activities and this can be reflected in the variety of equipment and materials.** The schools managed to go some way towards providing a balance of activities by:

✿ providing equipment and materials that encouraged children to move or be calm, to be noisy or quiet, to be involved individually or in small groups, or to experience novel or familiar activities;

✿ providing a variety of equipment and materials in each resource area.

### Equipment and Materials for Different Kinds of Activity

Equipment and materials that encouraged children to move around were found in most schools in the study. Movement was encouraged by large construction sets and blocks, imaginative play resources, puppets and home-corners and in moving between areas to link activities. The outdoor equipment, when and where it was available, encouraged movement. A calm atmosphere was induced by the provision of table-top puzzles and games, sand and water, creative materials, books and sewing.

In the schools a balance between noisy and quiet activities was provided for the children during the course of the day. The equipment that most frequently encouraged noisy activity was the large construction blocks and woodwork benches. When and where the climbing blocks, wheeled toys or musical instruments were available the children could be engaged noisily in the activity, while the sand, table-top equipment, creative materials, books and so on provided them with opportunities to withdraw and be quiet.

Professionals said that in order to meet the needs of four year olds opportunities should be provided to enable them to undertake activities individually or in small groups. The schools provided this balance by offering a range and variety of equipment, which could be used by children in either way. Children often began using the equipment individually and as their activity progressed they would invite others or be joined by other children. For example, books enabled children to browse on their own or to 'read' together in pairs or small groups. The climbing blocks, large construction sets and home-corner most frequently provided opportunities for collaboration, although other equipment like sand and water also encouraged group activity. Painting, junk models and making things, table-top equipment like puzzles or writing and drawing materials, which were often teacher-chosen, provided the most opportunities for solitary activity.

Although children are stimulated by new situations at this stage in their development they also need to feel secure. Professionals suggested that the materials provided should create a balance between the novel and the familiar. This was provided in the schools in the study by equipment and materials being available all the time and children having permanent access to them, for example, books, puzzles, pencils, paint, home corners and in some schools sand and water trays. Novelty was introduced by the addition of different articles, by offering a different medium or by changing the theme of the home corner. For example a set of nurses' uniforms had been purchased and were available in the home-corner. The school doctor had visited the previous day and interest had been revitalized in the home/hospital corner.

In some of the schools the introduction of something new or different stimulated an activity, for example, a daffodil was brought in to inspire a drawing or card-making activity. Hats, old boots, bones, ducks, caterpillars, snails and numerous other items provided a starting point for a theme. By observing children's response to the novelty provision, teachers were able to observe the child's interest and level of understanding and use this knowledge to plan future activity.

Often children introduced their own novelty to the classroom in the form of a favourite toy, an interesting object or something that had captured their imagination. Teachers used these opportunities to extend the child's learning, or the class' interest. For example, in one school at the end of playtime:

> a boy brought in a 'dandelion clock'. A discussion about the type of flower it had, why it looked like it did now involved a group of children. After an explanation of how it 'told the time', the children had to estimate what the time would be. The child who found it was then taken outside by the nursery nurse to 'blow it, to find out the time'.

## A Variety of Provision in Resource Areas

If areas of the classroom are equipped with a variety of resources children are provided with opportunities catering for a range of abilities and interests. Different resources stimulate ideas and extend children's learning. The guidelines suggested that different areas of the classroom could be equipped so that a balanced curriculum was provided.

### Natural materials
Natural materials could provide a variety of tactile and sensory experiences by including wood, peat, leaves, gravel, sawdust, earth and tea leaves in the resources, as well as sand and water, which were the most popular and most frequently provided by the schools in the study.

*Sand.* The guidelines suggest that variety can be provided by using wet or dry sand and different colours, sizes and shapes of sand tray. Some schools used commercially produced sand trays while others, particularly those on a limited budget but committed to providing variety and more access for children, used washing up bowls, tea trays, baby-baths and any other suitable container they could acquire. Although the nursery schools we visited had access to large, covered outdoor sandpits there were only a very few infant or primary schools that enjoyed such provision. Where a large sandpit was available outside children were able to stand or sit inside the pit, to use buckets and spades for large constructions, to feel the sand between their toes and to develop individual and group activities.

The guidelines suggested that activities in the dry sand could be changed by equipping the tray with different items like:

✿   sieves, colanders and tea-strainers for sifting;

✿ jugs, buckets, plastic and graded containers, plant pots and jelly moulds of different shapes and sizes to fill up and pour out;

✿ tubing of different sizes, funnels and wheels to pour through;

✿ rakes, trowels, various scoops, and spades to move the sand with;

✿ combs, sponges, sticks to make marks in the sand;

✿ stones, shells, pebbles, corks, pieces of wood, cones, feathers and so on to sort and to develop imaginative ideas;

✿ balances and magnifying glasses to encourage other maths and science concepts.

Similar experiences can be provided with sawdust, rice, salt or fine gravel as they have similar properties to dry sand. Wet sand can also be used with this equipment and comparisons can be made. Cars, small-world people and animals and flags can be introduced to enhance the provision.

In schools, trays with wet or dry sand were most commonly provided. Sometimes both would be available and occasionally leaves, peat or gravel were available instead. Lack of space often prevented teachers offering more equipment in the classroom. Where it was provided there was a variety of objects like sieves and small-world people to encourage different activities. Where the sand was part of the planned activities the following observations were made: 'the sand tray was half full with wet sand and no additional equipment. The children were able to make marks in it, feel it and squeeze it through their fingers'. In another classroom, 'the wet sand provided imaginative play with fences and small-world figures'. Where a teacher had planned 'shapes' for the half-termly theme, 'the wet sand tray was set up with buckets and spades of different shapes and sizes. These were castle-shaped, square and round buckets'. The sand activities were extended by another teacher's cards, which invited children to try to answer questions. For example: 'Can you make a tower that is as tall as 20 multi-link bricks? Write your name here if you have tried this challenge. Use dry and wet sand.'

*Water.* The guidelines suggest that variety can be offered to the children by providing water trays of different shapes, sizes and depths. Some schools used specially purchased trays but others used washing-up bowls, baby baths or old sinks. The equipment provided for water activities guided the kind of activities that took place. For example, baby baths with supporting materials like empty shampoo bottles and talcum powder containers, flannels and sponges or pretend washing powder encouraged doll-bathing or clothes-washing.

Assorted plastic containers like buckets, cups, beakers and bottles encourage different activities. If they comprise different sizes, shapes and volumes, with or without holes, early science and maths concepts can be explored. Other items suggested by the guidelines are sponges, corks, plasticine, different types of balls, plastic, wood, scoops, funnels, sieves, watering cans, tea pots, whisks, cones, hollow objects, hose and water wheels. If the water is situated outside it can be used to water plants, wash windows or equipment and 'paint' walls.

There were some interesting uses of the water trays. For example, one school had two trays: one provided free water activities for the children and the other provided teacher-chosen objects that would float or sink.

Sometimes three water trays were provided when equipment was shared between classes. This enabled different depths of water to be provided or to be used in different ways, for example, to wash the dolls, to use the water wheel, funnels and jugs or to have tea parties with teapots and cups and saucers.

Sometimes teachers provided coloured water to stimulate new activities and there were examples of using cold tea for tea-party activity, and jelly set in the water tray for tactile experiences. The addition of washing-up liquid to make bubbles, or cornflour or custard powder made interesting and stimulating changes in the equipment to encourage different activities. Most teachers felt that they used the sand and water for science activities but not as often as they should.

*Creative materials*
Creative materials can be provided in many different ways to stimulate the children's creative urges and provide endless opportunities for experimentation. The guidelines suggest that paper and card of different colours, shapes, sizes and textures should be provided. Some of the more unusual suggestions include fluorescent paper, corrugated cardboard and blotting paper. In the schools in the study there was a tremendous variety of paper and card, which included computer print-out, off-cuts of card and paper surplus to local business or industrial requirements. In one school 'antique' paper was made by soaking sugar paper in cold tea and allowing it to dry before use. Another teacher explained:

> In order to stimulate children to develop their activities different shapes of paper are introduced, for example, circular paper, little books, different coloured paper, postcards and paper and envelopes so they can write letters. Today there are circular sheets of plain paper in the drawer to which children have access. They find the circles of plain paper and decide for themselves to make butterflies. They also use the hole punch to make eyes, staples to reinforce the fold and string to make it 'fly' across the classroom. The children colour in patterns on the wings. The ideas are initiated by the children but stimulated by the materials available.

Variety can also be provided in the form of different mark-makers. For example, brushes of different lengths, thickness, shape and bristles can be provided to paint with. Household painting brushes, toothbrushes, shaving brushes and nailbrushes can be used with paint of different colours and textures. Paint can be thick or thin, or the texture changed by the addition of paste, sawdust or washing-up liquid. It may be available in liquid or powder form, ready mixed or for children to mix themselves. A variety of materials like commercial printing blocks, corks, bottles, cotton reels, sponges, hair rollers and pipe-cleaners can introduce new activities. Familiar painting activities can be offered to the children either on a table or on easels.

Felt-tip pens, pencil and wax crayons, charcoal, pencils, chalk and pastels provide variety and a choice of medium as well as different colour, thickness and hardness. As one teacher commented on the need for thick and thin pencils: 'they do not need thick ones at a younger age and thin ones when they get older. They need both all the way through. Pencil thickness is not age-related but actually serves a different purpose'. Most schools in the study offered children a variety of markers at different times throughout the year.

The guidelines suggest that different materials should be provided for collage and junk modelling. A variety of size, shape, colour and texture could be provided by boxes, cotton wool, material, ribbon, foam, lace, wood shavings, beads, buttons, eggshells, dried pulses and pasta, sweet papers, magazines, scraps of metal, natural materials like grasses, leaves, seeds, leather and fur. There should also be appropriate and different means of fixing them together such as adhesive of different kinds, Sellotape, paper clips, split pins, staples, elastic bands or string.

A variety of materials was used for making collages. The choice was often limited by the teacher. Where children were encouraged to mix their own paint under the watchful eye of the nursery nurse, there was often a lot of discussion involving the mixing of colours and attainment of textures to meet the child's requirements. Adhesive was generally freely available to the children and other means of attaching things such as Sellotape or paper clips were sometimes available.

The creative area can also provide blocks of salt or soap for carving, washable inks, clay, Plasticine, plaster of Paris, papier mâché, needlecraft and woodwork equipment. If all or some of these are provided throughout the week, term or year they offer a wealth of different experiences for the children. By ranging in colour, size and shape, familiar activities can become more stimulating and by varying the tools to work them with the children extend their experiences and expertise. For example, the needlecraft equipment can include a variety of fabrics or polystyrene trays, which can be used with large blunt-ended needles, ring hooks or different yarns, string, wool or ribbon.

Where children were given access to a variety of creative materials they were able to make choices. For example:

different materials were provided for making cards. The children had a choice of size and colour; they had a choice from old birthday cards, yellow or green paper or sticky shapes. The glue was either squeezed out of the container or used with a spatula. The children had access to scissors and paint and could choose what they wanted to use.

### Construction equipment

Interviewees and the guidelines suggested it was essential that areas should be provided where large and small construction kits and blocks could be used undisturbed and where it was not always necessary to pack them up at the end of every session. They should be made out of different materials like wood or plastic and reflect a selection of shapes and sizes so that mathematical relationships can be explored. They can also be used to extend activities with small world figures, play people, cars and train sets.

*Large construction equipment.* Bruce (1989) describes large blocks and construction kits as 'a mechanism towards mathematics, craft, design technology, drama, literature, history etc. They are a traditional but sometimes neglected, piece of classroom equipment …'. Building blocks balance and fit with each other and have always been part of traditional nursery equipment while construction kits join together or interlock and can often be used to make working models. Both kinds of equipment were found in the schools in the study. They were often newly acquired and provided as a direct attempt to meet the needs of the younger children being admitted to school. Often space was limited, so only a limited amount of large constructions could be built at any one time. However, observations revealed that both wooden and plastic blocks provided children with opportunities for collaborative and problem-solving activities even if there was a limited amount of equipment available. For example:

> In this classroom, there were no large wooden blocks, but there was a small amount of wooden construction equipment. Two boys spent a long time trying to make ramps for a car using two folding, collapsible wooden sections. They were trying to find a way to construct ramps without everything collapsing. They finally solved the problem by using blocks of Lego. Perhaps more apparatus would have dramatically extended this activity but would the challenge have been as great?

For some teachers the availability of this equipment contributed towards their craft, design and technology (CDT) plans. The children frequently built castles or rockets or constructed vehicles of various kinds such as buses or dust carts. Sometimes teachers extended the activity by providing other items such as a steering wheel, ramps or a hose-pipe. In another school where the four year olds had been busy on the theme of homes the following observations were made: 'out of doors the children constructed walls with various kinds of bricks. They tested them for strength, drew them and made models of them. Indoors another group of children collaborated to build a tall castle and then drew pictures of it using pencils and paper'. Construction sets like Quadro were very popular because they enabled children to build working models that they could use. For example, the home-corner had been set up as a dentist's surgery. The children used large sets to build a dentist's chair that could be moved and tilted. They built drills and so on with smaller construction sets.

Some schools had large soft blocks, which enabled children to build dens, houses and bridges to crawl in or wriggle under. The softness enabled high towers to be built safely. Collaborative play was generated and teacher intervention and suggestions prevented it from becoming 'just rough and tumble' games (see also Chapter 5).

*Small construction equipment.* Small construction blocks and kits were also regarded as important provision. There were many different kinds provided by schools, for example, Constructo-straws, Duplo, Stickle-bricks, Master-builder, Mobilo, Multi-link, Meccano and Playpax. Lego was the most popular and most commonly available with almost every school visited by the project team using it in some way or other. Often it was used for CDT, maths or science activities. For example, when a group of children built a boat they were encouraged to see if it would float, or how much cargo it could carry.

*The home-corner and role-play*

Equipment for the home-corner and role-playing should be of good quality, clean, attractively presented and available at all times. The guidelines suggested that a well-equipped home-corner would include things like sink units, cookers, washing machines, fridges, tables, chairs and beds. Smaller equipment like brushes for sweeping up, irons and ironing boards, washing lines and pegs, or a range of cooking utensils, teasets and cutlery, or TVs, telephones, clocks, books and magazines can be provided to change the focus of children's activities. Dolls should represent a multicultural society as well as there being baby dolls, which can be bathed.

In some of the schools the children organized the area into a home-corner even though the teachers intended it to be used as an opticians or pet shop. They enjoyed making food and inviting visitors for cups of tea. It was often a favourite area for the girls because it had 'high-heels and prams'. There were many examples of corners with painted views through an imaginary window outlined by curtains. Our observations revealed that many matching activities and opportunities for language development were provided in this area. Sometimes teachers were involved and through their interaction extended play. Often nursery nurses were involved in the play but most frequently the children developed their own activities and made links with other areas. For example, they collected books to read from the book-corner, used Lego to make a specifically required item or dough for extra food.

The permanent availability of the home-corner provided security for some children. Teachers often tried to stimulate changes in activities by equipping the area so that it was compatible with their plans or the termly theme. For example, depending on the resources provided, it could serve as a shop that might sell clothes, sweets, pets, toys, shoes or fish or as a bakery, tea shop or post office. Shoe shops were observed in school providing opportunities to practise, amongst other things, doing up buckles or shoe laces, pairing up shoes and noticing similarities and differences in a practical way.

Additional equipment encourages activity areas to be extended. For example, in one school there was a flower shop using real plants and specially selected equipment encouraged the development of a 'garden centre' and 'Interflora' section later in the term.

Other ideas suggested by the guidelines include a hospital, clinic or doctor's surgery, dentists, vets, hairdressers, castles, banks, fire stations, schools, launderettes, garages, bus or train stations, aeroplanes or airports, rockets and space stations or ships. Katz and Chard (1989) show how one area can be arranged to give children different options. In some of the schools teachers observed children's interests and the area became part of the planned learning environment. For example, some provided resources for haunted houses, jungles, dentists, doctors, under the sea, shoe shops and hairdressers. The researcher's notes describe the 'hospital provision' in one school:

> The theme for the younger children was 'ourselves'. The shared area was organized so that there was a baby clinic, a reception area, a hospital ward and a home corner. Genuine equipment was used, for example, small crutches, nurses' caps, information charts, which had been obtained from a hospital. The teachers felt that it was important that children were able to link the sequence of the play activities. All the way through there was great emphasis on the emergent reading and emergent number concepts that could be built on.

In another school:

> The area had been converted to a rocket launch pad with a large cardboard cylinder encasing a series of dials, wheels and lights. The teacher used the children's experience on this occasion to develop their imagination through language and encourage them to voice their fears of the dark.

Dressing up clothes also provide valuable opportunities to extend, vary and stimulate children's activities. Hats, gloves, handbags, scarves and jewellery stimulate children into different activities, while uniforms add reality to the play situation. The provision of multi-ethnic costumes helped some children to build on their previous experiences and others to be more aware of multicultural aspects of society.

*Books*

Books are widely available for most pupils of any age in school. They should be carefully selected, particularly for children of this age group, so that they reflect positive images of today's society and respond to individual stages of development and interests. A variety of books to cater for this can be provided by including fiction and non-fiction, different shapes and sizes, published and teacher- or child-produced books. For example, teachers were very concerned about using books to convey the meaning of print. This was achieved through attractive books, which could be used alone, discussed or read with other children or adults or could be used for large group story-times. Written material that could be referred to by the children like menus, invitations, birthday cards, recipe books, seed catalogues, telephone directories, *TV Times* and *Radio Times*, newspapers and so on were provided and used on a variety of appropriate occasions.

Teachers were concerned that the provision in the book-corner should foster a 'love of language'. They felt this could be achieved through good quality books as well as tape-recorders and taped stories or record players. Photograph albums, class or individual books made by the children provided many opportunities to enjoy and share language with others and become aware that print conveys meaning.

Most of the schools visited by the project team were well equipped with books and children used them whenever they felt like 'reading', when they wanted to be quiet as well as when they were asked to read to the teacher. Most children were involved in their school's reading schemes fairly early in the school year. Usually one scheme was predominant with other schemes backing it up or providing variety. Where more than one scheme was used the books were often colour-coded to show the level reached. Children were able to help themselves to any books with a red sticker which were kept in a red basket. Often the reading scheme chosen stimulated art and craft activities.

As HMI (GB.DES, 1989c) noted:

The work of under-fives in infant classes is often seriously constrained by the limited range of suitable equipment. The supply of books, if not the range, is usually satisfactory and the central library services run by LEAs often contribute significantly to maintaining an adequate supply. (para. 55)

*Table-top equipment*

Table-top equipment, games and jig-saws can provide a great variety of activities. It is not possible to list those which might be appropriate for use with young children as there are so many to choose from. The guidelines suggest that such equipment is useful for imaginative or fantasy play or manipulative play and should ensure progression for children. Many teachers had in fact developed their own games to meet the needs of their pupils (see p. 163). In the schools studied it was often table-top equipment that changed throughout the day. For example, in the morning the stimulus may be provided by a number game while in the afternoon it might be replaced by a language game or jig-saws. Often these were selected by teachers for specific purposes. One example is described in the researcher's notes: 'The teacher has made a set of parcels for a sorting activity. Small cartons of various sizes have been wrapped in four different colours of wrapping paper. The children have to sort them by their wrappers and their sizes.' Sometimes tables were left clear so that children were able to select their own equipment and materials. For example, as one child explained, 'I like the Lego best because you can make things. I like toys, paper and wood. They are all kept in the cupboard or drawers and we get them out ourselves.'

*Equipment for special interests*

Special interest equipment and materials relating to the termly themes were often provided. This also included specialist science equipment like magnets, magnifying glasses and pulleys or the computer and computer games. In the schools there was usually an 'interest table' and observation was encouraged by providing magnifying glasses. Sometimes special equipment was produced to enable children to maintain interest in an activity.

In one school the equipment available stimulated one child's specific activity. This had been inspired by the previous week's 'School Experience' which was a CDT project based on a story. Batteries, bulbs and a box of 'junk' were provided on a table. The following observations were made:

> One boy brought a doorbell push into school. He connected up batteries and bulbs to make the light work. He then linked this to the bell-push. He put the light inside a plastic bottle which he had cut the end off. The activity was developed by adding a metal 'motor' which spun when the current was switched on. He linked the motor and the light bulb and noticed that when the motor spun the light went out. By connecting the whole lot to the bell-push he was able to control the spinning motor ... Later in the day he linked up with children working with the construction blocks on the floor. They made a lighthouse complete with flashing light at the top.

*Musical instruments*

Music corners should be provided for children of this age to be able to experience listening to and investigating sounds. The guidelines state that children can be provided with a variety of experiences by encouraging them to use their voices, musical instruments and taped music. They should experience and appreciate rhythm, pitch and dynamics. They can be encouraged to sing traditional songs and nursery rhymes as well as new songs. Instruments can be home-made like shakers of different sorts, or commercially produced tuned and untuned percussion instruments. Tape-recorders, record players and radios provide variety in children's musical education.

The observations in schools showed that the music area was often neglected. Although children were given many opportunities to sing in large groups only a few were given opportunities to be aware of rhythm. For example:

(It is group time on the carpet.)
*Teacher*: Hands up if you've got two beats in your name.
(Three children are selected and asked to stand up.)
*Teacher*: Who is this?
*Children*: Jodie, Lisa, Gareth.
*They all chant*: Jo-die, Li-sa, Ga-reth.
*Teacher*: Let's clap their names.
(The children clap the rhythm and chant the three names.)

The activity develops by changing the order of chanting for example, Ga-reth, Jo-die, Li-saa and then including different children who have one beat or three beats to their names. The children manage it perfectly and the teacher comments 'Brilliant, you're all musicians in the making!'

Sometimes these kinds of activities were enhanced by using musical instruments. Often the quality and kind of instruments available were limited because they were shared with other classes or stored centrally or where they were available they were 'piled haphazardly on the window-sill'. A few teachers were aware that this area of the curriculum was neglected and provided regular opportunities for groups of children to use percussion instruments in the cloakroom or other corners to keep the noise level down in the classroom. The most frequent use of instruments of any kind by the children was when the class presented assemblies or concerts. There were only one or two schools in the study where children had unlimited access to tuned or untuned percussion instruments. Where they did the following observations were made:

a group of children have turned the home-corner in their class-rooms into a restaurant. The 'diners' wait patiently for their meal and the 'waiter' decides that some music would be appropriate. He enlists the help of two other children and takes them across the classroom to the music trolley. They select their instruments, a tambourine and triangle and return to the restaurant where they sing and play their instruments.

Musical provision was improved in some schools by home-made shakers, drums, coconut shells and other such improvised equipment. In these circumstances it was the teacher's commitment and expertise that encouraged the activity rather than the school's provision of equipment.

Tape-recorders and radios were seen in most schools. Headphones were often provided to encourage children to 'really listen'. However, it was clear that although this area was often carefully planned by the teacher, it was not always effective. Occasions were observed where children sat quietly apparently listening to a recording for a considerable length of time. When we asked them about the song or story they said they did not know because the machine was not working!

*Outdoor equipment*
Outdoor equipment in infant and primary schools could provide children with a variety of experiences. For example, the guidelines suggest that climbing frames, barrels, balls, ropes, wheeled toys and so on can provide different physical experiences. Variety of provision can be presented to the children by putting outdoors the equipment like paint easels and sand trays normally available indoors.

The nursery schools in the study were far more appropriately equipped than the infant and primary schools. As explained in Chapter 5, only a few schools offered four year olds access to outdoor equipment. It was an area that was receiving attention in some schools but improvement was limited due to a lack of funds and too few adults to provide outdoor activities safely.

However there were a few schools that were well equipped. The observations in one such school are described by the researcher:

Outside there were large wooden blocks, tunnels, barrels and wheeled toys. A group of children were engrossed in a 'complex game' with rules that were clear to them, if no-one else! They had arranged the blocks themselves and had to decide which holes to block up and which to leave free, where to put the tunnel and so on ...

**Variety Over a Period of Time**

Teachers have a tremendous choice of equipment and materials available to give children a variety of experiences. It is not possible for everything to be offered all at the same time so classrooms are often arranged so that there is a choice during the day, during the week or during the term as explained in Chapter 5. When a limited amount of space is available it is even more important to restrict the access to some of the equipment and make changes as and when necessary. It is important that teachers understand that different materials promote different learning opportunities so that they can plan for changes based on children's interests, skills, development and progression as well as themes over a period of time.

## Selecting and Funding Appropriate Equipment

An evaluation conducted in one authority (Pollard, 1989) found that teachers felt that equipment was usually 'adequate or better' in most resource areas although science and outdoor equipment were rated as poor. Bingham (1988) found that schools were providing more nursery-type equipment; there were more sand and water trays, more construction and play equipment as a result of early admission in another authority.

Some of the schools visited by the project team had a long tradition of early admission, others had recently adopted the policy. Where changes had been made towards more appropriate provision for younger children, new equipment had been bought to encourage more 'structured' provision and to offer more constructional play activities. It was presented so that children could use it independently. The practitioners emphasized that equipment suitable for use with the age group was *gradually* being built up. For example, sets of interesting things to display like collections of shiny things, stones or shells, as well as apparatus to vary the activities offered in the sand, like collections of different sieves, buckets or scoops.

If the equipment is to be built up gradually it needs to be durable. This means that it is often expensive and requires extra funding. Other items are consumable but, as one teacher commented, having four year olds in school means that 'the paper is used more quickly'. In the schools studied, additional equipment and materials for four year olds were funded in various ways:

- ✿ through the LEA;
- ✿ through capitation;
- ✿ through parental help;
- ✿ through other agencies and contacts;
- ✿ by teachers making their own.

**Through the LEA**

Some authorities, particularly where early admission was a recent and planned policy, provided extra funds through capitation or special grants. In these schools headteachers were able to report that there had been a great improvement in equipment and resources in the last few years. Often, however, the extra funds were withdrawn once the policy had become established. HMI made similar remarks: 'additional funding was available for schools admitting four year olds into reception classes for the first time. Amounts varied from £200 to £800 depending on the number of children admitted' (GB.DES, 1989c, para. 42).

In some authorities there were 'bulk purchasing schemes' to ensure that *all* schools received some suitable, durable equipment without having to justify it through capitation allowances. Some LEAs were able to provide resource banks from which teachers could borrow equipment. This was especially useful to help teachers evaluate the suitability of an expensive piece of equipment before purchasing it.

In one of the authorities where additional funding, bulk purchasing schemes and resource banks were available the following observations were made in one school.

> The half set of large construction blocks is an example of the extra equipment bought specially when younger children were first admitted. The first year the policy was changed the four year olds had a lot spent on them. They had extra sand and water trays, large and small bricks. In the current year there are some new construction blocks and jig-saws but there has been less money to spend. At first the LEA allocated special funds and recommended it to be spent on bricks. They specified that it should *not* be spent on things for older children.

Advisers or advisory teachers and headteachers often decide what special equipment should be available as a county policy. Sometimes additional resources are available 'on loan' to schools. Science, CDT and other specialist equipment, which schools may not have access to, is provided by a central pool of resources that can be shared by schools throughout the year. As one headteacher explained:

> We decided to merge the National Curriculum with resources used in the reception classes. Some of the LEA materials are being piloted and are on loan for a while. For example early years CDT materials are currently on loan from the advisory teacher and being used in the reception class. They will be returned later in the term for use in another school.

A range and variety of books can be provided by using the school library service. This is particularly useful for reference materials supporting a theme. Some schools in the study obtained extra equipment and materials because schools had been closed down or combined with others.

## Through Capitation

In many of the schools in the study there was only limited, if any, extra funding from the authority. Equipment and materials for the youngest children was provided through the usual capitation.

Sometimes, where the youngest were admitted early at the discretion of the head they were not actually included in capitation. Even so, good quality equipment and adequate materials were available because the head was sympathetic to the needs of four year olds and attempts were made to provide equipment and materials appropriately.

Improved provision was achieved in some schools by pooling or sharing resources. When this was the case it was usually stored centrally and shared with the older children. For this to work effectively there needed to be some kind of organization or timetabling so that it was used by as many children and as much as possible. If such arrangements were made the equipment was available when required and teachers could plan activities accordingly.

Often 'pooled' equipment was organized by the teachers with areas of responsibility. For example, one school provided access to musical instruments more frequently than most because the teacher of the four year olds was the music coordinator. The money allocated to her because of her responsibility was used to buy instruments, which were stored in the four year olds' classroom. Where specialist science equipment was available, the four year olds had access to these items when there was a whole-school approach and they were included in the planned allocation of resources.

Similarly books, reading schemes or maths schemes were often selected by the teacher with responsibility for that area. This was considered to encourage continuity throughout the school; where there was an early years coordinator the equipment and materials were organized for the nursery and first year unit.

Sometimes equipment was pooled because two classes had amalgamated and teachers were team teaching, or because areas had been created for two or more classes to share equipment. Where such changes had been tried the teacher commented: 'it's an excellent idea financially because you no longer need two of everything'.

The decision about how the available money should be spent usually lies with the headteacher and varies according to school organization.

In the schools studied the project team found several different arrangements being made. Here are a few examples:

- ✿ The headteacher bought everything centrally because it was felt that this avoided favouritism and duplication of equipment. This led to the provision of shared resources and the four year olds were 'no better or worse off than anyone else'.
- ✿ The headteacher ordered everything after discussion with class teachers.
- ✿ The headteacher ordered resources after taking the whole school's needs, including the youngest children, into account. Often there was a focus on different areas each year, for example, books one year and science equipment another year.
- ✿ The teachers with posts of responsibility selected and organized the equipment and materials throughout the school. For example, one person selected and organized all the maths equipment and the early years coordinator arranged all the nursery and first year equipment.
- ✿ General equipment like pencils, paper and so on was ordered by the headteacher and teachers put in a list of requirements based on the themes they would be covering.
- ✿ Class teachers were given their own money to spend as they wished. Where this was the case one teacher with four year olds commented 'a large part of my requisition has been spent on play equipment'.

There was an awareness amongst headteachers and teachers that resources were being eroded. Quality equipment had been provided but extensive use through sharing with other classes and the extra wear and tear when used by younger children were causes for concern. It was feared that capitation at the present level would not be sufficient to allow stocks to be replenished at an appropriate rate. Headteachers were particularly aware that additional funding was needed for equipment to meet the requirements of the National Curriculum. When the fieldwork of the present study was being done LMS was still an unknown quantity in most authorities and in pilot form in a few authorities. Headteachers were concerned that they might have less money to spend on replacing equipment as it might have to be allocated for other things.

### Through Parental Help

The majority of the classes received active help from parents in the form of money donated by bodies like the PRA, Friends of the School and the School Fund. The money had usually been provided through fund-raising activities like jumble sales, dances and discos, treasure-hunts, nature trails, fashion shows and so on. The money raised in this way was usually allocated for specific items like computers, construction blocks, storage sheds, play-houses, climbing frames, sand and water trays and dolls.

In a few schools, however, such contributions were not so forthcoming. Parents were not able either financially or personally to provide help. The teachers found that *they*, rather than the parents, had to organize events, which added to their work load. This also means that funds are only raised on a small scale; but everything helps in a disadvantaged area. In this LEA capitation through the authority was low and, because of the poverty of the parents, fund-raising was minimal.

Headteachers and teachers were very appreciative of financial help but parents also provided valuable home-made equipment and materials. For example, much of the home-corner equipment was made by parents. This was often done at home because of their own interest in sewing or woodwork and their involvement with the school. Sometimes groups of children worked with parents in school to extend the range of equipment and materials that were available. For example, in one school:

> There were houses made out of cardboard boxes, which had been provided and organized by parents but painted by the children. Windows, doors and roofs had been added in appropriate colours to match the reading scheme. To extend the equipment available for the children's language activities one of the parents made appropriately dressed rag-dolls. These were accessible to the children at all times and particularly popular at the beginning of the year.

Parents also contributed toys, jig-saw puzzles and games no longer needed at home. Junk materials, like yoghurt pots, boxes, material, wood off-cuts and so on, were collected by parents to keep the constant demand supplied.


## Through Other Agencies and Contacts

In schools with generous funding, and especially in schools with limited funds, additional equipment and materials for children under statutory age were provided by 'teachers begging, borrowing or stealing' from any of the local contacts they had. This included such things as the following:

✿   Personal contact with local business and industry. Often products that were surplus to their requirements or waste, like computer print-out, boxes, card off-cuts, paper, packaging of various kinds for use in collages, were useful in school. In one area this was well organized with an established Play Resource Centre. This was a Community Programme Project sponsored by the (then) Manpower Services Commission. The Centre offers materials to member groups such as playgroups, schools and handicapped centres. The aim is to collect safe surplus materials from local business premises and recycle it for use as play materials. A leaflet publicizes their activities as 'learn and play with things thrown away'. Personnel are on hand to give demonstrations and creative workshop ideas and links are established and maintained between suppliers and establishments using the surplus materials.

✿  Using personnel on training courses at local colleges. In some areas schools are able to provide the raw materials such as wood, and a plan or drawing to show what they would like built. The students make the equipment to the schools' specification. This is called Community Industry and provides a link between students learning a trade and the schools. In one school, for example, they made 'all the stuff for our home-corner'. This included ironing boards, cots, mirrors, sink unit, cooker, a stand for the dressing-up clothes, cupboards and stools. A telephone box had been made in another school, and when it was their turn again they would ask for a puppet theatre to be made.

✿  Borrowing equipment from museums, libraries, hospitals, farms and so on.

✿  Using old electrical or musical apparatus from jumble sales so that children can investigate how they work. Needless to say they should never be plugged in to the electricity supply!

✿  Children bringing interesting objects they found in the garden or on holiday, sharing their pets and collecting materials for art and craft activities, like junk models and collages.

## Teachers Make their Own

Teachers often produced home-made cards, games and other equipment so that individual children's needs can be met. Their contributions to extending the range and variety of equipment and to the presentation of materials were quite considerable. For example, pencils were kept in attractive pots that had been neatly covered in plastic. This had been done by teachers in their own time. The following examples were also observed:

✿  Empty bottles, shampoo, Fairy Liquid and so on for use in the home-corner had been patiently collected from teachers' own homes. Collections of 'broken equipment' like old keyboards were saved so that children could investigate how they work.

✿ Display items for 'special effect' home-corners and labels for activity areas, drawers and storage were all made by teachers in their own time.

✿ Language and number games as described previously (p. 163). Teachers also covered boxes to introduce novelty factors for different reasons. One teacher covered a box to represent 'buried treasure' to give stimulus to a flagging theme, another covered boxes of different sizes for matching and sorting activities and another had a black box for children to guess what was inside by the noise it made.

A typical example of the level of involvement of teachers with four year olds in their classes is described in the researcher's notes:

All the equipment and materials are of good quality. Many of them have been made for use by children according to their needs. The teachers tended to do this in directed time. They made work cards to go with the submarine area. Boxes were covered and coded 'with symbols' to show what was in them. There was a home-made map of an island with fish, bridges, rivers and seas. In another area a teacher-made matching game was available.

## Conclusion

Although the interviewees recognized that the equipment and materials available for use in reception classes often reflected the amount of funding available, the provision of appropriate equipment and materials was a crucial factor in providing an 'extended nursery curriculum' for these young children. Schools were gradually building up sufficient, appropriate, good quality items. With children's access to a wide range of equipment and materials available it is important that the teacher's selection is made with great care. Classes sharing or exchanging equipment can provide variety for children; funding through the PTA may help to provide some of the quality, but most important of all is the children's opportunity to use the equipment in a situation that encourages independence, confidence and security. Appropriate provision is only a starting point from which appropriate practice can develop.

# 9 Staffing

If provision in school is to be suitable for four year olds **an appropriate ratio of adults to children is crucial.** Children of this age need a sufficient number of adults to help them feel secure and confident and to practise their use of language, which is developing rapidly at this age. The findings from the study support the view that an appropriate ratio is one that allows adults to interact with the children and be involved with their activities, observing them as individuals and intervening at the right moment to extend their learning.

Concern was expressed, both in interviews with professionals and in LEA guidelines, that there should be appropriate adult–child ratios in classes containing four year olds in school. It was emphasized that the adults employed in these classes should be trained and experienced in working with this age group. Trained adults were needed to enhance the learning opportunities provided by children's play and to encourage language development.

Other studies have stressed the need for more adults. For example, teachers involved in Pascal's research (*TES*, 30.9.88) said they 'needed full-time trained ancillary help'. This was a higher priority for them than INSET (in-service education of teachers) or additional equipment for the children. Stevenson (1988) acknowledges that child–adult ratios are high in reception classes and highlights the need for more adults on hand 'who are aware of and have had appropriate training to be able to cater for the needs of these children'.

From the teachers involved in the study the most desperate cry was for 'another pair of hands more than anything else'. Lack of adult help imposes severe restrictions on practice, and teachers may find themselves working in a way that is limited to just 'catering physically for so many active bodies'.

## Staffing Ratios

The Select Committee was concerned about the factors contributing to quality provision for under-fives and claimed that 'the staffing ratio of child to adult is a particularly important one' (House of Commons, 1988, para. 5.9). They continued by recommending that in authorities where four year olds are in reception classes 'steps be taken ... to bring all their reception classes up to the required standard, in particular to establish an appropriate staffing ratio' (para. 7.15).

## LEA Policies

Some authorities admitting four year olds to their schools' infant or primary classes have attempted to provide an appropriate staffing ratio. This has been achieved by including the youngest children in the staffing allocation for the school even though the children are not of statutory age. Several different arrangements have been made; for example, in one authority: 'teaching staff and nursery assistance will be allocated for the summer-born age group. This means that there will be additional staffing for the summer-born children on the basis of 2 adults to 28 summer-born children. One adult is a teacher, the other a nursery nurse'. It was the intention of this authority that additional staffing would ease the admission of four year olds into school. In addition to the extra staffing, a programme of in-service training would be available for teachers who had four year olds in their classes.

Other authorities provided funding and allocated nursery nurses or ancillary helpers for each reception class with four year olds for all or some days of the week. For example, 'some additional staffing' in one authority comprised, 0.3 of a teacher's time for two terms and 0.5 of a nursery nurse's time for three terms. There were claims from another authority that '75 per cent of the early admission classes have a full-time nursery nurse and six per.cent have a part-time nursery nurse; if qualified help is not available there is usually a part-time classroom ancillary'.

There were recommendations from advisers in a different authority that the headteacher and any part-time staff should not be included when calculating the number of staff to work with this age group. The adult–child ratio should be 1:13 with there being not more than two nursery nurses to every teacher.

Where authorities have not been so generous the adults working with the youngest children can feel that early admission is a way of providing 'nursery education' on the cheap. This was particularly the case in authorities where four year olds were admitted to infant classes 'almost overnight' with no extra funding, resources or extra staffing for the schools. For some of these schools the passage of time has alleviated a few of the difficulties with teachers finding support in in-service training and headteachers making changes in staffing arrangements. However, the deployment of extra adults to work with this age group can affect the availability of ancillary help for teachers of older children. This can cause friction in the staffroom unless there is a whole-school commitment to providing appropriate staffing ratios for the youngest children. (Whole-school commitment is discussed further in Chapter 10.)

In some authorities the funding has been made available but the recruitment of staff has proved difficult (*Teacher*, 14 November, 1988). It was noted in the present study that difficulties were still occurring in replacing not only suitable teachers but also trained ancillary helpers. Teacher shortages continue to be a problem and it has been suggested that one authority may 'close the nurseries rather than send primary-aged children home' (*TES*, 14.7.89).

Depending on the LEA's formula for funding, there may well be limitations on providing additional staffing in infant and primary schools. At the time of writing (1990) it is only possible to speculate what influence the Local Management of Schools (LMS) may have. When the aggregated school budget is used for staffing requirements the effect of employing expensive experienced staff, especially in smaller schools, is still unknown. The confusion is seen in one school governor's comment:

> 'the governors and the headteacher have to decide where to spend the money. In the report [from the LEA] it says something about pupil–teacher ratios; one teacher to 20 children age 4+, one teacher to 24 children for 5+ and 6+. More cash will be available for the younger children but no-one knows yet how it will work.

Other adults involved in the education of this age group agonized over the possibility of funding two ancillary helpers for the price of one experienced teacher or whether to persuade the Parent–Teacher Association (PTA) to pay a salary. There was concern that a change in financing might change the attitude to four year olds completely. It is possible that those holding the purse strings may feel 'that the four year olds don't have to be there, so we won't pay anything for them'. Some of the schools in the study were fortunate in appearing to benefit under the new arrangements. As one headteacher explained, 'There will be a general assistant full-time in each of the two reception classes. At the moment the general assistant is shared between them'.

## Recommended Staffing Ratios

There are obvious difficulties in providing appropriate activities without enough adults available to talk to and interact with these young children. Large classes and insufficient adults make it impossible to provide quality learning experiences. 'It is difficult', interviewees explained, 'to implement a nursery style curriculum without nursery style resourcing'.

This was also noted by HMI who said: 'Conditions associated with ... better quality education in nursery schools and classes include: a narrower age band of children; better adult/child ratios; ... and more teachers experienced in teaching three and four year old children' (GC.DES, 1989b, para. 6). In a nursery school visited by the project team the following observations were made by the researchers:

The nursery is well staffed. The teachers and nursery nurses work full-time and the staffing has remained fairly stable. There are six classes of 28–30 children, with a teacher and two nursery nurses in each class. This makes an average teacher–child ratio of 1:29 and an adult–child ratio of 1:9 or 10. There is also a headteacher and a teacher with special responsibility for parent involvement.

The nursery nurses are in the school from 8.30 a.m. till 3.45 p.m., which means they are there in time for team meetings and planning sessions before the children arrive. The nursery nurses are very much part of the team. In fact the headteacher emphasized that the staff work as a *team*. The head said that it is important to be well staffed for this age group. She had recently visited a reception class in a school in another authority, where the teacher was 'on her knees' trying to provide appropriately for the youngest children without another adult to help her. The head commented that four year olds still need cuddles, reassurance and 'support for their very being'. Therefore sufficient adults are essential for this age group.

The difference in resourcing between nursery and infant classes, often *within the same school*, was also noted in the HMI survey (GB.DES, 1989c). For example, in schools with a nursery class and an infant class with four year olds, it is possible for the nursery class to have appropriate staffing ratios and resources while the four year olds nearby do not enjoy such provision. The contrast between nursery and reception class staffing allocations was also noticed. It was not uncommon to find reception classes with adult–child ratios of 1:26 or 1:28 for the majority of the week. Here are two examples of staffing ratios in reception classes:

There are 52 children in the reception unit. They are in two groups and each group has its own teacher and base. A non-teaching assistant is allocated for two mornings a week. She spends a morning with each reception teacher. There is usually a full-time YTS [Youth Training Scheme] student attached to the unit but today she was absent. During the morning there was a parent helping in the classroom, in the afternoon the dinner lady stayed to help.

In another school

There are three classes with 28–31 children and a teacher in each class. They share a part-time teacher for approximately half the week and ancillary helper for part of the morning and part of the afternoon.

The staffing ratio is probably the greatest discriminator between nursery and infant classrooms. Research studies have shown that in the nursery the recommended staffing ratio is '1:13 but in practice it is usually nearer 1:10 ... In the infant department, however, the permitted ratio jumps to 1:33 ... though the average is 1:22 and most reception classes are not more than 1:28' (McCail, 1989, p. 15).

## Improving Staffing Ratios

There is no doubt that there is a wide gap between the appropriate staffing enjoyed in nursery schools and classes and the situation found in infant or primary schools. In the study some of the latter had established adult–child ratios moving towards levels found in nursery environments. A better staffing ratio had been achieved in some schools for part, if not all, of the week. This had been made possible through either the LEA policy or commitment from the headteachers.

### LEA policy

It has already been noted above that some authorities allocated extra teachers for this age group or a nursery nurse to each reception class. This enabled some of the schools to provide a teacher–pupil ratio of 1:26 and an adult–child ratio of 1:13. The benefits of this are acknowledged by HMI who noticed signs of improvement for some four year olds in school. They also noted that the 'greatest benefits have accrued where LEAs have provided sufficient teachers and other adult staff who are suitable trained and experienced in working with this age group' (GB.DES, 1989b, para. 8).

### Headteachers' commitment

Interviewees explained how headteachers had a crucial role to play in improving staffing levels. It was the headteacher who could give a lead in recognizing the importance of providing appropriately and acknowledging the difficulties in accommodating these younger children in reception classes. Through the headteacher the school could be organized to reflect the needs of the youngest children. They could and should be given the best staffing ratio and the most experienced teachers.

Adult assistance was more freely available where headteachers had been supportive and committed to trying to provide more appropriate staffing ratios. They had achieved this by:

✿   allocating part-time teachers to work with this age group;
✿   allocating nursery nurses to work with these children;
✿   allocating non-teaching assistants (NTAs) to work with four year olds;
✿   using voluntary helpers in the classroom.

*Allocation of part-time teachers*

Some schools allocated peripatetic teachers, bilingual teachers work-ing with children for whom English is not their first language, CURT (county unattached relief teachers), Section 11 teachers, headteachers and deputy headteachers without class responsibility to 'help out' with the youngest children. One example observed in the study is described below:

> The school is well staffed with extra teachers because the pupil in-take is 100 per cent Asian. English is rarely, if ever, spoken at home. In the reception class there are 32 children who began school in September at the age of four. There is a full-time teacher and a nursery nurse. The class also has a relief teacher who spends half of the week with them. A 'floating' teacher joins the team for one afternoon and for half an hour on Friday during 'library time'. The teacher–child ratio is thus reduced to 1:16 or less for half the week; and the adult–child ratio varies from 1:16 to 1:11.

*Allocation of nursery nurses*

When and where nursery nurses are available they are 'very highly prized'. This was clearly demonstrated by one headteacher who felt obliged to send the youngest children home when strike action took the nursery nurses out of the classroom. The amount of time for which nursery nurses are allocated to the youngest children varies con-siderably. For example, some work full-time with the youngest class at the expense of the older classes. Others work with the youngest child-ren for only part of the week or divide their time between several re-ception classes.

Sometimes extra classroom helpers, either qualified nursery nurses or non-teaching assistants, are appointed to work with children with special educational needs. These helpers were often observed to be in-volved in activities with their 'special' child and a small group of main-stream children.

*Allocation of non-teaching assistants*

Non-teaching assistants (NTAs) are employed in many schools. Their time is usually divided between all the classes in the school. In some schools the headteacher allocated them to work specifically with the four year olds to help provide an appropriate adult–child ratio. This was not regarded as being ideal because often these classroom helpers were also 'welfare' assistants who could be called away to other classes to deal with children who were feeling unwell.

One school used their NTA in the following way:

> She spends five mornings a week in school. There are eight classes so the reception children normally have her help for one morning

out of eight. Towards the end of the summer term she spends more time in the reception class 'because they need help when the nursery children visit them'. In September she spends all her time in the reception class to help settle in the children who have come from the nursery. She has been an NTA for just over a year now. She said she 'loves it', and there is never time to be bored because she is involved throughout the school and 'it is very interesting'.

### Using voluntary helpers

Interviewees suggested that parents, students and other members of the community could help in providing appropriate adult–child ratios. The SMAP team (Bennett, 1987) found that the quality and variety of the curriculum was limited by adult–child ratios as high as 1:30 and called for more qualified help. When this was not forthcoming some schools overcame difficulties by involving parents and other adults from the community to help.

*(1) Parents.* Professionals suggested that parents could be encouraged to come into school to improve the adult–child ratio. They could help in all manner of ways, from washing paint-pots to being involved in children's activities or passing on their own special skills.

In practice parents were found helping in the classroom in a variety of ways; some did 'household tasks' like washing the Lego or sorting the jig-saws with the children. Sometimes parents were to be found just sitting in the classroom and being 'available to talk with the children'. Other parents were involved with the children in activities initiated by the teacher or by themselves (see Chapter 5).

Increased parental involvement has helped to bring about a more desirable adult–child ratio in some schools. For example:

> In one school where two teachers were assisted by a nursery nurse, a student and two parents in the morning and another teacher in the afternoon, the staffing ratios improved dramatically. The teacher–child ratio was 1:35 in the morning but the adult–child ratio was 1:11 with parental help. The afternoon staffing ratio was also more appropriate than the 1:35 official allocation because of the use of a part-time teacher. The teachers in this school were aware that 'these ratios have improved because of the support of the head'. They held hopes that next year a permanent teacher and extra classroom would become available because of a 'conscious decision being made to keep the adult–child ratio down'.

*(2) Students.* Students also helped in the classroom. For some, such as trainee nursery nurses and teachers, this was part of their

training. For others, like those in YTS or school students, it was work experience.

Students usually work with small groups of children. Sometimes they have their own assignments to complete, such as observation of children for child studies or special activities relating to specific curriculum areas.

*(3) Other members of the community.* Other members of the community provided regular help in a few classrooms. For example, 'a retired lady telephoned the school and volunteered to help for a "couple of afternoons a week" because she had time on her hands. The teacher with whom she worked commented, "She comes in twice a week to listen to stories. Her detached patience is invaluable"'.

There was, however, a word of caution from our interviewees. They reminded the team that there is an optimum number of adults for working with young children. They felt that too many adults could be detrimental to the learning environment. This was also reported in earlier research (Clift *et al.*, 1980). In the present study, some staff felt that if there are too many adults present young children may miss out on opportunities to play freely without intervention. It was considered that children need to 'play alone sometimes and have the freedom to indulge in their own language with their peers. Sometimes they stop talking when an adult approaches'.

However, the majority of four year olds' classrooms were unlikely to have more than the optimum number of adults. Information gathered on an in-service course for headteachers and teachers revealed that, in that authority, there was very little adult help for teachers with four year olds in their classes so it was not surprising that these teachers were saying: 'I would like to see a nursery nurse or school helper full-time in a class of four year olds. With 28 to 30 children it is difficult to do each one justice.'

Even in schools where teachers were committed to providing appropriately for the younger children and wanted to implement changes in their classroom organization and teaching approach, the staffing ratio was often a constraining factor in bringing about such changes. As one teacher explained: 'There is insufficient adult help to give me time for the changes I would like to make. I would like to arrange activity areas in the classroom and have more time for observation of children.'

The desperate need for more adults to work with these children is recognized by some school governors. One whole-heartedly agreed with involving other people in the classroom, particularly parents, but would consider 'almost anybody to get the ratio down'.

## Qualifications and Training

### Qualified Staff

The interviewees were concerned about the lack of suitably qualified teachers working with the youngest children. They felt that many teachers with four year olds in their classes lacked a real understanding of child development in this age group. Some teachers did not know how children of this age learn, and failed to see the potential in the various activities and materials. It was hoped that increased opportunities for in-service courses would raise awareness in the profession and help those who had not benefited from early years or nursery training. Government funding being channelled in this direction was welcomed.

*Teachers' qualifications and experience*
Most of the interviewees stressed that it was **'important that teachers of this age group were qualified and experienced'**. It must be remembered that the participants in the schools involved in the study had been pointed out as examples of providing appropriately for this age group so it is not surprising that the majority of these teachers had appropriate backgrounds, in terms of an infant training, which, for some, included the nursery age as well. Others had worked in playgroups at some stage of their careers, which they felt had 'extended their experience'.

Very few of the teachers were making use of the subject specialisms they had pursued during their initial training. One example was the teacher who had specialized in art and now had 'responsibility for science throughout the nursery, infant and lower juniors'.

Most of the teachers working with the youngest children were experienced in working with four year olds. They enjoyed this age group and had chosen to teach these children. Some teachers, both those with and those without infant or nursery training, had found in-service courses helpful. The few teachers who had previously taught older children or worked in different environments commented that 'teaching younger children is very demanding physically'. It was only now 'after nursery experience and several years with that age group' that they were 'feeling confident'. A headteacher went as far as saying that even though she had an infant training initially and had participated in in-service courses for this age group recently, she 'sometimes forgot just how young these children are'.

*Nursery nurse qualifications*
In the guidelines collected from authorities and in the interviews with professionals there was concern that **the expertise of nursery nurses should be recognized and valued.** They had been trained to

work with this age group and proper use should be made of their expertise and time in the classroom.

As the National Nursery Examining Board (NNEB) explains in their syllabus, the training course covers:

✿ children's growth and development;
✿ child observation;
✿ physical development and keeping children healthy;
✿ cognitive development and learning through play;
✿ emotional development;
✿ social relationships.

This should enable students, when they qualify, to contribute to the planning and organization of activities and to be involved with the children in carrying them out. They should be able to contribute to the care and welfare of children and to liaise with other adults such as parents and social workers.

The roles and deployment of nursery nurses working with four year olds were wide-ranging. For example, some nursery nurses ran the nursery group of an early years unit under the supervision of the reception teacher, while others spent only a few hours a week working with the youngest children (see Chapter 10).

*Other classroom assistants*
Some LEAs specified a certain level of academic achievement for people applying to be non-teaching assistants. In some areas it is difficult to recruit qualified help, so untrained ancillaries are fulfilling the role. They are useful as another pair of hands and sometimes their expertise is particularly appreciated. Even though they usually have no formal qualifications a few are bilingual and are 'invaluable as interpreters'.

**In-service Training**

In-service courses could help teachers who had neither initial training nor experience with this age group. Many teachers are uncertain about which activities to provide and even more unsure about why they should provide them (Staniland, 1986; Drummond, 1987). Dowling (1988) states: 'teachers need help in clarifying their ideologies and support with the practicalities of their work' (p. 4).

The professionals involved in the study, with its focus on appropriate practice, were committed, qualified and experienced. Many of the headteachers and teachers were undertaking, or had completed, BEd and MEd degrees with a focus on 'children's play', 'observing children' and so on. They had attended a variety of courses and conferences, visited other schools, joined in quality workshop sessions and taken up practical suggestions.

The participants in the in-service initiatives studied in the project (see Chapter 11) were just as committed to providing appropriately for the youngest children but were not always trained or experienced in working with them. Only a few of them had taken initial training courses that included the nursery age group; the majority were trained to teach the infant or the infant–junior age range and one in four had no primary training at all.

Interviewees expressed the view that every teacher should spend some time with the youngest children so that they understand the importance of the first few weeks in school. All courses, both initial training and in-service for all primary teachers, should include a component devoted to the nursery age. Child development is very important and should be a major part of educational training.

In-service training can play a role in increasing and developing teamwork in school. The contributions nursery nurses can make, for example, should be understood and appreciated.

Nursery nurses felt that 'there was very little in-service' for them, although they could do some in their own time. Since then new funding arrangements, Grants for Education Support and Training 1991–92, (GEST) include INSET for non-teaching assistants. They still regret the fact that they do not have opportunities to visit other schools. Even when their school is visited by other staff it is 'only the teachers' who return the visit to other schools. They would appreciate seeing how nursery nurse expertise is deployed in other schools. In a few schools there was a move towards inviting nursery nurses to share not only early years unit meetings but also in-service training sessions. These were often school-based training days.

The early years teachers felt that for teams to work more effectively together, attending courses as a team would be beneficial. This would, and should, include the headteacher, the teachers and the nursery nurses. The value of this idea is encapsulated in a teacher's reply when asked about any difficulties encountered in making adjustments for her class of four year olds. She said she had no difficulties because 'the headteacher had previously been on the same course so she was very supportive'.

During the study opportunities to attend conferences and courses for the early years were prolific. Teachers' interest in and dedication to providing the most appropriate experiences for their young charges has to be applauded. The courses and conferences were well supported and often over-subscribed. A range of subjects was covered, often including school management and the curriculum. Towards the end of the study the emphasis changed to include the National Curriculum and assessment procedures.

## Choice of Teacher

Some of the interviews and the LEA guidelines suggested that probationary teachers should not work with this age group. This was because 'particular skills and experiences were required' in what was described as a 'very difficult job'. A few guidelines emphasized that what is important is the quality of the teachers' personality and teaching ability. They should understand the range of normal child development and how children learn.

Governors will become more involved in the selection of staff. The governors interviewed realized that the quality of the early years teacher was 'incredibly important'. They held the view that qualifications and experience were important but 'Manner, demeanour and approachability' were also important in early years education. Characteristics such as 'being able to talk to children as people' were an asset. When appointments were being made by some governors an infant teacher with a family would be more likely to be their choice because 'they usually have a better understanding of young children'. One governor found it difficult to say what it was they were really looking for but said 'I'll know it when I see it'.

# Conclusion

It seems that the greatest deficiency in provision for four year olds in infant classes is in the staffing levels. Increased staffing would enable teachers to meet children's individual needs more effectively. The most appropriate curriculum for these young children is individualized. 'No child can be seen as average, and the classroom should reflect the wide variety of educational needs found within it' (Kernig, 1986, p. 42). Is it realistic to expect a teacher to achieve this aim without a nursery staffing allocation, without the help of qualified assistants or without training and experience for themselves?

Pupil–teacher ratios should be in line with nursery recommendations. Teachers trained and experienced in early years education and full-time ancillary support should be available. Adult–child ratios are improved further when voluntary helpers are encouraged to spend time in the classroom.

To be committed to providing appropriately with regard to staffing is difficult, particularly in a climate of staff shortages and untrained teachers. More adults are needed to provide the quantity and more training is needed to provide the quality in early years education. Support from both within and outside the school is essential.

# PART FOUR

## Support

If practice and provision for four year olds in infant classes is to be more appropriate, schools need all the support available to make and sustain the necessary adjustments. Consideration should be given to sources of support within and outside the school.

# 10 Support within the School

During the interviews with professionals, the view was frequently expressed that there seemed to be a general lack of support from politicians, the media and the general public for the development of early years education. The early years tended to be held in low esteem and therefore failed to attract the necessary commitment and funding. It was hoped that the recent focus on the under-fives by a House of Commons Select Committee in 1988 and a government inquiry in 1989 would help raise the profile of this section of the community and all those involved in it. On a practical level, the interviewees suggested that support could be provided or improved at all levels of the education service from the classroom to the local authority. This would help to give teachers the confidence they needed to make effective changes.

This chapter considers the roles and relationships involved in working together as a team in the classroom and in the school as a whole.

It is important that everyone involved with the reception class works together to achieve similar aims. Nursery education involves team-work, co-operation and collaboration and these are no less important when working with children of nursery age in school. However, a team spirit may be more difficult to achieve in infant or primary schools because staff working with four year olds often feel under pressure from parents, from teachers further up the school and some-times from a headteacher who is unsympathetic to the needs of very young children.

# The Class Teacher

Professionals taking part in the study emphasized three aspects of the class teacher's role that are particularly important when providing ap-propriately for four year olds. Such a teacher needs to be an early years 'expert', able to lead a team and able to communicate effectively with other people.

### The Early Years Expert

The class teacher is a trained professional who is expected to be an expert in providing educational experiences for the pupils. Reception teachers in particular need to be proficient in easing children into school and enabling them to develop a wide range of competencies. Their distinctiveness lies in what Pascal calls 'the complexity of the task they are faced with – their specialism is that of being a generalist, catering across the curriculum, being able to integrate and meet a wide range of developmental needs and involve a wide range of people in doing so' (Pascal, 1989, p. 8). It is important that **teachers of four year olds should have an understanding of early years education** so that they are able to respond appropriately to child-ren's learning needs.

### Leading the Team

Appropriate provision for four year olds requires that the teacher has some form of qualified help, preferably a full-time, trained nursery nurse (see Chapter 9). In schools that have tried to improve adult ra-tios for this age group the teacher is likely to have some ancillary help (whether trained or untrained) and perhaps volunteer parent helpers working in the classroom for at least part of the time. **The class teacher is thus the leader of a team and, as such, needs man-**

**agement and communication skills to perform this role suc-
cessfully.**

Team leadership is something for which the primary teacher is unlikely to have been trained. Professionals interviewed said that initial
training was 'falling down' in providing guidance in this respect. In
fact, as the Select Committee pointed out, *nursery* teachers are 'the
only members of the teaching profession who from their first day as a
probationer must be seen as a team leader working with other professionals and para-professionals ...' (House of Commons, 1988, para.
5.15).

The schools in the study employed a variety of 'teams' to work with
the youngest children. For example:

✿ in an age four reception class (all English as a second language) : a
class teacher, a full-time nursery nurse and a one-third 'support'
teacher;

✿ in an age four reception unit (equivalent to two classes) : two class
teachers, a full-time YTS assistant, a two-tenths non-teaching assistant and several parent helpers as and when available.

When there is more than one class teacher in the team, one of them
is usually designated the leader. One school was unusual in having an
early years coordinator who had no class but who was responsible for
coordinating the nursery and the two reception classes and for liaising
with the local playgroup.

One of the tasks of a team leader is to have regular meetings with
the team. The teams all held regular meetings in order to:

✿ plan, discuss and evaluate the work of the class or unit;
✿ share ideas;
✿ discuss problems and difficulties;
✿ discuss the needs and progress of individual children;
✿ communicate information about the rest of the school.

Here is a description of one such meeting as recorded in the researcher's notes:

> Members of the team [the teachers and nursery nurses of the two
> reception classes and the nursery] meet approximately once a
> week. At the beginning of the term they discuss the development of
> a class theme or project. It is now well into the summer term and
> the first subject on the agenda is 'transition'. The team have been
> preparing letters and booklets for induction to the nursery class.
> Home visits and arrangements with the 'mother-tongue' support
> teacher are discussed. The team then move on to evaluate their
> project on 'Living Things', commenting on its strengths and

weaknesses, and highlighting areas that have been left out or were found 'too much'. They realize that the display element is quite demanding and is tending to become the main focus of their attention, so they decide in future to concentrate more on what the *children* want to do.

Another task of the team leader is to deploy the various members of the team. In some cases, team meetings provide the forum for deciding what the members of the team are going to do. In others, the teacher designates tasks to the rest of the team. The following example illustrates the way in which one reception teacher organized tasks:

> The team consists of a class teacher, a nursery nurse, a support teacher and, for part of the year, two student teachers from the local training college. At the beginning of the term, the class teacher draws up a flow-chart of the activities that centre around a particular theme. The other members of the team select which activities they would like to take responsibility for. They then develop these activities according to their own ideas (and the children's interests) within the theme. The class teacher believes that this allows individual team members to utilize their own skills and interests to the best advantage.

In very small schools it is possible for the entire staff to function as a close-knit team with a special interest in the youngest children. One such team consisted of a headteacher, a class teacher and a nursery nurse in a school of 42 children aged from four to nine. The children were grouped into two classes, one infant and one junior. All the staff were nursery trained and had had nursery teaching experience. An activity-based approach was adopted throughout the age range and both classes shared the same theme. As the teacher explained, 'Because this is a small school we all discuss everything as a team.'

Dowling (1988) suggests that in the nursery some team meetings could include other members of staff, such as the caretaker and dinner ladies. This idea might usefully be taken up, when appropriate, in the reception class. Informal talks with lunchtime supervisors and cleaners revealed that they appreciated being included in discussions about school matters and sometimes had useful contributions to make from their own perspectives. In one school, for example, the women who supervised the playground at lunchtimes said that 'generally the younger children cope very well but difficulties arise because there is nothing much for them to do. Things like skipping ropes and bean bags would be useful. The supervisors could then organize some activities and play with the children.' The cleaner also felt some responsibility for the care and welfare of the children and commented on how her job had changed with the admission of younger pupils. She said that:

> it was more difficult now because young children used such a lot of things like glue and wax crayons, which are very hard to remove from the floor, especially when they get trodden in. She often chatted to the teacher at the end of the day and knew she appreciated the problem. With such a lot of children in the room it was impossible to prevent spills, but it was also important to keep the floor hygienic and safe.

The views of ancillaries such as these are worth taking into account when trying to work together in providing effectively for young children. The people in question had opportunities to communicate their views informally to the teacher at the beginning or end of the afternoon session. Feeling that their opinions were respected and perhaps discussed and acted upon enhanced working relationships in the common cause of providing for young children.

## Communicating with Others

Leading a team calls for interpersonal skills, both in terms of negotiating good relationships and in communicating with people.

Professionals at all levels stressed that **teachers working with four year olds in schools need to be able to articulate and, if necessary, justify good early years practice with confidence to others.** Indeed, some LEA guidelines state quite clearly that early years teachers need to be 'public relations officers', particularly with regard to parents. HMI are adamant that an important aspect of the role of the teacher is 'to explain to parents what the school is seeking to achieve and to help them to extend their children's learning' (GB.DES, 1989c, para. 11). This is not easy, and even the most experienced and dedicated teachers may have difficulty in justifying their practices to others. Drummond (1989b) attributes this difficulty to a lack of any clear pedagogy to support practice, resulting in 'a hole at the centre of the early years universe'. This means that practitioners may be unable to speak out in defence of the basic principles of early childhood education because they are unsure as to 'what these principles are, what values they are based on and how they can most effectively be expressed' (ibid.).

Teachers employed various strategies for explaining what they and the children were doing. One teacher wrote out the daily timetable and a description of the current theme on posters, which she pinned on the wall outside the classroom door for the information of parents, students, visitors and so on. Inside the classroom, activities were assigned to areas and an explanation of them was pinned on the wall near each area. For example:

> The 'listening area' was described as the place where children could explore and compare sounds. They could work with ideas such as fast and slow, loud and soft, long and short and so on. They could also try out rhythms. They could select story tapes to listen to on the cassette player that they could work themselves. They could also bring tapes from home if they wanted to.

Most reception teachers made arrangements for parents to come into the classroom, both on appointed days and informally (see Chapter 3). In a deliberate attempt to explain what they were doing, one school held a series of 'Open Evenings' and also encouraged parents to come into the classroom at any time, either to help out or just to talk about their child. Other schools held Open Evenings *and* Open Days so that parents could not only hear about what went on in school but also see the activities in progress. As one teacher explained: 'We have three Open Days a year for the parents to come into the school. With the reception classes we also have evening sessions with the parents to explain things like reading and number activities. They have a practical workshop and a talk'. A reception teacher described how she used a typical Open Day:

> When the parents come in I explain things like how we use certain materials or why we do baking. If a parent says 'Why does my child not have a reading book?' I explain what the child is doing and they soon understand. I show them the child's own reading book and I find parents prefer this to reading schemes because the children make them themselves. I explain the different stages the children work through and the importance of the child understanding rather than learning by rote. We make lots of the materials the children use and I think the parents appreciate the time we spend.

## Other Classroom Staff

**The support of other staff in the team is crucial in providing appropriately for four year olds in school.** The key figures here are the nursery nurses or ancillaries who work regularly alongside the teacher.

## The Nursery Nurse

Professionals interviewed pointed out that **nursery nurses have received two years training and their expertise should be valued and used to the full**. They should not be used merely to clear up and tidy the classroom but should be involved in activities, in following up ideas and in discussions with the children. In this way the teacher and nursery nurse could work together as 'partners' in providing an appropriate environment for young children's learning.

The guidelines collected from LEAs adopted a similar stance, recognizing that nursery nurses are trained people whose role should complement that of the teacher. The nursery nurse should support the teacher and share in providing appropriate experiences for the children. Their training has allowed them to develop observation skills, which could be used to assess how individual children respond to activities. They are also able to attend to the children's health and welfare.

Evidence that nursery nurses are often under-deployed in schools was recently reported by HMI (GB.DES, 1989c) who found that:

> a significant number worked predominantly in a supervisory and servicing capacity which did not use their experience and expertise to maximum effect. In the best circumstances, the invaluable assistance given to the teacher in helping to prepare and implement the work underlines the need to make the most of this ancillary provision. (para. 35).

Nursery nurses in the schools studies were asked how they saw their role in the reception class. From the researcher's notes, one said that:

> she felt she had made good use of her training and that she had skills that teachers may not have, such as medical awareness and observational skills. She saw her role as very much a partnership with the teacher – she was involved in planning but also suggested ideas and organized some activities in her own way. She and the teacher discussed things such as the organization of the classroom, the types of activities provided and the development of individual children.

In another school, nursery nurses spent a year full-time with the reception classes and then moved on to other infant classes before returning to the youngest children. The researcher noted that: 'they felt much more involved as members of the team in the reception classes, because there they were free to develop the activities for which they were responsible'.

The ways in which nursery nurses were allocated responsibility varied with the class teacher. One was assigned to those activities for which she seemed to have a special aptitude and was said by the teacher to be 'particularly good with practical maths'. Another was able to choose activities from the teacher's overall plan and then develop them according to her own ideas.

Observations of nursery nurses at work in the classroom revealed differences in the ways they were deployed. Some were more involved in planning and record-keeping than others. Their role also differed with regard to whole-class activities, such as story and rhymes. In some classes these activities were led by the teacher while the nursery nurse finished clearing up. In others, the nursery nurse took a regular turn at leading the whole class while the teacher was engaged in clearing up, preparing for the next session or talking to parents. In some schools the nursery nurse was appointed with responsibility towards children with special requirements. For example, a child with a tracheotomy was allocated extra nursery nurse support. Several schools with a very high proportion of children for whom English was not their first language had the benefit of nursery nurses who were bilingual.

In some schools, especially those with a nursery class, the nursery nurse moved on *with* the children to reception and beyond. This provided continuity, not only for the children, but also for the nursery nurse who was able to note the 'tremendous progress' young pupils can make. Continuity is difficult to achieve if the nursery nurse's time has to be shared between classes or if the post is a part-time one. One nursery nurse explained that:

> the part-time nature of her job and the fact that she also spent time with other classes made it difficult to be involved in planning activities and seeing them through. In her absence the children moved on to other things. Consequently she felt that her training was not being utilized and that almost anyone could do her job.

This example clearly demonstrates that if professional skills and expertise are to be properly used, **the nursery nurse's appointment to a reception class should, wherever possible, be a full-time one.**

## Non-teaching Assistants

Reception classes with full-time NNEB support were still very much in a minority at the time of the study. In the face of severe financial constraints some LEAs, in an attempt to recognize the need for more adults in classes with four year olds, recommended the use of full-time or part-time ancillaries who were not necessarily trained and who cost less to employ.

Several of the schools in the study fell into this category. In most cases the assistant was shared between more than one class so that support in any one reception class was part-time. For example, in one school the reception teacher had an assistant for two-tenths of the week, in another for five-tenths, and it was not necessarily always the same assistant.

The assistants might divide their time between several reception classes or between reception and other age groups in the school. This affected the degree to which they could be involved in any one class and their role within it. As one assistant said: 'I don't feel I'm a member of the reception team – I'm only in there one morning out of eight.' By contrast, an assistant in another school, who spent 50 per cent of the week with one reception class, regularly took responsibility for certain group activities in a way similar to the nursery nurses described earlier.

The assistants' involvement with group activities varied from class to class because they tended to help out wherever another pair of hands was most needed. They were often seen finishing the clearing-up at the end of a session while the teacher took the whole class for story. Asked how she saw her role, one assistant said that:

> she was 'more of a mum than the teachers' and liked giving the children a cuddle when they needed one: she helped with classroom activities and she also spent a lot of time helping the children with things like shoes and coats; she tended to notice their physical health and they went crying to her when something was wrong.

## Voluntary Helpers

In addition to any regular paid support they might have in the classroom, the schools welcomed a regular commitment from volunteers such as parents, retired folk and young people on the YTS. It was the parents, however, who formed the majority of voluntary helpers in these schools.

### Parent Helpers

The professionals interviewed recommended that **parents should be involved as helpers in the classroom.** They could be a useful additional resource, providing a much-needed boost to adult ratios. Some interviewees believed that it was enough for the parent helpers simply to *be* there, thus not only providing an extra adult for the children but also adding to an atmosphere of warmth and informality in the classroom. Others felt that better use could be made of parents' time by giving them specific things to do under the teacher's direction.

The issue of parental involvement in the classroom is a controversial one, since it can give rise to ambivalent feelings on the part of the parents and the professionals (Beck, 1989). The recruitment of parent helpers and decisions about their participation must be handled sensitively if feelings of jealousy, suspicion and resentment are to be avoided.

Most of the schools encouraged parents to help in the classroom and several had a deliberate policy, especially with regard to the reception class. An invitation to help was issued at the start of the school year, usually in the form of a letter from the teacher or headteacher. Parent helpers were usually placed with their child's class at first. Those who continued to help for several years were then likely to be placed where most needed.

The timetabling of parental help depended on the parents and/or the school. Some schools accepted help on a regular basis, say for one or two specific half-days per week. One school invited parents in on Tuesday afternoons; on arrival they were assigned to whichever classes had requested help. In other schools, parents came in whenever they were available, depending on work-shifts or whether they could find someone to mind their toddler or baby. This had the disadvantage that the class teacher was unable to plan ahead in order to make the most of the extra help. Some mothers said that if a crèche could be organized at the school they would be able to help more often.

In reception classes parents assisted in all kinds of ways (see Chapter 9). However, the deployment of parents to certain tasks is a matter that requires sensitive treatment and mutual understanding. Beck (1989) reported that, while parents found it acceptable for their peers to help with swimming, school trips and special events, they were not always happy to see parents involved with maths, science and language activities, which they perceived as being 'academic subjects' for which teachers had received training. On the other hand, both teachers and parents appreciated the benefit of help in relieving teachers of the more menial tasks so that they were able to spend more time with the children.

The extent of the parent helper's involvement as a member of the team is also a matter for sensitivity and tact. Schools tried to make parents feel welcome by, for example, offering them a hot drink at playtime, although parents were not usually expected to use the staffroom. The helpers felt they had good relationships with the class teacher in so far as they could pass on their comments and know they were being listened to. However, it is important that both teachers and parents see that confidentiality is observed. Parent helpers were not usually involved in planning and evaluation or in discussions about individual children.

Here is an example of how one school managed the involvement of parents in the reception class.

> The school serves several growing estates of modern suburban development. Parents come in when they can and, in consultation with the reception teacher, decide what they are going to do. Some like to work with group activities, while others prefer the more menial classroom tasks. The teacher tries to accommodate their choices and also capitalizes on their special aptitudes and interests. Sometimes there are two or three parents in the room, at other times there are none. During our observations, one parent helper was involved with a group of children making models out of wood, another took a group into the school garden to hunt for minibeasts. A third parent helped with a computer game. Her husband had also been in to help with a woodwork activity. He wanted to help more often but found it difficult to fit in with his job. Parents with a particular interest are also encouraged to come in from time to time to talk to the children. On one occasion, a mother who is keen on gardening came specially to show the children how to create a flowerbed and plant seeds. This formed part of a developing project about 'The Environment'.

The involvement of parents as classroom helpers tends to be short term. A few discover a special interest in working with children and go on to become general assistants or take nursery nurse training. Others give up because of family commitments or return to work elsewhere. Most schools found that after the beginning of the year parental involvement gradually diminished.

One way to make up for this loss might be to encourage other members of the community, especially retired people with time on their hands, to help in the classroom. These people may be able to offer a more sustained involvement over a longer period than busy young parents. They may have much to offer and, in return, feel valued for the contribution they make. In one school, for example:

> An elderly lady comes into the reception class at least once a fortnight (more if she can) to help with reading. She sits with children in the 'quiet corner' and reads or listens to them as required. She also helps with the library books, which children select to take home, and contributes to their reading record. She is very attached to what she refers to as 'her class' and highly appreciates the opportunity to be involved.

# The Headteacher and Other Teachers in the School

In a broader sense, the 'team' working with the youngest children must include the headteacher and other teachers in the school. The professionals interviewed pointed out that teachers of older children, and indeed some headteachers, are not always sympathetic to the needs of the youngest children or to their teacher's role. They recommended that **a whole-school approach should be adopted towards early admission, with a policy for appropriate provision being developed with all members of staff.** It should be recognized that the four year olds are part of the school community and that their needs should be acknowledged and understood throughout the school.

A whole-school approach might also bring benefits not just for the reception class but also for the rest of the school. As Weir (1988) explains, responding more effectively to the four year olds 'might manifestly affect and influence for the better the whole of the infant/primary curriculum' (p. 16).

The interviewees were of the firm opinion that headteachers could provide this approach by ensuring that the youngest children are part of the whole-school community, providing support for teachers with four year olds in their class, having concern for transition and continuity and explaining appropriate policy and practice to teacher colleagues and parents.

### Ensuring that Four Year Olds are Part of the School Community

Headteachers taking part in the study said that they definitely regarded their four-year-old pupils as part of the school community. Most of them tried to show this by making conscious efforts both to include the youngest classes in corporate school events and to prevent their feeling isolated from the rest of the school. In some respects a narrow path has to be walked between treating the youngest children appropriately and at the same time not isolating them.

Two schools had taken deliberate steps to make the youngest children and their staff feel less isolated from the rest of the school by:

- ✿ transferring the four year olds from their former classroom at one end of the building to an 'early years unit' in the main body of the school;
- ✿ including the early years teachers in staff discussions and decision-making on issues concerning the rest of the school.

Conscious attempts to show that the four year olds were a part of the school community meant that the youngest classes were included in school projects and special events.

Most of the schools had special events throughout the year, such as fêtes, fairs and other fund-raising activities, to which all the children and their parents were invited. In addition, some staff organized events linked to certain aspects of the curriculum, such as 'Book Week', 'Maths Week' and so on. During the study, one school introduced a new 'school experience in CDT' in which everyone, including the four year olds, was involved.

This is an urban infant school with a high incidence of social need. For two weeks of the summer term the whole school was involved in a CDT programme based on Roald Dahl's story *The Enormous Crocodile*. Each class contributed to the designing and building of a huge set in the hall in which the story could be acted out. The set included working models, and the focus of the children's activities was on how to make them work. Each class discussed the story and put forward ideas for making it 'happen'. This resulted in an agreed plan being drawn up for the design. The set, complete with models, was then constructed by the children with help from the staff and a few parents. Each class contributed to the various stages in developing the project. The four year olds in the reception class helped construct the framework for all the large animals in the story, such as the crocodile and the hippopotamus. They worked out how to make the crocodile's jaws open and shut by using hinges, and they also made the 'crocodile palm-tree' out of wood and paper. When the project was finished, *all* the classes had a turn at enacting the story and trying out the various devices, such as pressure pads, buttons, switches and magnets, to make the models work.

Four year olds in the study contributed to displays on walls and tables in school halls, foyers and corridors. Headteachers believed that this helped the children to understand what each can do. As one headteacher said, 'The older children appreciate the nursery's contribution and the younger children's work is given value.'

Sometimes, instead of the youngest children being drawn into whole-school activities, the rest of the school is drawn into an initiative begun with the four year olds. For example, several heads considered that the approach used with the youngest children could also be used to advantage with older pupils. Thus a 'play-based' or 'activity-based' curriculum was adopted throughout the school, in one case up to age 11. This not only contributed to continuity and integration between the age groups; it also avoided the idea that play is only for 'the little ones' (see Chapter 5).

The recommended practice of exempting the youngest children from whole-school 'fixtures' such as playtime, lunchtime and assembly carries with it a risk of isolating these children and their staff from the rest of the school (see Chapter 3). While it is desirable to retain separate arrangements for playtime for as long as possible, it is probably advisable to introduce the four year olds gradually to assembly as the school year progresses. Here is an example of how a large urban infant school managed it:

> For the first half of the year the three reception classes did not attend school assemblies but held their own 'assemblies' in their classrooms. During the second term the head and staff agreed that these children were tending to become isolated from the rest of the school and their teachers 'never crossed paths' with other teachers. They decided to try a compromise. The reception children were introduced to school assembly once a week, remaining for the first 15 minutes only. This was so successful that they gradually increased their attendance to every day, but only for the first quarter of an hour. The head plans next year to begin this during the first term, perhaps no more than fortnightly to start with. She said that this gradual introduction to whole-school activities 'helps to engender a community feeling in the school'.

## Providing Support for Teachers with Four Year Olds

An understanding headteacher is likely to be the most valuable source of support a teacher of four year olds can have. It is the responsibility of the headteacher, together with the governing body, not only to define an appropriate curriculum for this age group but also to make the practical arrangements for it to be carried through. This requires that there is the highest quality of provision possible with regard to the deployment of staff and the organization of the physical environment. To this end, headteachers will need to be aware of appropriate adult–child ratios, which teachers are likely to be most suitable for the age group and how ancillary support may best be deployed. They will also be sensitive to the in-service needs of the staff involved (see Chapter 11). They will need to organize the size and age composition of the admission classes, bearing in mind the vulnerability of the youngest children. They will also be responsible for the sympathetic management of timetabling and the allocation of space, equipment and materials.

Reception teachers reported that their headteachers supported them with extra resources. As one explained, 'We're lucky here because the head is concerned about this age group and gets us plenty of things for them.' One teacher described how the headteacher was 'always fighting for extra help for us'. Another pointed out that she received the lion's share of ancillary time, although there was only one general assistant for the whole (primary) school and this meant that she was entirely without help for three days of the week.

Clearly, headteachers find their task easier if they have the backing of a supportive LEA, but in many cases this is not so and headteachers were constantly struggling to obtain scarce resources for their schools. Several said they hoped that LMS would enable them to improve matters in the future. On the other hand, there was one aspect of headteacher support that was greatly valued by teachers and that does not require backing from the authority or anyone else. It may be called 'moral' support. As one teacher explained: 'Leadership is so important. Teachers can't be good at their jobs if they feel isolated; they need support from the top.'

Moral support was much appreciated and helped to increase self-esteem in what was sometimes perceived to be a low-status job. It was also of particular importance when teachers wanted to make changes in their classrooms. The support of headteachers who took time to listen to their staff and encourage their efforts was highly prized.

The effectiveness of the headteacher's support will be greatly influenced by his or her own expertise in the field of early years education. The professionals interviewed considered it essential that the headteacher should have a knowledge of this field and, preferably, experience of teaching young children. A headteacher who does not understand the needs of the younger pupils may not see early admission as an issue and may not acknowledge its special problems. As one reception teacher told us, 'He doesn't understand. As long as we're coping he thinks we're OK.'

A headteacher who is not trained or experienced in this age group may seek support from the LEA, the advisory service or INSET. Indeed, the interviewees recommended that headteachers should participate in the same or similar INSET initiatives as their staff. Some LEAs actively encourage this practice.

On the other hand, it is extremely difficult for an enlightened headteacher to provide support for the youngest classes if the teachers themselves are not understanding and sympathetic to the needs of their pupils. As one headteacher on an INSET course explained, 'I have to work within the structures that teachers set up. I try to break these down as much as possible without undermining my staff – but ideas are entrenched! '

Headteachers whose training had included under-fives admitted that this affected their attitude towards the younger children. It could also influence the older pupils because they tended to favour the use of a play-based or 'active learning' approach throughout the school. A primary headteacher whose training had not included the early years was recorded in the researcher's notes to have said that 'he left the infant department in "the tender care of the deputy head who is trained for this age group and is very supportive of the teachers". However, he spent 50 per cent of his time working in the classrooms and spent two story-time sessions a week with the reception class.' Several head-teachers were timetabled to teach the youngest classes, although it was not always easy to abide by this. The headteacher of one large urban school with a high incidence of social need reported that 'she tried to teach all the classes in the school at least once a week but it was not always possible because of other demands, which sometimes "blew up" without any warning'.

Nor is it easy for headteachers of very small schools to teach in the reception class because they usually have a class themselves, often consisting of the junior age range. They also have to fit in school ad-ministration, interviews with parents and so on, and secretarial help tends to be minimal. They may be able to arrange to exchange classes with the infant teacher from time to time. On the other hand, head-teachers of small schools are able to be in close contact with all their pupils and know each one by name. As the headteacher of a two-class rural primary school explained: 'The advantage of working in such a small school is that we all know each other and there is a good atmos-phere.'

## Having Concern for Transition and Continuity

A headteacher is unlikely to perceive the reception year is isolation. The children are already on their way through the school and the con-cerned headteacher will try to ensure a smooth passage. This means giving consideration to the various points of transition into, up through and out of the school. It also means taking account of their experiences before entry and after moving on.

Procedures relating to entry and to transition from home, pre-school and nursery have already been discussed (see Chapter 3). With regard to continuity within the school, several headteachers had made conscious attempts to improve matters by appointing an early years coordinator with responsibility for the three to five age range. In one school, for example, this responsibility covered a nursery class for three year olds, a reception class for four year olds and a mixed-age class for four and five year olds. The post-holder's main task was to coordinate the curriculum for these children. This headteacher felt strongly that if the nursery curriculum is treated separately from the rest of the school there is a danger that the capabilities of the youn-gest children will be underestimated. A coordinated curriculum with a continuous system of record-keeping helps to avoid this problem.

On transfer from reception to the middle infant year, headteachers of schools with multiple-form entry tried as far as possible to keep classes as they were so that children stayed with the same peer group. Flexibility allowed individuals to transfer to another class if it was considered necessary. It was not always possible, however, to maintain the same groups right through the school because year groups fluctuate in number and classes have to be tailored to suit staffing. This often leads to the formation of classes with an age range of more than one year – a common feature in the primary sector, especially in small schools.

## Explaining Appropriate Policy and Practice to Others

The professionals interviewed said that it is the headteacher's responsibility to support the teacher in explaining what is appropriate provision and practice for four year olds and to resist pressures to focus on more formal teacher-directed activities.

Unsupportive colleagues may accord reception teachers low status or put pressure on them to keep the children quiet and 'get them on' ready for the next class. With the advent of National Assessment at seven, they might also pressurize them to start young children on more formal programmes with visible end-products. It must be made clear to them that the reception teacher is not 'just baby-sitting' and the children are not 'messing about' when activities are in progress.

Some headteachers felt that all their staff did have an understanding of the youngest children's needs. In very small schools, for example, it is possible for teachers to discuss everything as a team and everyone is likely to be in regular contact with the whole age range. In larger schools this may not happen unless deliberate steps are taken. Teachers with four year olds in their class may have to explain why their pupils need special conditions, concessions and resources. In particular, as the Bedfordshire Pilot Project revealed (Thomas, 1987), teachers may have to justify their approach to colleagues who do not understand the value of play. To avoid this situation, one headteacher said that she chose her staff very carefully so that they were able to fit in with the school's play-based philosophy. If their training had not included the under-fives, she encouraged them to attend INSET courses. Other strategies that helped towards a general understanding of the younger pupils included:

✿ asking teachers to take responsibility for different age groups rather than staying with the same one from year to year;
✿ having regular staff meetings, which included early years staff;
✿ adopting an activity-based approach across the whole age range in the school (see Chapter 5).

Reception teachers were particularly appreciative of help from colleagues who had posts of curriculum responsibility. Curriculum coordinators have a special role to play in servicing the needs of the four year olds. The professionals interviewed considered it **particularly important for teachers with responsibility for certain aspects of the curriculum to be conversant with early childhood development and to include the youngest children in their overall scheme for the school.**

In the schools studied, coordinators of maths, English and science were all engaged at the time in reappraising their schemes of work ready for the start of the National Curriculum. This had involved them in a series of discussions with the rest of the staff and a period of in-service training. They all said they were taking account of the under-fives, and some were also including the nursery class where there was one. In the infant schools, most of these post-holders had gained experience of working with four year olds because they were either teaching or had at some time taught the reception class. However, this is less likely to be the case in all-through primary schools, where the subject coordinator's training and experience may not have extended to the younger end of the age range.

Parents often see a sharp distinction between nursery education and what they believe to be the 'real learning' that should take place once the child enters the reception class (Cleave *et al.*, 1982; Collinson and Bennett, 1986). The introduction of the National Curriculum and National Assessment at seven is likely to strengthen the view that children should have three full years of infant education. This makes it even more imperative that parents appreciate appropriate early years practice and the sound educational principles on which it is based. This requires that headteachers are themselves committed to these principles so that they do not give in to fears of losing pupils to schools with a more 'formal' approach.

It is important that schools and parents work together in the interests of their child's education, and this requires that each side must be prepared to *listen* to the other as well as to explain. Communication is a two-way process; it works in both directions. A very real difficulty is that channels of communication between home and school may be blocked by huge differences in attitudes and expectations, especially in areas of social deprivation. As Hurst (1987) explains, for parents who are the victims of disadvantage or discrimination, 'the deployment of professional expertise and knowledge can, if not sensitively handled, further weaken the self-esteem and confidence of parents' (p. 98). Communication may also be hindered by language differences. Multi-ethnic schools, for example, may need to take account of several home languages when making initial contacts, and the help of bilingual staff and parents can be invaluable in doing this effectively.

The headteacher has the task not only of communicating early years practice to parents but also of communicating it in a manner that is sensitive to the particular needs of the families the school serves. In this respect each school will be different. Here are examples of how the heads of two very different schools in the study tried to communicate to parents what their four year olds do in school.

*A large infant school with a multi-ethnic population*
Most of the children came from families whose mother tongue was not English. The families were first-generation Asian immigrants speaking a total of seven different languages. Five of the languages were used in paper communications between school and home. The headteacher felt that there was a need to bring parents and school closer together. Parents' meetings were tried in the evenings but no-one turned up, so it was decided to invite parents into the classrooms during the day so that they could see what their children were doing. Videos were used to explain the purpose behind the activities, there were photographs of special events and projects, and the staff were on hand to answer questions and hold discussions. The teachers in turn were invited to the mosques in the neighbourhood where most of their pupils went to study the Koran during the evenings and on Saturdays. This brought home to them the realization that by the end of the reception year these children were not only grappling with English in school but were reciting the Koran in Arabic. Added to the mother tongue spoken at home, this made a total of three languages spoken from the age of five.

*An urban primary school with a mix of long-established families and newly-arrived young professionals*
When the children started school, their parents received a booklet about the school. After a month or so, the headteacher held a meeting with the parents to explain the approach used in the reception classes. Parents were then encouraged to go into the classrooms and 'be four years old' with the activities. They were acquainted with the words their children would use, such as 'more and less', 'set and subset' and so on. The headteacher invited parents to make comments so that there was feedback for the school. One mother interviewed in the study said she appreciated having the activities explained. She had been a bit concerned at first that the children were doing 'too much playing', but because she had been into school she realized now how things worked – even though it looked as though they were playing they were really learning. Her husband added that he wished school had been like that when he was a boy!

## Parents and Governors

**The support of parents and governors is particularly relevant in the light of recent legislation,** which is intended to give them a greater role in the management of the school. It is therefore important that they understand what the staff are trying to do and are supportive of their efforts, especially where younger children are being admitted to a system traditionally oriented towards pupils of statutory school age. It is also important that those holding the purse-strings are sympathetic to the needs of these younger pupils and help to resource them accordingly.

People have certain expectations of what should go on in schools, often based on their own experiences. There is a need for the community at large to recognize what is appropriate provision and practice for four year olds and to be persuaded away from notions of formal skills and schemes of work. Parents and governors who are well-informed and supportive could play a crucial role in this respect.

## Parental Support

Headteachers and teachers felt that on the whole parents were supportive of their efforts with the four year olds. Support was given in a variety of ways and some of these have already been discussed elsewhere in this report: helping settle their child into school (see Chapter 3); attending parents' evenings, workshops and 'open' sessions (see above); and helping in the classroom (see above).

Other ways in which parents were supportive included:

✿ fund-raising – through fêtes, jumble sales and PTA activities;
✿ helping on children's outings, walks and trips;
✿ helping out when something specific needed doing in school – cutting up card, photocopying, making booklets for the children to use, lifting paving stones to enable a flower-bed to be made, assisting with special projects;
✿ attending school plays, concerts and assemblies;
✿ bringing their children into and fetching them from the classroom, thus affording opportunities for talking with staff and seeing their child busy with the activities;
✿ participating in shared or paired learning schemes.

There are a number of points to be made about the various forms of support listed above. Firstly, the extent to which parents were engaged in them varied considerably from school to school. For example, fund-raising provided a major boost to resources in some areas, while in others it was simply not possible. As one headteacher explained, 'Most of our families haven't got much so we can't do anything on a big scale. We only ask for help with essentials, never with frills.' Secondly, invitations to parents to help in school met with varying degrees of response. In the best circumstances the parents were

described as 'very supportive – they are very interes'
children are doing'. Thirdly, it is interesting to note
items in the list entail not merely support but also ₹
in children's learning. Much has been written in
parents working as 'partners' with the school in the.
tion. Hurst (1987), for example, sees partnership as 'prou... .
greatest single opportunity for educational advance open to teachers
today' (p. 109). Partnership in this sense is particularly important for
the parents of children with special needs. Some of the schools had
adapted their usual arrangements for parental involvement with these
pupils in mind. For example:

> in one school arrangements for involving parents had evolved over
> several years into a situation where parents were encouraged to
> spend time in the classroom and share the child's learning. Regular
> contact with parents with younger children provided valuable op-
> portunities for discussing concerns and perhaps identifying special
> needs. Support could then be offered from an early age. After ad-
> mission, the parents of children with special needs were invited to
> regular consultations with the headteacher and all those who
> worked with their child. Progress was discussed, and together they
> agreed on a further plan of activities. The activities were based on
> the school's curriculum, and the staff ensured that the necessary
> materials and support were made available.

Other instances of partnership in action were seen most commonly in
shared or 'paired' reading schemes. Reading tends to be the area of
the curriculum most favoured for parental involvement of this kind. A
recent NFER survey (Jowett and Baginsky, 1988) revealed that home–
school reading schemes were in operation on a substantial scale in 44
LEAs, compared with only ten having schemes in other curricular
areas.

Shared reading schemes encountered in the present study involved
parents in reading with their children at home and sometimes at
school as well. Such schemes usually included some kind of preparation for parents, often in the form of booklets and workshops to explain the purpose behind the scheme. Professionals in the study were
anxious to point out that while it is desirable to involve parents in their
children's learning, it is essential that they understand the reasons behind the activities. Here is a typical example of one such scheme in
operation in an infant school:

> Before starting school, careful links are established between home
> and school. In the term prior to entry, parents and children spend a
> session together in school when they are encouraged to choose a
> book to take home and share together. From time to time reading

workshops are held for all parents. Books are attractively displayed in the school and are accessible at all times. Book corners with a settee, cushions, carpet and soft toys encourage the reader to linger and browse. Any book may be borrowed and taken home in a special 'book bag' accompanied by a parent/teacher reading diary. Most children have three books in their possession at any one time. A wide choice of titles covering a range of abilities is available, and the school bookshop and book club encourage ownership of favourite books.

For schemes like this to operate effectively, it is essential that good relationships are established between home and school, and this may not be easy. Support, like communication, is a two-way process and the parents may themselves be relying on the school for support.

To help draw parents and school closer together in an atmosphere of mutual support, some headteachers with space available had set aside a room exclusively for the use of parents. In one nursery school, for example, parents could call in for a cup of tea and a chat, and visit their child's classroom. As the headteacher pointed out, to make this idea work effectively, it is necessary that a member of staff has responsibility for the room and 'cherishes' it. It is important to ensure that the room is used to the full, and this entails finding out the parents' needs and wishes. There can be barriers to overcome, which may prevent some parents from coming into the school at all.

In one primary school in the study, a similar 'Parents' Room' was being set up on a community basis. While the school provided the facilities, other organizations, such as the local health authority and the social services made available personnel such as nurses and outreach workers. The intention was to find out what parents wanted and then to develop workshop sessions, which would include school-oriented issues and eventually discussions about the curriculum.

Clearly, if such schemes are to operate successfully, much thought and consideration must be given to the purposes of the Parents' Room and the ways in which it may be used, and to establishing a close dialogue between the users of the room and the staff of the school in which it is situated.

## School Governors

Most of the schools in the study considered their governing bodies to be generally supportive of their efforts with the youngest pupils. Governors who were rated as 'very supportive' not only listened to what the headteacher and staff had to say and backed up their proposals but also involved themselves in the life of the school by:

✿ accepting invitations to special occasions such as concerts and plays;

✿ sharing their special expertise or interest with the children by giving talks;

✿ attending regular events like assembly;

✿ helping out with classroom activities.

When necessary, they made active representations to the LEA by passing on the requests and concerns of the staff, responding to papers and generally making their views known.

The chairpersons of such bodies saw themselves as 'the guiding light' in supporting the school, pushing for the achievements of its aims and ensuring that the children got 'the best possible education'. Their governor colleagues were well informed, with at least one non-teaching representative having substantial experience of working with young children.

Not all the schools in the study were so fortunate. Several expressed grave concern at the governors' lack of interest, especially in the light of the increased responsibilities thrust upon them by the 1988 Education Reform Act. To improve matters, one headteacher had invited governors to spend time in the school to see what was going on. Although they stayed only an hour, she felt that this was 'a breakthrough' in building up a relationship between the school and its governing body.

By the time the project ended (1990), governors were only beginning to get to grips with their new role. This included taking on responsibility for school finances under LMS, staff appointments and curricular aims. **In schools with early admission, the support of the governing body with its increased financial responsibilities could prove to be critical for the under-fives.** A recent HMI survey of quality for four year olds in primary classes (GB.DES, 1989c) found that only about half the schools managed their resources satisfactorily, and few schools had an overall resourcing policy that recognized the distinctive needs of this age group. An informed governing body with an understanding of the aims of early years education could do much to ensure that any available funding is used appropriately, for example in the appointment of ancillary help (see Chapter 9) and the purchase of suitable equipment and materials (see Chapter 8). One school in the study had already piloted LMS and the governors were looking forward to 'the challenges the real thing' would bring. However, with the current trend towards taking schools into the marketplace, it is important that educational issues are not swamped in the pursuit of financial enterprise.

It is the task of governing bodies in schools with early admissions to work with the headteacher and the senior management team in establishing a policy with regard to pupils under five. To do this, they will need to identify the priorities, set objectives and evaluate and revise policy in the light of what has been achieved.

The present study has shown that in order to carry out this task, members of the governing body must

✿   be interested and committed to early years education;
✿   understand the needs of these younger pupils;
✿   go into the school regularly and participate in activities;
✿   manage the finances with due consideration for appropriate staffing, equipment and materials for these children;
✿   take positive action to secure the best possible provision for this age group.

## Conclusion

Successful provision for early admission requires support throughout the school community.

Adults in the early years classroom should work as a team under the teacher's leadership. The teacher needs to be proficient in early years education and possess good team management and communication skills. To promote team involvement and continuity, ancillary helpers should spend as much time as possible with the same class. Where nursery nurses are available they should work in partnership with the teacher and make full use of their training and expertise. Regular voluntary support from parents and other members of the community can be a valuable resource; good relationships are essential.

To ensure the full support of other teachers in the school, a whole-school approach is recommended which recognizes that the youngest pupils are part of the school community. In treating them appropriately, care must be taken not to isolate the children or their staff from the rest of the school. The headteacher can support them by understanding their needs, explaining appropriate policy and practice to others and, if necessary, justifying it to those who are unsympathetic. The headteacher should have a knowledge of early years education and experience of teaching children under five.

To avoid undue pressure towards formal learning, it is important that parents and governors understand and support the needs of children admitted early to school. The governing body should work with the school to establish a policy for these pupils and take steps to ensure that their needs are being met.

# 11 Support from Outside the School

This chapter moves on to consider ways in which sources beyond the school might provide support for teachers of four year olds. Various levels of support are considered, ranging from self-help groups to the LEA. A wide range of potential sources is discussed including links with other agencies, initial and in-service training, the advisory service, LEA policies and guidelines, and the role of elected members and officers. The project's studies of LEA guidelines and selected INSET initiatives are described in detail.

## Links with Other Agencies

Interviewees recommended that **schools with early admissions should, wherever possible, make links with other agencies working for the health, safety, care and support of young children and their families.** Close links could be established with, for example, special needs teams, the schools psychological service, the school health service, the social services, the police and community support schemes. Workers in these agencies have a wealth of knowledge and skills that could be drawn upon. Barrett (1986) suggests that inter-professional seminars and workshops be set up to discuss ideas and share expertise.

Across the country as a whole there is a variety of day care provision for the under-fives in both the statutory and voluntary sectors, but availability varies tremendously from place to place. Education is only one of the services available and there have been repeated calls (Pugh, 1989) for coordination between the different departments responsible. So far, no national policy has materialized although local initiatives have been made by some authorities. Probably the best-known of these is Strathclyde where the management of under-fives services is centralized under one department (Pugh, 1989).

Schools, however, are ideally placed to forge links with other agencies in their own authority or locality. Those with a concern for transition and continuity prior to school entry liaise with personnel in pre-school playgroups and day care. Once the children are in school, there are opportunities for liaison with medical officers, social workers and so on. In their recent report on education for four year olds (GB.DES, 1989c), HMI applaud links with health visitors, school nurses, educational welfare officers and educational psychologists. They give the following example: 'In one school, the meeting for parents, prior to the children's admission, was attended by the school nurse who explained the range of assessments that she would make during the child's first year' (para. 17).

Schools in the present study referred to their links with home–school liaison officers, special needs support staff, speech therapists, road safety officers and the police. For example, one LEA appointed home–school liaison officers on an area basis and each officer made regular visits to parents in the area. In another authority, special needs support staff were organized into area-based teams. Schools were visited regularly, meetings took place between the headteacher and the team coordinator and children who were considered to have special needs were 'carefully monitored'.

Speech therapists were in great demand among the schools, but their availability was very variable. In an authority where speech therapists worked in hospitals, clinics *and* schools, parents were advised that 'children who have speech and language difficulties and have not seen a speech therapist before starting school, should be brought to the notice of the headteacher as soon as possible'. A school with a rather high incidence of pupils with speech difficulties organized therapy for them after their post-admission medicals. In another LEA, schools greatly valued the support they received from speech therapists working on a private basis with children in the nursery but deplored the fact that there was no provision from four onwards.

Some schools praised the support of the local authority's Road Safety Officer whose job is to educate on all aspects of road safety through regular liaison with schools and local groups. A few schools had established regular contact with the police in their area and invited members of the local constabulary into the school to alert pupils to the dangers of drugs and of talking to strangers.

It is important that schools have positive attitudes towards other agencies if they are to make the most of their support. Personnel who regularly visit the school, such as the doctor, nurse or educational psychologist, might perhaps be invited to share the staffroom so that easy informal relationships with the staff are encouraged. Support works in both directions. Schools also have a wealth of expertise and experience to offer, and it is worth considering how this might be used to support others in the community who work with young children.

## Other Schools

**The use of other schools as a means of support was widely recommended** by the professionals interviewed. Schools could function as resource centres and, in certain cases, provide examples of good practice or act as a stimulus for others to try out fresh ideas.

Resource centres support other schools in their locality by acting as 'banks' from which equipment and materials can be borrowed. These centres are especially useful for small schools where it is impractical or too expensive to buy in the larger or more costly equipment. It also affords teachers the opportunity to try out certain items in their own school before deciding whether to buy them.

Teachers often feel isolated within their own classrooms and are eager to see for themselves how other teachers manage and how they deal with problems. Visits to selected schools were sometimes arranged by the advisory team. Exchange visits between reception and nursery staff, both within and between schools, were said to be particularly beneficial. Visiting other schools to observe them in action often entails obtaining supply cover and this is expensive. It is important, therefore, to ensure that the staff being released are able to make maximum use of their visits. Advisers responsible for organizing visits made the following points:

✿ individual members of staff differ in their levels of experience, understanding and development; visits will therefore need to be matched to their specific requirements;

✿ visiting staff need to be clear about what it is they are looking for in the visited school;

✿ the organizer should be fully conversant with the visitor's school and the one being visited; follow-up support with opportunities to discuss, try out and evaluate ideas is essential.

Staff in schools that provided examples of appropriate early years practice not only received lots of visitors but were also likely to share their ideas by giving talks in other schools, teachers' centres and colleges. Although they were quite willing to do all these things, some of them pointed out that this did not mean they had 'got everything right' themselves. They too sometimes felt in need of support.

## Professional and Self-help Groups

Interviewees stressed **the need for staff working with four year olds in school to have opportunities to meet with other early years practitioners.** This could help overcome feelings of isolation, allow ideas and experiences to be shared and provide a forum for discussion. This might be achieved by joining a professional organization such as BAECE (British Association for Early Childhood Education) or ECHO (Early Childhood Organization), which offers opportunities for teachers, students, nursery nurses, advisers and parents to come together. Professional organizations are not only a source of support but can provide a 'voice' for their members.

Opportunities to meet with colleagues from other schools could also be afforded through local groups, often set up by the members themselves as self-help or support groups. These sometimes began in a small way with a group of colleagues meeting informally after school to share similar concerns. Successful ventures of this kind often became more structured as time went on, with a planned programme involving speakers from outside the group. These groups could thus become a very valuable form of in-service support and training. As Barrett (1986) explains, teachers are so involved in what they are doing that they need opportunities to separate themselves from it in order to 'see' what is going on. They therefore need opportunities to think and talk objectively about their practice and the reasons behind it. In the present study, such groups were particularly appreciated by staff in small schools because they afforded them the rare opportunity to talk with their peers.

Support groups may consist of staff with similar roles (for example all teachers) or a mixture of roles (such as teachers and nursery nurses). When the group first meets, it may take time for individual members to overcome shyness and summon up the confidence to speak in front of the others. This can be especially true in mixed groups where, for example, a nursery nurse may feel intimidated by the presence of teachers. While mixed support groups were agreed to be beneficial for sharing expertise, it was also pointed out that there may be occasions when nursery nurses (and perhaps teachers too) need to meet separately in order to feel that they can speak their minds more freely.

To encourage and sustain this useful form of support, there are at least two points worth considering:

✿   Ways need to be found of putting more early years staff in touch with each other both within and between LEAs. Perhaps the advisory team could help in this regard.

✿   Members of support groups usually meet in their own time and together they constitute a powerful resource for staff development. Consideration should be given as to whether some non-contact time could be provided for this purpose: this might also include visits to other schools (see above).

## Initial Teacher Training

Most of the teachers observed had trained initially to teach children from three or four years of age. However, they are quite untypical of reception teachers generally, many of whom are teaching four year olds without having had either training or experience in the age group

(GB.DES, 1988, 1989c). Many training courses defined as 'infant' cover an age range from *five*. However, even teachers with infant training pointed out that it was easy to forget how young these children really are, and teachers who had worked mainly with older infants said they sometimes found it difficult to adjust to the under-fives.

The interviewees stressed **the importance of early years training for teachers of children admitted below the statutory age.** They also pointed out that certain aspects of the teacher's role, such as assessment and accountability, have assumed increasing relevance in recent years, and the student teacher needs to be trained accordingly. From their comments and from the many examples discussed throughout this book, it is clear that particular attention needs to be given in initial training to the following.

*Understanding early childhood development*
This is essential if the teacher is to be capable of planning an appropriate curriculum and matching tasks to the needs of individual children (see Chapter 5).

*Explaining good practice to others*
Communication skills are vital so that teachers can, if necessary, justify their practices with confidence and argue for much-needed resources; they need to be able to articulate good practice and explain it clearly to their colleagues, to parents and governors, to workers from other agencies, to students and visitors (see Chapters 5 and 10).

*Leading a team*
The teacher requires some grounding in management and inter-personal skills in order to work effectively with other adults in the classroom and develop effective links with parents (see Chapters 3, 5 and 10).

*Observing children and evaluating their progress*
Teachers need observation skills and an understanding of how to use the observations they make; more attention needs to be given to ways of recording children's progress and understanding the purpose of such records (see Chapters 5 and 6).

All of the above are important factors of initial training that need continual updating through in-service support. There are, however, a number of difficulties to be overcome if relevant training is to be provided.

First, there is the problem, clearly described by Drummond (1989b), that educationists lack any real shared perception of how the early years curriculum, its content and principles of procedure are to be represented. She argues that, although practitioners are undoubtedly influenced by the traditions handed down by the early 20th century philanthropists and educationists, they often have difficulty in defining exactly what it is they have inherited (see Chapter 4).

Secondly, this state of affairs is not helped by the fact that there is a shortage of early years specialists to train the teachers. This is due largely to the closure of many training institutions and a reduction in early years specialist courses during attempts to rationalize teacher education in the 1970s.

Thirdly, there is the difficulty of timetabling priorities. Child development courses are being squeezed out of initial training by the CATE (Council for the Accreditation of Teacher Training) regulations, which require students to spend the equivalent of at least two years on a chosen main subject. Main subject courses are largely academic rather than pedagogic in content, and early years education does not qualify as a main subject. Student time is to be further eroded by the recent government requirement for trainee primary teachers to spend 100 hours on science and design and technology in addition to 100 hours each on mathematics and English. Student teachers encountered in infant classes during the present study commented on the lack of child development theory in their courses and considered that their training should have been of a much more practical nature. These comments echo the views expressed by probationary primary teachers taking part in an HMI survey in 1987. Asked whether they thought they were well prepared to teach children under five, 37 per cent considered the question inappropriate for the course they had followed (presumably because they had trained to teach older age groups). Of the rest, six in ten felt that they were not adequately equipped for teaching such young children. The report concluded that 'in view of the fact that many four year olds are currently admitted into reception classes and that teachers who train to teach older children may find themselves in charge of reception classes, preparation to teach under five year olds should feature to a greater degree in the training of a higher proportion of primary teachers' (GB.DES, 1988, para. 3.32).

Professionals taking part in the present study stressed **the importance of selecting the most appropriate candidates for teacher training in the first place.** Selection must take account of personal qualities as well as academic aptitude, and these are not easy to assess during the traditional interview. Dowling (1988) suggests that alternative selection schemes should be considered. She describes a particular example where candidates spent a full day undertaking written responses on personal qualities, intellectual and attitudinal tasks; took part in leaderless discussion groups and a specially devised, simulated teaching task; and also had a traditional interview. As Dowling points out, methods like these need careful monitoring over time.

Clearly the task facing those responsible for early years training is formidable. They need to provide a relevant and practical course, firmly grounded in developmental theory, which takes account of the rapidly changing context of education. Furthermore, they need to deliver the course to carefully selected students in the face of ever-increasing competition for time and resources, while at the same time boosting their own level of expertise and experience. The importance of their role in early childhood education cannot be overestimated.


## In-service Training

The discussion of initial training has shown that there are serious gaps that in-service education will have to fill if schools are to provide more appropriately for children admitted below the statutory age. **There is a need for INSET courses to help teachers to clarify what they believe and to support their practice; to help teachers who are uncertain about what to provide and why they should provide it.** Particular attention needs to be paid to the topics identified as essential to early years practice – observing children and evaluating their progress, developing links with parents and working with other adults in the classroom.

Providers of in-service initiatives have the task of not only updating initial early years training to suit the changing context, but also of plugging gaps in initial courses covering such a wide age range (3 to 11) that relatively little attention can be paid to the needs of children under five. An even greater challenge to INSET providers lies in the fact that many teachers who now have four year olds in their classes trained initially to teach older children (see above).

These difficulties were recognized by the 1986 House of Commons Select Committee, who called for a 'special programme of training for infant teachers who are for the first time teaching, or are soon to teach, children of three or just four years of age' (House of Commons, 1986, para. 13.26). Very few LEAs actually arranged a coordinated programme of INSET prior to admitting younger children; the majority set up initiatives gradually when the children were already in school. Recently, however, there has been a substantial increase in INSET provision for teachers of under-fives. This has been helped by new arrangements for INSET funding under which training for teachers of four year olds in primary classes became a national priority in the LEA Training Grants Scheme (LEATGS) from April 1989, with further developments to follow under Grants for Education Support and Training (GEST) (see Chapter 9).

The precise focus of INSET initiatives needs to be tailored to suit the users. Staff vary in their requirements, depending not only on their own training and experience but on the policy and provision in the LEA and in the school. INSET should therefore be available at various levels to suit the requirements of the staff. For example, at the time of the present study one LEA with annual admission was still at the stage of 'raising awareness' among teachers of the needs of four year olds and of good practice in meeting these needs. In another LEA an evaluation study carried out by the authority revealed the need for INSET at different levels: day courses for headteachers on the organizational implications, and more substantial courses for all staff on curriculum theory to support their practice. (Examples of four INSET initiatives serving different levels of need are discussed below and described in the Appendix.)

## INSET Provision

There is tremendous variation in INSET provision from one authority to the next. In 1986, LEAs with early admissions ranged in provision from six authorities with no courses at all for teachers of four year olds to one with a total of 64 initiatives, including those based at a newly established Early Childhood Centre in the area (Sharp, 1989). While many authorities provided INSET for 'the early years' (three to five or seven), it was the LEAs that had recently adopted a policy of annual admission, together with those running carefully monitored pilot schemes, which organized courses specifically for teachers with four year olds in primary classes. At that time, awareness of the need for INSET support for these teachers was gradually increasing and there were plans to expand when the anticipated LEATGS arrangements came into effect.

Setting up INSET programmes in an LEA is usually the responsibility of the advisory service. But not all LEAs have early years specialists on their advisory staff (see below). The HMI survey (GB.DES, 1989c) found that LEAs with 'appropriate and co-ordinated arrangements' tended to be those where early years advisers were available and able to influence the planning and provision. In the best practice, follow-up support was also provided, usually in the form of visits by an advisory teacher to staff who had participated in the INSET (see below).

The professionals interviewed advocated that **LEAs should co-operate more with initial training establishments in providing INSET at all levels, but especially longer courses on the theory behind the practice.** Some of the LEAs participating in the study had organized a structured programme of INSET beginning with a basic 'survival' course run by the advisory team for teachers lacking experience with under-fives, and moving on to courses at various levels bought in by the authority from a local training college. Between them, the LEA and the training establishment were thus able to cater for a wide variety of needs and offer in-service support ranging from the short and purely practical to the longer and more theoretical award-bearing courses.

Abbott (1987) describes the range of INSET initiatives provided by one teacher-training institution. At the time, these ranged from short, non-award bearing courses to diplomas in early childhood education and advanced courses leading to the awards of BEd, BPhil, MEd or MPhil. Nationally, provision is very variable and within institutions courses are continually being updated and amended. In recent years there has been a move in many teacher training establishments towards a more modular approach to INSET. This allows teachers to plan their own 'menu' of courses and provides a structure from certificate through diploma to BEd and MEd levels in early years courses. It also allows non-teachers (such as nursery nurses) to embark on advanced training. Some courses are particularly innovative; for example, one teacher-training establishment was planning a multi-professional diploma course to be studied part-time over two years by teachers, health visitors, social workers and staff from voluntary agencies.

For many schools, there is no training institution within a realistic travelling distance and this means that the main burden of providing INSET falls on the advisory team who may already be over-stretched. To provide more INSET opportunities, some advisers involve early years teachers and headteachers in leading courses or sessions. To assist matters further, the interviewees suggested that LEAs might collaborate more with each other to share expertise. They might also draw on the expertise of professionals from various agencies. One example of shared expertise to provide in-service support is:

> a recently published learning pack (Drummond *et al.*, 1989) for people who work with young children in all types of provision. The pack was prepared by a group of professionals from teacher training, nursery nursing, the advisory service, the Preschool Playgroups Association and the National Children's Bureau. It includes contributions from teachers, parents and others working with young children and their families.

## The Users of INSET

Despite the increase in early years INSET initiatives, considerable inequalities of opportunity existed during the study. These resulted partly from differences in location and accessibility and partly from whether provision extended to practitioners other than teachers.

**INSET must be accessible to those who want to use it.** The interviewees suggested that there should be deliberate attempts to improve accessibility in rural areas, perhaps by setting up more early childhood centres.

The time, as well as the place, must be convenient. Many INSET initiatives take place out of school hours and staff with young children of
their own may find it difficult to attend. The school year must also be
taken into account. Some day-time courses beginning in September
start so early in the term that they clash with schools' attempts to give
new entrants a staggered start. Staff said they were unable to attend
because the children had not had time enough to settle in at school
and any interruptions to their routine at this critical stage were to be
avoided. Most of the teachers, however, were involved in school-based
early years INSET, much of it prompted by the need to revise their
curricula prior to the introduction of the National Curriculum.

Teachers in the very small schools were fortunate in being able to
obtain supply cover fairly easily. This meant that in a two-teacher,
rural primary school, for example, the infant teacher was able to attend courses to suit her various roles as deputy head, class teacher and
area coordinator for certain subjects.

**The participation of headteachers in their staff's INSET was
considered to be particularly important for headteachers of
primary schools whose training and experience may not have
included under-fives.** The headteacher of one school in the study
was responsible for organizing a course for headteachers and their reception teachers. She felt that this would enable the headteachers to
support their staff and not regard the reception class as 'an easy op-
tion'.

In 1986, just over half of the LEAs employing nursery nurses or ancillary helpers in infant classes provided some INSET for them (Sharp,
1988). This was generally at a reduced level from that offered to teachers. Unfortunately, although some LEAs make their own provision,
these staff were not eligible under the LEATGS. However, this has
now been made possible under the new GEST arrangements
(GB.DES, 1990c).

In the present study, non-teaching assistants and sometimes parent
helpers were included in general invitations to take up INSET opportunities. Many of them had under-fives of their own, which limited
their take-up of after school opportunities. They were therefore more
likely to take part in school-based INSET days.

### Four Examples of Early Years INSET

During the school year 1988–89 we visited four very different in-service initiatives in various parts of the country. The initiatives illustrate
attempts at different levels to meet the needs of practitioners working
with young children including four year olds in school. Details are
given in the Appendix.

The initiatives were selected from the vast range available and consisted of:

✿ a one-day LEA course on equipment and materials for the early years curriculum;

✿ a series of ongoing support groups organized by teachers in conjunction with the advisory team in a shire county;

✿ a one-term (50 hours) practical course provided for an LEA by a college of education;

✿ a six-month (80 hours) course offered by an institute of education to staff in the surrounding authorities.

Teachers commenting generally on their experience of early years INSET said that they had particularly appreciated the opportunity it afforded of meeting with colleagues from other schools. It had also sharpened their awareness and given them the confidence to follow up ideas. In looking back over their recent involvement in the initiatives studied, teachers made the following comments.

✿ Working with teachers from other schools (and sometimes from other LEAs) had given them a 'great boost' because it was interesting to see how others worked and to hear about their experiences. Sharing problems and ideas was very valuable because 'it helps you to realize you are not as isolated as you feel'.

✿ Their confidence in themselves had been strengthened when the INSET reinforced some of the things they were already doing. It had also helped them to realize that in the course of their normal classroom practice they were already covering some aspects of the National Curriculum that had been worrying them.

✿ They felt more confident about trying out new ideas and making changes in their schools or classrooms.

✿ They were now more inclined to stand back and think about their own practice. INSET had also made them stop and look more carefully at what individual children were doing.

✿ They were more able to explain or defend their practice and articulate it to others (special mention was made of critical parents, and unsympathetic colleagues 'in the junior department').

✿ Their appetites had been whetted for more INSET. For example, on completion of one course, members wanted to follow it up with a higher level course devoted to topics that had only been 'scratched on the surface', such as gender and multicultural issues.

✿ They were likely to take a more active role in INSET in the future, for example one member now chaired the support group in her own area.

We wanted to know whether teachers had, as a result of attending INSET, made any changes to their classroom practice. To this end, participants in the two courses and one of the support groups visited were sent a short questionnaire asking whether they had made any changes, whether they had experienced any difficulties in making changes and whether there were any further changes they wanted to make in their class or school. The replies received from those teaching four year olds ($n = 20$) are particularly relevant. All but three of these teachers had initially trained to work with older children (from five or above).

### Changes made since attending INSET

Changes made since attending early years INSET seemed to reflect changes in philosophy. Teachers said they were much more aware of the 'need to start with the child'. They were committed to giving their pupils more choice and more involvement in decision-making in the classroom. They were committed to organizing the class on more 'nursery-like' lines, giving the children time for exploration and discovery. They had become more aware of equal opportunities for their pupils, especially with regard to gender. One of the three whose initial course had included four year olds said that INSET had reinforced her earlier training, which by now had 'begun to wear a bit thin'.

All 20 teachers reported that they had made specific changes relating to staffing, the physical environment and/or their teaching approach. These included:

- ✿ pressing for more ancillary help and increasing the number of adults in the classroom by involving parents and YTS students as helpers;
- ✿ changing to team-teaching;
- ✿ creating more space by changing classrooms and removing some of the tables and chairs;
- ✿ encouraging more freedom of movement by arranging the classroom more flexibly;
- ✿ making more provision for structured play and providing more equipment, particularly for construction activities;
- ✿ making equipment and materials accessible and available to the children, who also learned to put it away;
- ✿ providing a wider variety of activities that were always available, for example changing the home-corner into a shop or a milk-float, and having the water tray and a range of natural and unusual materials permanently to hand;
- ✿ adopting a less formal approach and a more play-oriented day;
- ✿ encouraging more small group activities;
- ✿ reviewing the ways in which children communicate their experiences, focusing on their oral language and extending their vocabulary;
- ✿ making more use of child observation to inform practice.

Of course, it is not possible to attribute these changes solely to the influence of recent INSET initiatives. Change may be encouraged by many other factors, including the personalities, relationships, attitudes and resources peculiar to each school. It is also important to note that such changes do not necessarily happen suddenly. As a member of the ongoing support group pointed out, 'All these changes have taken us two years.'

*Difficulties and obstacles encountered in making changes*
Six of the teachers said they encountered no difficulties in making changes. This was attributed largely to the fact that the headteacher was understanding, colleagues were tolerant and the continued support of their INSET group gave them confidence.

The remaining 14 teachers identified similar obstacles. These were:

✿   lack of trained ancillary help, space and equipment;
✿   opposition to young children moving about in a mixed-age class;
✿   the 'entrenched' attitudes of colleagues and parents which could be difficult to change;
✿   lack of self-confidence: teachers felt guilty about 'just sitting back and observing', and often wondered 'whether the changes would work'.

*Further changes teachers wanted to make*
Six teachers said they planned no further changes, two of them preferring to 'keep an open mind' about next year's new entrants who might have different needs. The other 14 teachers hoped to improve their admission procedures, develop better links with local pre-school settings attended by the children and involve parents more in the classroom. They intended to improve the physical environment by creating more space and making better access to the outdoors. They also wanted to introduce more small group activities and give children more opportunities for choice and investigative play.

## The LEA Advisory Service

Where children are admitted early to school, LEA advisory services can play a vital role by supporting practice and providing in-service opportunities for those working with younger pupils. In the study, the kinds of support offered and their influence on practitioners were found to be very variable between the LEAs involved. Some advisory teams had made strenuous efforts on behalf of four year olds and their teachers. These included:

✿  organizing a range of early years INSET initiatives;
✿  establishing an early childhood centre;
✿  setting up resource banks;
✿  convening working groups for a specific purpose: for example, to draft guidelines for teachers of young children or to produce booklets for guidance on specific topics;
✿  monitoring and evaluating a pilot scheme for early admission;
✿  liaising with LEA officers over the resourcing and implementation of policy;
✿  presenting papers to the Education Committee, for example, on the need for better provision for children admitted early to school;
✿  appointing additional support in the form of advisory teachers.

In addition, professionals suggested that the advisory service could take a more active role in publicizing good practice, not only within their own LEA but to other authorities, so that ideas and expertise could be more widely shared.

### Advisers

The interviewees stressed that, **wherever possible, advisers and inspectors should have expertise in early years education** so that they understand and are sympathetic to the needs of these children. However, at the time of the study some LEAs had no early years adviser, either because under-fives in school were considered to be the responsibility of the primary adviser or because the post had been allowed to lapse. Others had appointed temporary extra advisory support during the induction of a new early admissions policy, but this was expected to be discontinued after the first year or two.

A further difficulty is that the role of advisers is changing. In addition to their specialist responsibilities, advisers often have a more generalist role that transcends specific age-ranges or curriculum areas. They may also have pastoral responsibility for a group of schools. The advisers interviewed expressed concern about the government's call for advisers to take on a more 'inspectorial' role with regard to monitoring the National Curriculum as it gets underway in the schools. They anticipated that they would probably have to shed the 'support' aspect of their work and this in turn could create a need for more advisory teachers.

### Advisory Teachers

**The appointment of early years advisory teachers was widely recommended** by professionals and by the 1988 Select Committee (although this may not be possible under the new arrangements for LMS). The 1986 NFER survey on four year olds (Sharp, 1988) found that a quarter of LEAs with annual admission had appointed, or were about to appoint, early years advisory teachers. However, it can be difficult to recruit advisory teachers because of the general dearth of early years specialists. Also, in the case of secondment, schools are sometimes reluctant to 'lose' their best teachers from the classroom, especially in these times of teacher shortages.

Not all the LEAs involved in the study had advisory teachers. Of those that did, only one appointed them on a permanent basis, the rest regarding them as a temporary measure to support the induction of a new annual admission policy. In the best example of the latter:

> a county with a recently adopted policy of early admission appointed a team of six advisory teachers to support reception teachers, many of whom were teaching four year olds for the first time. The advisory teachers worked closely with the two primary advisers and had regular meetings with them. Originally seconded from their schools for one year, the scheme proved so successful that the team was retained for a second year. The county was divided into 12 administrative areas and each advisory teacher was assigned two areas. A comprehensive INSET programme was mounted, with a series of short, practical 'twilight' courses provided by the team. The purpose of these courses in the first instance was to help raise morale and give teachers 'coping strategies'. Later, the courses were developed to include aspects of the curriculum, teaching approach and assessment. Advisory teachers found that course members particularly valued the opportunity for group discussion: small groups gave individuals the confidence to contribute to the discussion and encouraged them to think about their practice. The team anticipated that teachers would eventually feel the need for more theory to support their practice and would then be ready to take advantage of the longer (10-week) day-time courses on offer.
>
> The advisory teachers described their role as a dual one of supporting and advising. They visited teachers in their classrooms and arranged for them to see other teachers in action. They worked on a 'person-to-person' basis, provided teachers with on-the-spot comments and advice on how to develop ideas. They felt they were 'agents of change', gradually raising awareness and improving teachers' confidence in their own ability.

These and other advisory teachers in the study had undertaken a range of tasks including:

✿ setting up and/or leading local INSET initiatives and support groups, sometimes in collaboration with a teacher or headteacher;

- ✿ organizing resource centres where teachers could borrow equipment and materials;
- ✿ visiting teachers in their classrooms to offer support, feedback and advice – this was considered to be very valuable but required a 'lot of bodies' to carry it out sensitively and effectively;
- ✿ providing a 'willing ear' for teachers to sound off to or confide in;
- ✿ arranging for teachers to visit other schools;
- ✿ contributing towards documents to guide practice, or papers making representations to the Education Committee.

Advisory teachers commented on the importance of building up good relationships with teachers. This takes time; temporary (one-year) secondments may be too short to allow this to happen.

Advisory teachers other than those for the early years may also offer support to staff working with young children. For example, some LEAs appoint an advisory teacher to work with under-fives with special educational needs. At the time of the study, advisory teachers to support the introduction of the National Curriculum were also much in evidence. However, recent changes in LEA budgets and financial responsibilities make the future funding of advisory teachers uncertain.

## On the Receiving End

Individuals vary in the use they make of the support offered. Take-up is likely to vary according to whether users perceive the offer to be relevant to their needs and whether they are willing to avail themselves of it. An investigation into the take-up of advisory support in one authority (Pollard, 1989) found that headteachers made more use of advisers, whereas teachers made more use of advisory teachers and peer support groups. The same study also found that staff in large schools made most use of advisers, INSET and support groups, while small schools made most use of advisory teachers. Not surprisingly, staff in newly established classes for four year olds made more use of *all* forms of advisory support than their colleagues in schools with a tradition of early admission.

Teachers' actual experiences of support offered by the advisory service differ enormously, even where well-planned schemes are underway. The following comments indicate the extremes reported in the study:

An early years specialist was appointed two years ago, but there are 70 schools in her area so she has only visited us once so far.

The adviser runs INSET courses for teachers and nursery nurses at the early childhood centre. We attended an eight-week course and this led to the production of guidelines for the early years.

# LEA Guidelines

## The Need for Guidelines

The interviewees were unanimous that **LEAs with early admission should provide guidelines for teachers with four year olds in their classes.** A strong reason for providing guidelines is that when policies are changed, reception teachers with younger pupils are often unsure of where they belong. As some of them explained, they feel 'at the join', somewhere between nursery and primary but not belonging entirely to either. A similar point is made by Weir (1988) who argues that few schools with four year olds seem to be sure whether early admission is a means of extending forms of nursery provision, or whether it is deliberately directed to the earlier introduction of infant education. It is important, therefore, that LEAs make the position of their reception teachers clear.

The HMI report (GB.DES, 1989c) supports this view, stating that:

schools that admit four year olds to primary classes require LEA guidance on the most appropriate ways of working with young children in these circumstances. Based upon that guidance, the schools need to formulate curricular policies and guidelines which provide for continuity and progression in learning from three or four onwards in order to meet the immediate learning requirements of the youngest children and to prepare them for subsequent stages of their education. (para. 44)

## Availability of Guidelines

Relatively few LEAs provide written guidelines for schools with early admissions, although there are signs of a growing awareness that they are needed. The 1986 NFER survey (Sharp, 1988) revealed that fewer than a third of LEAs with annual admission had produced such guidance. Since then progress appears to have been slow. In 1988–89, as part of this project, another survey was carried out. This time 87 authorities in England and Wales known to admit children of rising-five or younger, were approached for any guidelines they might have produced for teachers working with four year olds. Guidelines were received from 24 LEAs, three having completed them very recently. A further nine LEAs indicated that they were hoping to prepare guidelines in the near future.

The guidelines fell into three groups: those with a distinct nursery emphasis, those written specifically for infant teachers and those for teachers of young children in either situation. A few authorities produced two sets of guidelines: one for nursery teachers and the other for infant teachers of four year olds. HMI (GB.DES, 1989c) found that among the 14 LEAs in their survey, those with significant nursery provision had guidelines setting out aims and objectives for under-fives but had not adapted them for use with their four year olds in primary classes.

It would, therefore, appear that a valuable source of potential guidance for infant teachers is being overlooked. If nursery guidance exists, perhaps it could be more widely offered to primary schools, at least as a basis on which to build.

## Preparation of Guidelines

Most of the existing guidelines had been prepared by working groups. The groups consisted mainly of advisers, headteachers and teachers from primary, infant and nursery schools, although a few also included nursery nurses and playgroup staff. Occasionally, guidelines were the product of an in-service course.

All but one of the LEAs had produced their guidelines *after* the admission policy had been changed. In some cases this was after a period of many years. While guidance specifically for teachers of four year olds in primary classes tended to be produced by LEAs where the policy change was recent, a few had been prepared in the last year or so by authorities with a long tradition of early admission. This indicates a general growing awareness of the need to give this age group special consideration, even in areas where teachers have been tempted to say, 'What's so special about four year olds? We've always done it this way!'

The guidance documents varied considerably in presentation, ranging from a few pages of thought-provoking questions to substantial booklets of practical suggestions for the teacher.

## Content of Guidelines

The guidelines were studied in some detail and their content has been incorporated into the preceding chapters of this book. By and large, there was considerable agreement between the documents and the views expressed by interviewees on the issues associated with providing appropriately for four year olds.

The needs of this age group were defined in the guidelines in terms of the more general needs of young children (and indeed all human beings) for love and security, praise and recognition, new experiences and responsibilities; and the more specific needs associated with their combined physical, intellectual, social and emotional development (see Chapter 2).

Needs were articulated in relation to the physical resources and arrangements required to meet these needs; the need for flexible entry procedures (Chapter 3), suitable facilities (Chapter 7) and adequate staffing (Chapter 9). All the guidelines advocated a practical activity-based curriculum reflecting and extending the best in nursery practice (see Chapter 5). Play was perceived to be the vehicle through which learning occurs, although some guidelines preferred to use the term 'activity' instead of play. The roles of the various adults involved were seen as crucial in enabling the curriculum to be implemented and developed. For example, the teacher was seen as 'an enabler' for the children, a manager of the learning environment and a public relations officer to liaise with parents and community; the nursery nurse was seen as a carer for the children and a support for curriculum development; and parents were seen as partners in their children's education (see Chapters 9 and 10). There were differences, however, in the way the actual content of the curriculum was expressed. Differences were also noted in the amount of guidance offered on record-keeping and assessment (see Chapter 6).

To assist LEAs who may be planning guidelines, two very different examples are outlined below. Both of them are provided by LEAs with a recently adopted policy of annual admission and are directed specifically at teachers of four year olds in primary classes. They were provided by two of the LEAs whose schools were followed up in the study.

*Example 1*
This document is a working paper consisting of questions intended to provoke thought and discussion about provision for very young children in school. The paper begins by setting out the authority's policy on admission, but the bulk is concerned with making provision for them. Provision is considered through a series of questions under the following headings:

✿ learning through relationships: prior to school, at admission, parental participation and exchange of information, playgroups, other agencies, other adults outside school, the local community, adults in school;
✿ learning through first-hand experience: moving and manipulating, curiosity and motivation, imagining and imitating, observing and

discovering, expressing, discriminating and appreciating, general points;
✿ talking, listening, understanding and thinking;
✿ organization: starting school, flexible routines, teaching and practising, organization of the day, organization of the classroom;
✿ checking children's thinking and development;
✿ the quality of the teacher.

*Example 2*

This document is a 40-page booklet of 'notes for guidance'. It begins with an outline of the authority's policy on admission and then makes recommendations on appropriate provision and practice under the following headings: staffing; the class; accommodation; overall environment; classroom/curriculum; organization of space and time; materials and resources; teaching style and method; planning, assessment and record-keeping; and in-service training.

These are followed by a checklist of points for teachers and headteachers that may need further development and consideration, including the role of parents and governors and liaison with support services.

Appendices contain:

✿ a detailed list of the skills relating to children's cognitive, social, emotional and physical development;
✿ a description of eight areas of experience with particular reference to the four-year-old child;
✿ notes on transition to school;
✿ the role of the nursery nurse;
✿ suggested basic equipment for classes of young children and a list of suppliers.

Other LEAs' guidelines for teachers of four year olds included:

✿ webs to show how the activities relate to certain curriculum areas or skills;
✿ diagrams to illustrate how themes or projects might be developed;
✿ frameworks for the development of aspects of the curriculum, such as language and literacy;
✿ specimen planning sheets and record forms;
✿ safety precautions in the use of climbing apparatus;
✿ lists of useful reading.

The variety of guidance documents, both in content and presentation, reflects the need for each LEA to produce guidelines that meet the requirements of its own schools. One authority's guidelines are not necessarily appropriate in another LEA. Within each document there should also be flexibility to allow schools to respond to their own local needs.

### Dissemination of Guidelines

**If LEA guidelines are to serve any useful purpose it is important that they reach the people for whom they are intended.** Although some of the headteachers in the study were actively involved in drafting guidelines for their authority, and staff in several schools had been involved through attendance at an in-service course or working group, copies of the guidelines did not always reach the schools that had contributed to them.

A survey carried out by one authority (Pollard, 1989) found that staff in schools with newly established classes of four year olds were more aware of the LEA's guidelines than staff in schools with a tradition of early admission. The HMI survey (GB.DES, 1989c) also revealed the patchiness of schools' response in LEAs where guidelines existed. Clearly there is a responsibility on the part of LEAs not only to provide written guidance for schools with early admissions, but to make sure that it reaches the staff involved.

## LEA Policy and Implementation

The interviewees stressed that **a coherent, well-thought-through admission policy is essential, and an informed Education Committee and officers are invaluable in helping put such a policy into effect.**

The HMI report (GB.DES, 1989c) noted that 'some LEAs have yet to adopt clear admission policies'. It also pointed out that authorities need 'to recognize the resource and curricular implications of admitting four year olds to the primary school' (para. 46). The present study confirmed that some authorities had changed their admission policy at very short notice without any prior planning and resourcing. To our knowledge, only one LEA at that time had prepared a detailed step-by-step outline of policy and resourcing well in advance of lowering the admission age.

The 1986 NFER survey (Sharp, 1988) explored the level of resourcing for four year olds in primary classes in 56 LEAs with a policy of annual admission. The survey found that most of the LEAs provided full capitation for these children although they were not obliged by law to do so. On the other hand, only five of the authorities came close to meeting all the 1986 Select Committee's recommendations regarding class size, ancillary help and part-time admission (House of Commons, 1986). More recently, however, the introduction of LMS has shifted much of the responsibility for financial management from the authority to individual schools, thus enabling them to have more control in selecting their own priorities.

Policy statements are sometimes incorporated into guidelines documents. Usually, the authority's policy on early admission is clearly stated at the beginning and is followed by details for schools on the provision of a suitable environment and curriculum for these young pupils. Policy statements usually stipulate the age at which children may be admitted, special arrangements such as part-time admission and details of any extra resourcing. For example, one such statement announced that children could be admitted from the beginning of the school year in which they became five, but went on to explain that if parents wanted their child to be admitted later it would not prejudice their right to a place for that child at a particular school. Another statement affirmed the Education Committee's support for the principle that the education of the youngest children must be suited to their age and stage of development, and pledged additional staffing, a programme of in-service training and funds for full capitation.

The more detailed policy statements also set out clear criteria for provision in schools. These statements stipulated, for example, that a school could admit children early provided that:

❁ the physical conditions and 'teaching programme' were appropriate;
❁ early admissions did not create over-large classes;
❁ places were available for children of statutory age moving into the area during the school year;
❁ children younger than rising-five attended part-time;
❁ four year olds were not placed in vertically grouped classes with children aged six or seven (except where there was no alternative, such as in a small village school);
❁ a generous share of available ancillary help was allocated to classes containing four year olds;
❁ children in nursery classes had at least one complete year in the nursery before being moved into an infants class.

All these criteria accord with the general picture of 'appropriateness' confirmed in the study and provide schools with a sound basis from which to proceed.

## Education Committee and Officers

Members of the education service interviewed pointed out that appropriate provision for early admission can be achieved more speedily and effectively if there is someone on the Education Committee and among the officers who is understanding of and sympathetic to the needs of young children. Such a person is invaluable in providing a much needed 'voice' for early years education and arguing for appropriate resourcing. Professionals in several of the LEAs involved in the study praised individuals, among both elected members and education officers, for their efforts in supporting the introduction and implementation of new policies, resourcing and guidelines for the admission of four year olds to school.

A difficulty is that perceived priorities can alter with a change of council and even the best-laid plans, especially in a non-statutory area like the education of the under-fives, may be shelved (*TES*, 12.5.89). It is crucial, therefore, that early years education is not allowed to become a political football and that everyone, including politicians and the public at large, understands the importance of providing appropriately for children who are on the threshold of their educational careers and indeed their lives.

# Conclusion

Schools with early admission should be able to draw on external sources of support both locally and in the wider community.

To promote mutual support, schools with children under five should seek links with other agencies working with young children and their families so that knowledge and expertise can be shared. Schools can also assist each other by acting as resource centres or sharing ideas. To avoid a sense of isolation, adults working with under-fives should have opportunities to meet with others through professional or self-help groups.

Training institutions have a vital role to play in ensuring a supply of suitable trained staff with specialist knowledge and skills. These are needed not only to maintain the classrooms of today but to redress the shortage of early years trainers for the future. Institutions can also collaborate with LEAs to provide much-needed in-service support. There is a continuing demand for accessible INSET courses for teachers not previously trained in the age group, to plug gaps in earlier training and to offer theory to underpin practice. LEA advisory services should make full use of advisers and inspectors with early years expertise and should, if possible, enlist the help of specialist advisory teachers.

All LEAs with early admission should have a coherent policy, with a well-informed Education Committee and officers to help put it into effect. They should provide clear guidelines for teachers with four year olds in their classes and ensure that the guidelines reach the people for whom they are intended.

# PART FIVE

## Summary and Recommendations

When the main principles of the preceding chapters are drawn together, they offer both a summary and a list of recommendations for practice, provision and support for children admitted early to infant schooling.

# 12 A Framework for Action

Since the study was carried out, the admission of four year olds to school has been caught between pressure for more places and cuts in finances. Demand for more daytime provision for under-fives has continued as firms have tried to attract mothers back to work. At the same time, early admission policies in some LEAs have been threatened by cutbacks due to rate-capping and the introduction of the community charge. These have been blamed for proposals in at least two authorities with little or no state nursery provision to raise the school starting age from four to five (*Guardian*, 13.11.90, p. 27; *TES*, 16.11.90, p. 8). Also, as LMS gets underway, individual schools may reconsider whether they should continue to admit children below the statutory age.

Most of the professionals interviewed in the study believed that ideally four year olds should be in nursery rather than infant classes. However, while the number of nursery places continues to fall far short of demand and children are admitted early to infant classes, every effort must be made to ensure that their needs are suitably catered for.

This final chapter pulls together the main principles of appropriate provision and practice discussed in this book. Drawing on all the sources of evidence used in the study, including statements about what ideally should be provided and our observations of what succeeded in practice, it offers a framework of recommendations to assist policy-makers, course providers and practitioners to improve provision, practice and support in schools admitting four year olds.

The principles articulated in these recommendations are based on educationists' beliefs about what young children, and four year olds in particular, are like (see Chapter 3). For example, four year olds are described as active and energetic, questioning and curious. They are developing rapidly, not only physically and mentally but socially and emotionally as well, and range widely in ability. Yet they still operate very much as individuals and need a lot of adult attention; with four year olds it is 'Me, now'. Because four year olds are like this, they have certain requirements that make educational provision and practice appropriate or otherwise. However, these requirements do not begin at four and cease with the fifth birthday. Four is part of a continuous period of very rapid development from birth to seven. Therefore much of what is said of four year olds also holds true for children from the age of three to five or more.

Implicit in our recommendations are the changes and adjustments schools need to make if they are to be suitable learning environments for children below statutory age. These statements therefore have particular relevance for school governing bodies and all those responsible for holding the purse strings under the new arrangements for the Local Management of Schools (LMS). Schools cannot be satisfactory places for under-fives unless they have suitable resources; teachers cannot offer appropriate practice if the physical provision is inadequate. On the other hand, no amount of resourcing will be sufficient unless the adults involved are committed to the task facing them. In the end, good practice must depend to a large extent on the expertise and dedication of individuals. Furthermore, if changes are to be made and commitment sustained, these individuals and their schools need as much support as possible.

The recommendations (like the chapters) are organized into three groups relating to appropriate practice, appropriate provision and support.

# Towards Appropriate Practice

## Admission and Entry (Chapter 3)

✿ A gradual introduction with sensitive treatment from the adults involved is essential to a smooth transition to school.

✿ Links should be developed with the child's parents and family before admission and relevant information exchanged; children and their families should be encouraged to visit the school; home visiting is widely recommended.

✿ Entry should be staggered over a period of time so that children can be admitted individually or in small groups.

✿ Attendance should be part-time at first; arrangements should be flexible to suit the needs of individual children.

✿ Arrival and leaving times should be flexible and vary from the rest of the school to avoid the crush; there should be a calm start to the day.

✿ Children should be introduced sensitively and gradually to school routines such as assembly, lunch and playtimes.

## The Activities (Chapter 4)

✿ The activities (learning experiences) should be of sufficient range and variety to promote a broad and balanced curriculum.

✿ There should be continuity between appropriate activities for children under five and the requirements of the National Curriculum; school curriculum planning should include the youngest pupils in the school.

✿ The curriculum should be an integrated one, not compartmentalized into separate subject areas:
  ❀ activities should be multidisciplinary;
  ❀ all areas of the curriculum should be covered.

✿ There should be a balance between activities of different kinds: group and individual, mobile and calm, noisy and quiet, novel and familiar.

✿ Activity areas should be clearly defined, and at the same time carefully sited to allow natural links to be made between them.

✿ Situations should be created that offer a challenge and can be developed and extended by the children or adults.

✿ Use should be made of the wider environment both inside and outside the school.

❂ Activities should:
  ❀ be flexible enough to take account of a wide range of experience and ability;
  ❀ be appropriate to the needs of individual children;
  ❀ be relevant and meaningful for the child;
  ❀ allow for individual progress and extension.
❂ Provision should allow for the simultaneous development of activity and language; there should be opportunities for children to share their experiences and to talk about what they are doing while they are doing it.

## Teaching Approach (Chapter 5)

❂ A play approach should be adopted:
  ❀ play should not be taken to mean the opposite to 'work';
  ❀ the value of play should be acknowledged, understood and communicated by everyone concerned;
  ❀ play is not the prerogative of the youngest pupils but can be used as an approach throughout the school.
❂ Teachers should have clear aims and intentions, both for the activities and for the child:
  ❀ they should plan an environment that allows children to proceed at their own level and pace;
  ❀ tasks should be matched to the individual child.
❂ Timetabling should be flexible with the minimum of interruptions to children's activities; there should be some overall pattern to the day or session to give children a sense of time and help them feel secure.
❂ Although children of this age operate mainly as individuals, opportunities should be provided for group activity:
  ❀ children should be brought together from time to time for stories and discussions;
  ❀ groups should be small rather than whole-class;
  ❀ frequent opportunities should be provided for small group activity and collaboration in spontaneous groups and pairs.
❂ Learning should be based on active, first-hand experiences:
  ❀ children should have opportunities to explore, experiment, investigate, try out things for themselves and make 'mistakes';
  ❀ they should be encouraged to look and observe, and become familiar with the use of the written word around them even before they can read:
  ❀ the emphasis should be on the processes rather than products of learning;
  ❀ dependence on commercial schemes should be avoided.

✿ The teacher should 'start from where the child is', taking account of the child's pre-school experience and levels of confidence and competence.

✿ Adults should intervene sensitively in children's activities in order to develop and extend their learning:

    ❀ the adult needs to observe the child so as to know when and how best to intervene;

    ❀ adults also need to judge when not to intervene.

✿ An appropriate approach is one that recognizes children's interests and builds upon them:

    ❀ there should be a balance between adult-initiated and child-initiated activities;

    ❀ children should have opportunities to make choices and decisions and to take some responsibility for their learning;

    ❀ control of activities should be negotiated with children rather than imposed upon them.

## Monitoring and Recording Progress (Chapter 6)

✿ Monitoring and record-keeping procedures should take account of the whole child: physical, social and emotional as well as cognitive aspects of development must be considered because all aspects are interrelated.

✿ All schools should have procedures for monitoring children's progress from the start:

    ❀ LEAs should assist schools in developing their monitoring and recording procedures;

    ❀ records that run through the school should share a common language so that misinterpretations are kept to the minimum.

✿ Monitoring procedures must take account of the diversity of young children's development and pre-school experience.

✿ Monitoring should be a continuous process, carried out by observation during the course of children's normal activities; it is essential that adults have time to observe and assess as part of the ongoing development of the curriculum.

✿ Monitoring should be team-based involving teachers, nursery nurses, ancillary helpers, the parents and the child.

✿ Good record-keeping is essential, both to evaluate the curriculum and to assess children's progress; the emphasis should be on the child's own progress rather than on the child's position in relation to other children.

✿ The purposes of records, who will have access to them and the uses to which they will be put, should be made clear to all involved.

# Towards Appropriate Provision

### Space (Chapter 7)

✿ The outdoor space should be safe and secure, and an extension of the indoor learning environment; it should have adequate storage facilities and surfaces of different types (grassed and hard).

✿ The provision should allow children to move freely between indoors and outdoors.

✿ Toilets and sinks should be readily accessible.

✿ The youngest classes in the school should have the most available space; non-essential classroom furniture can be removed to increase space.

✿ Furniture and fittings should be of suitable height and size so that children can use them independently.

✿ The indoor space should have recesses and open areas; tables and storage units can be used creatively to break up space and provide areas for different kinds of activity; floor surfaces should be of different types (especially carpet for quiet activities and non-slip tiles for wet or messy activities).

### Equipment and Materials (Chapter 8)

✿ Equipment and materials should be of good quality (with limited resources quality is more important than quantity); they should be clean and attractively presented and consist, where appropriate, of real objects rather than toy imitations.

✿ Equipment and materials should be sufficient in quantity for children to be able to develop and complete an activity, and for several children to use them at the same time.

✿ Equipment and materials should be easily accessible so that children can use them safely and independently; they should be clearly labelled so that children can service their own activities and put things away when they have finished with them.

✿ A range of equipment and materials should be provided that:
  ❁ is appropriate to the different levels of young children's ability and experience;
  ❁ provides opportunities for multidisciplinary activities and allows for individual progression;
  ❁ reflects a multicultural society and promotes equal opportunities for children of different gender, race and culture.

✿ A variety of equipment and materials should be provided that:
  ❁ allows for a balance of different kinds of activity;
  ❁ covers all areas of the curriculum;

❀ includes the following types of materials (and the equipment to go with them): natural, creative, constructional, domestic and role-play, table-top, musical and sound-making, listening and books, special interest, outdoor.

## Staffing (Chapter 9)

❀ Adult–child ratios should be as high as possible, preferably in line with nursery recommendations of 2:26 (one teacher and one nursery nurse to 26 children).
❀ Teachers should be trained and experienced in early years education.
❀ Full-time ancillary support should be available; ancillary workers should be trained and preferably hold a nursery nursing qualification.
❀ Adult–child ratios can be improved by encouraging voluntary helpers (especially parents) into the classroom.

# Sources of Support

## Support Within the School (Chapter 10)

❀ Teachers with four year olds in their classes should have an understanding of early years education and be able to articulate and justify appropriate practice to others; they should possess the skills needed to lead a team and to establish good relationships with parents and other professionals.
❀ The support of the other team members is essential; ideally the teacher should work in partnership with a qualified nursery nurse whose professional training and experience should be used to the full; ideally, classroom ancillaries should spend as much time as possible with the same class so that they can be more involved with the work of the team.
❀ Early admission should be a whole-school issue, with a policy for appropriate provision developed with all members of staff; it should be recognized that the youngest pupils are part of the school community, and their needs should be acknowledged and understood throughout the school.
❀ Headteachers with under-fives in their schools should have a knowledge of early years education and experience of teaching children of this age.
❀ Headteachers should take the lead in supporting staff working with four year olds by:

    ❁ ensuring that fours are part of the school community;

    ❁ being aware of appropriate class size and age range, and sensitive to the need for suitable timetabling, staffing and re-sourcing;

    ❁ explaining appropriate policy and practice to others;

    ❁ having regard for the in-service needs of early years teachers and their teams;

    ❁ offering moral support and encouragement.

✿ Other teachers in the school should understand the needs of the younger children and appreciate why they require extra staffing and resources; all teachers should spend some time in the youngest classes; curriculum coordinators should be conversant with early childhood development and include the youngest children in their overall schemes for the school.

✿ The support of parents is essential:

    ❁ parents and teachers need to understand that they both have a valued and valuable contribution to make to the children's education;

    ❁ parents can also provide an additional adult resource and should be encouraged to help in the classroom.

✿ Parents and governors should have some understanding of what the staff are trying to do for four year olds and be supportive of their efforts; those responsible for the budget should be sympathetic to the needs of younger pupils and resource them accordingly; the governing body should work with the headteacher and senior management team to establish a policy with regard to pupils under five.

## Support from Outside the School (Chapter 11)

✿ Schools with early admissions should seek links with other agencies working with young children and their families.

✿ Staff working with four year olds should have opportunities to meet with other early years practitioners through professional and self-support groups.

✿ Other schools can be useful as resource centres and, in certain cases, can provide examples of good practice or act as a stimulus for fresh ideas.

✿ Initial training for intending teachers of young children should:

    ❁ refer to the whole of the three to eight age range;

    ❁ pay particular attention to early childhood development and to the skills required for leading a team, explaining good practice to others, and observing children and evaluating their progress;

❀ take special care in the selection of appropriate candidates for early years training.

✿ In-service initiatives are needed to update or fill gaps in the initial training of adults working with four year olds:

❀ various levels of INSET (from short 'survival' initiatives to more substantial award-bearing courses) are required to suit different needs;

❀ LEAs should co-operate more with initial training establishments, especially in providing longer courses on the theory underpinning good practice;

❀ courses should be accessible to staff in rural areas;

❀ headteachers should, where possible, attend the same courses as their staff so that they have a common basis for discussion;

❀ more INSET opportunities should also be available to nursery nurses and other regular classroom helpers. (Recent changes under GEST (1991–92) now allow in-service funding for nursery nurses and non-specialist advisers with responsibility for under-fives.)

✿ LEA advisory services should take a more active role in publicizing good practice and sharing ideas and expertise, both within and between authorities:

❀ ideally, there should be at least one adviser in the authority with early years training and experience;

❀ if possible, early years advisory teachers should be appointed to support schools with four year olds.

✿ LEAs should provide guidelines for teachers with four year olds in their classes and ensure that the guidelines reach the people for whom they are intended.

✿ LEAs with early admissions should have a clearly thought-through policy; well-informed Education Committee members and officers can be invaluable in helping to put the policy into practice.

## Conclusion

When trying to meet the needs of children admitted early to infant classes, the question that should perhaps be asked is not 'Are four year olds ready for school?' but 'Is the school ready for four year olds?' We hope that this book will prove to be useful in helping to answer this question.

# Appendix

# Four Examples of Early Years INSET

## 1. An Early Years Creative Curriculum Circus

This consisted of a display of equipment, materials and activities that was circulated around the authority.

*Aims*
To create ideas for setting up learning environments for young children and to offer suggestions on the wide range of activities and materials available.

*Provider*
The LEA of a largely rural county with an established policy of annual admission at four. The circus was organized by the County Under Fives Development Officer (Education), a primary adviser and the early years support team.

*Duration*
One day (10.00 a.m. to 4.30 p.m.), repeated at seven different locations around the county from late September to early October.

*Venue*
The equipment and activities were transported in a large van to each of seven areas where they were set up in the hall of a school or college.

*Participants*
The course was intended for 'everyone working with our youngest children in schools, nurseries and playgroups, for parents, teachers, playgroup leaders, assistants, nursery nurses, carers, minders ...'. A half-day's supply cover could be applied for where necessary. The 'circus' attracted a steady flow of visitors and was attended by a variety of early years practitioners, especially reception teachers, and also students from local colleges and pupils intending to make careers in child care and education.

*Content*
Equipment, materials and suggestions for their use were set out in activity areas: sand, water, table and floor activities, music, books, imaginative play, craft and design, modelling, cooking. Each area contained a variety of equipment, much of which could be improvised without great expense. Each area comprised a range of materials with suggestions for using them and extending children's language and skills. Support materials for adults were both hand-made and commercial, and included activity cards, leaflets, handbooks, and resource packs.

In addition to the activity areas, there was a display organized by the PPA, an exposition of the work of the schools psychological service and suggestions for involving parents in their child's learning. Attention was also drawn to a resource centre sponsored by the (then) Manpower Services Commission for the use of those working with children and disabled groups. The aim of the centre was to recycle safe waste collected from local businesses for use as activity materials. Based on the premise that industry throws away tons of materials daily and that children and other community groups need materials for play and creative use, the resource centre provided a link between the two. In exchange for a small annual membership fee, groups were offered an extensive range of materials, and a member of staff was available to give workshop demonstrations of their possibilities.

*Methods*
Adults were encouraged to participate in activities and explore ideas. Many took photographs of the displays, and members of the early years curriculum team were on hand to give demonstrations and answer questions.

*Follow-up*
Although there were no formal plans for follow-up sessions, course attenders were invited to register their INSET needs and preferences on a checklist. On the basis of these preferences an early years 'day' (with supply cover) and a number of after-school workshops would be arranged. There were also opportunities for teachers to indicate whether they would like help in their school with certain aspects of the curriculum such as music. In addition, teachers in this LEA would be able to apply to take a new early years course being planned by a college of higher education in a neighbouring county. This would be a one-year course of 20 sessions for which teachers would be given half-day release. The course would lead to a Certificate in Advanced Professional Studies and could count towards a modular degree.

## 2. Early Years Staff Support Groups

*Aims*
To provide educational support for teachers and nursery nurses working with young children.

*Provider*
The groups were organized by school staff in conjunction with the advisory service in a shire county with a recent policy of annual admission. There were five groups, one in each area of the county. Each group had an organizing committee, and representatives from the committees met with the early years adviser to plan the programme. The groups worked on similar themes but tackled them in their own way according to the needs of the group. The themes were established at a day conference and evaluated at the end of the year. County-wide courses were organized by the advisory team to support and develop the work of the groups.

*Duration*
The groups were ongoing and each met about three times a term during the evenings. Headteachers were encouraged to cover for staff to visit other schools during the day from time to time.

*Venue*
Groups met in schools and occasionally in members' homes for planning purposes. Workshop activities and talks by visiting speakers were held in teachers' centres or schools.

*Participants*
Originally intended for teachers of four year olds, group membership was extended to those working with children aged three to eight. Members were mostly teachers, headteachers and nursery nurses, but membership was flexible and some groups were also attended by governors and playgroup personnel. Group attendance averaged 30 to 40, with guest speakers attracting audiences of 60 to 80. At the time of the study, attendance was having to compete with demands from National Curriculum courses.

*Content*
The overall themes for one year were 'observation' and 'key experiences'. One group decided to concentrate on sand and water play for a term. At the first meeting, a visiting speaker set the scene by describing observations of children engaged in sand and water activities. The second meeting took the form of a workshop in which members explored the use of sand and other natural substances, such as gravel, peat, sawdust, wood shavings, split peas, wood, twigs and clay. After

trying out ideas with small groups of children in their classrooms, members came together at the third meeting to share their findings. As a result of all this, the group produced a booklet of activities, skills and observations generated by sand and water play.

*Methods*
Meetings took the form of workshops and discussions to explore chosen themes. These were led by members of the advisory team, curriculum support teachers or group committee members and were supplemented with talks by visiting speakers. The term's work was sometimes drawn together in a booklet or a display, which could also form the basis for further development.

*Follow-up*
The groups generated an ongoing programme of in-service support. At the end of the year it was generally agreed that the groups had sustained the interest of their members in early education and had helped to enhance its profile. Issues had been raised to which members were able to respond as people who really 'know how it is' – based on first-hand experience. Classrooms were being opened up to visiting teachers and this was helping to 'break down barriers'. During the following year, two members of each group were expecting to attend a county-wide course for ten half-days to study the principles of the early years curriculum and to carry out observations in schools. It was hoped that they would then describe their experiences to colleagues at a day conference on the subject.

# 3. A Ten-week Course on Four Year Olds in School

*Aims*
The course was described as a 'practical' one and was intended to give teachers 'the opportunity to share experiences, examine appropriate practice and discuss issues of concern with a view to developing existing practices and teaching skills'.

*Provider*
A faculty of in-service studies at a college of higher education. The course, which was presented by a senior lecturer, was bought in by LEAs for their reception teachers. The course was flexible to meet the needs of staff in different areas: some of the user LEAs had a long tradition of early admission while others had recently changed their policy to admit four year olds.

*Duration*
Ten weekly sessions throughout a term. The timing of the sessions depended on supply cover; for example, one authority provided cover for half a day per week, so sessions were held from 1.30 p.m. to 6.30 p.m.

*Venue*
Depended on the location of the course users. For example, in one LEA the course was based at the area in-service and conference centre.

*Participants*
The course was intended for 'teachers of four year olds in early years classes'. When observed during the study, sessions were attended by 20 teachers from one LEA with early admission. Some of the teachers had reception classes of four year olds, others had mixed-age classes from four to seven.

*Content*
This varied from term to term to meet the needs of the participants. When observed, the course programme had been modified to suit teachers from an LEA with a carefully planned policy and guidance on early admission. The course included a consideration of the following topics:

- transition and starting school;
- parental involvement;
- a curriculum for four year olds;
- classroom organization and management;
- early language and literacy;
- early mathematical development;
- early science and technology;
- creativity;
- curriculum planning;
- assessment and record-keeping;
- issues in early education.

While retaining broadly similar themes, the emphasis varied according to the group, and previous groups had concentrated on such topics as the needs of four year olds, using the environment, learning through play and working with other adults in the classroom.

*Methods*
The course tutor drew on the expertise of other professionals, such as HMI, researchers, college lecturers and a seconded nursery head-teacher to give talks and workshops or to lead some of the sessions.

Course members took part in group activities, such as mapping the early years curriculum on to the National Curriculum subject areas. They watched videos of individual children and were encouraged to carry out observations of children in their own classrooms. Discussions were held and visits made to a number of schools.

### Follow-up
The course qualified as a module for a Diploma in Advanced Studies in Education (DASIE). It tended to give teachers 'a taste for INSET' and they could apply to attend further part-time and full-time courses provided by the college in nursery and infant education.

## 4. A Six-month Course on Early Years Education

### Aims
The course was intended for teachers who 'would like to work collaboratively to explore questions of curriculum content, method and evaluation', and was expected to enhance their personal and professional development.

### Provider
An institute of education. The course tutor was a senior lecturer at the institute. Places on the course were bought by some of the neighbouring LEAs or were paid for from schools' INSET budgets. The course was flexible to meet the needs of the participants and was based on members' first-hand experiences in the classroom. It encouraged members to examine their practice and build on their own expertise and skills.

### Duration
One day per week (9.30 a.m. to 4.00 p.m.) for 15 weeks during term-time from November to April – a total of 80 hours.

### Venue
The course was based at the institute and members travelled there from the surrounding LEAs.

### Participants
Approximately 20 teachers (headteachers, class teachers and support teachers) of children aged four to six. When observed in the study, the course was attended by teachers from three LEAs.

### Content
The course centred on three main questions:

✿   what principles do we draw on as we plan the early years curriculum?
✿   how best can we achieve our intentions for children's learning?
✿   how will we know if we are effective?

The course details were determined by the members who were encouraged to investigate the topics that interested them most. Topics were selected from a list including:

✿   children's play;
✿   children's spoken language;
✿   multicultural and anti-racist provision;
✿   problem-solving activities;
✿   gender issues;
✿   reading and writing in the early years.

Other topics were added by members. The course observed in the study considered:

✿   the learning environment of school;
✿   observation;
✿   self-evaluation: looking at our own learning;
✿   language at home and at school;
✿   analysing talk in the classroom;
✿   different kinds of play;
✿   early literacy;
✿   problem-solving;
✿   organization: rules, regulations and routines;
✿   group-work in the curriculum;
✿   monitoring and assessment.

*Methods*
An emphasis on the ways in which teachers can learn from each other and, through small group discussion, support each other's learning. Members were expected to 'share their growing insights into their own practice and to create for themselves a supportive but questioning climate of enquiry'. They were required to carry out classroom-based work of various kinds in preparation for each meeting. During the course, members were involved in workshop activities, lectures, seminars and discussions, and were expected to undertake a certain amount of background reading. From time to time, outside speakers were invited to talk on some of the topics. At the end of the course there was a review period of four consecutive days during which members gave presentations on a project carried out in their own schools.

They also evaluated the course in terms of its value for themselves, their schools and their LEAs.

*Qualification*
The successful completion of the course led to the award of a Certificate of Further Professional Study.

# References

ABBOTT, L. (1987). 'INSET for teachers of young children: current provision and future possibilities'. In: *Four Year Olds in School: Policy and Practice.* Slough: NFER/SCDC.

ATKIN, J. (1981). 'Is play quite the thing?', *Times Educational Supplement*, No. 3404, 25 September, p. 50.

ATKIN, J. (1988). The National Curriculum and four year olds. Paper prepared for the National Curriculum Cross-curricular Working Group (unpublished).

BAKER, K. (1989). 'Another crusade that must be won' (IBM Education lecture), *Times Educational Supplement*, No. 3804, 26 May, pp. A20–1.

BARRETT, G. (1986). *Starting School: An Evaluation of the Experience.* London: Assistant Masters and Mistresses Association.

BAYLISS, S. (1989). 'The state of play', *Times Educational Supplement*, 14 July.

BECK, K. (1989). 'Parental involvement in school: some dilemmas'. *Education 3–13*, 17, 3, 10–12.

BENNETT, D. (1987). 'The aims of teachers and parents for children in their first year at school'. In: *Four Year Olds in School: Policy and Practice.* Slough: NFER/SCDC.

BENNETT, N. (1989). 'For starters', *Times Educational Supplement*, No. 3803, 19 May, p. B2.

BENNETT, N. and KELL, J. (1989). *A Good Start? Four Year Olds in Infant Schools.* Oxford: Blackwell Education.

BINGHAM, C. (1988). Exploration and experiences: children and teachers (unpublished secondment report).

BLACKBURNE, L. and SPENCER, D. (1989). 'Tory win provokes nursery fears'. *Times Educational Supplement*, No. 3802, 12 May, p. A5.

BLATCHFORD, P. (1989). *Playtime in the Primary School.* Windsor: NFER-NELSON.

BLENKIN, G.M. and KELLY, A.V. (Eds) (1987). *Early Childhood Education: A Developmental Curriculum.* London: Paul Chapman.

BOORMAN, P. (1987). 'The contributions of physical activity to development in the early years'. In: BLENKIN, G.M. and KELLY, A.V. (Eds) *Early Childhood Education. A Developmental Curriculum.* London: Paul Chapman.

BREDEKAMP, S. (Ed.) (1986). *Developmentally Appropriate Practice.* Washington, DC: National Association for the Education of Young Children.

BREDEKAMP, S. and SHEPARD, L. (1989). 'How best to protect children from inappropriate school expectations, practices and policies', *Young Children*, 44, 3.

BROADHEAD, P. (1989). 'Rough and tumble play', *Child Education*, September, 11.

BROWNE, N. and FRANCE, P. (Eds) (1986). *Untying the Apron Strings*. Milton Keynes: Open University Press.

BRUCE, T. (1987). *Early Childhood Education*. London: Hodder and Stoughton.

BRUCE, T. (1989). 'Constructive play', *Child Education*, May, 25–8.

BRUCE, T. and GURA, P. (1988). The value of block play in the early childhood curriculum. Paper for NFER Conference *Four Year Olds in School: Research and Practice* (unpublished).

CAMPBELL, R.J. and NEILL, S.St.J. (1990). Thirteen Hundred and Thirty Days. Final report of a pilot study of teacher time in Key Stage I commissioned by the AMMA. University of Warwick, Department of Education, Policy Analysis Unit.

CLARK, M. (1988). *Children Under Five: Educational Research and Evidence*. London: Gordon and Breach.

CLARK, M., BARR, J. and DEWHIRST, W. (1986). 'Early education of children with communication problems: particularly those from ethnic minorities', *Educational Review*, Offset Publication No. 3. University of Birmingham.

CLEAVE, S., BARKER LUNN, J. and SHARP, C. (1985). 'LEA policy on admission to infant/first school', *Educational Research*, 27, 1, 40–3.

CLEAVE, S. and BROWN, S. (1989). *Four Year Olds in School – Meeting their Needs*. Slough: NFER.

CLEAVE, S., JOWETT, S. and BATE, M. (1982). *And So To School: A Study of Continuity from Pre-school to Infant School*. Windsor: NFER-NELSON.

CLIFT, P., CLEAVE, S. and GRIFFIN, M. (1980). *The Aims, Role and Deployment of Staff in the Nursery*. Windsor: NFER-NELSON.

COLLINSON, J. and BENNETT, D. (1986). An Interim Report at the End of the First Year of the Small Authorities Project in Early Childhood (unpublished).

COX, D. (1987). *A Survey of Speech Therapy Services for Children with Particular Reference to Special Education*. London: Voluntary Organisations Communication and Language (VOCAL).

CROCKER, A.C. (1988). 'Are some gifted children at risk because of their infant school experience?', *Education Today*, 38, 3, 49–54.

CURTIS, A. (1986). *A Curriculum for the Pre-school Child*. Windsor: NFER-NELSON.

DAVID, T. (1990). *Under Five – Under-educated?* Milton Keynes: Open University Press.

DAVIS, D. (1989). 'Encounters with Harpo Marx in the Wendy House', *Education 3–13*, 17, 3, 55–9.

DESFORGES, C. (1989). 'Getting down to bases', *Times Educational Supplement*, 24 April, p. B2.

DOE, B. (1989). 'Rumbold lightens load for weary governors', *Times Educational Supplement*, No. 3804, 26 May, p. 1.

DOWLING, M. (1988). *Education 3 to 5: A Teachers' Handbook.* London: Paul Chapman.

DRUMMOND, M.J. (1987). 'Afterword – Is There a Way Forward?' In: *Four Year Olds in School: Policy and Practice.* Slough: NFER/SCDC.

DRUMMONS, M.J. (1988). British–Irish seminar: the educational needs of four and five year olds. A review (unpublished).

DRUMMOND, M.J. (1989a). 'Learning about gender in primary schools'. In: LANG, P. (Ed.) *Thinking About ... Personal and Social Education in Primary and Middle Schools.* London: Blackwell.

DRUMMOND, M.J. (1989b) 'Early Years in Education: Contemporary Challenges'. In: DESFORGES, C. (Ed.) *Early Childhood Education. British Journal of Educational Psychology*, Monograph Series No. 4.

DRUMMOND, M.J., PUGH, G. and LALLY, M. (Eds) (1989). *Working with Children: Developing a Curriculum for the Early Years.* National Children's Bureau/Nottingham Educational Supplies.

EARLY YEARS CURRICULUM GROUP (1989). *Early Childhood Education: The Early Years Curriculum and the National Curriculum.* Stoke-on-Trent: Trentham Books.

GALLAHUE, D. (1982). *Understanding Motor Development in Children.* New York: Wiley.

GHAYE, A. and PASCAL, C. (1988). 'Four year old children in reception classes: participant perceptions and practice', *Start: An Occasional Paper.* Worcester College of Higher Education.

GREAT BRITAIN. DEPARTMENT OF EDUCATION AND SCIENCE (1985a). *Better Schools.* Cmnd. 9469. London: HMSO.

GREAT BRITAIN. DEPARTMENT OF EDUCATION AND SCIENCE (1985b). *The Curriculum from 5 to 16.* London: HMSO.

GREAT BRITAIN. DEPARTMENT OF EDUCATION AND SCIENCE (1985c). *The Quality of Provision for the Young Child in the Primary School. The Four Year Old in School.* Regional Course Document. London: DES.

GREAT BRITAIN. DEPARTMENT OF EDUCATION AND SCIENCE (1988). *The New Teacher in School.* A Survey by HM Inspectors in England and Wales 1987. London: HMSO.

GREAT BRITAIN. DEPARTMENT OF EDUCATION AND SCIENCE. (1989a). *Standards in Education 1987–1988.* The Annual Report of HM Senior Chief Inspector of Schools. London: DES.

GREAT BRITAIN. DEPARTMENT OF EDUCATION AND SCIENCE (1989b). *Aspects of Primary Education: The Education of Children Under Five.* London: HMSO.

GREAT BRITAIN. DEPARTMENT OF EDUCATION AND SCIENCE (1989c). *A Survey of the Quality of Education for Four Year Olds in Primary Classes.* Report by HMI. London: DES (339/89/NS).

GREAT BRITAIN. DEPARTMENT OF EDUCATION AND SCIENCE (1989d). *The Implementation of the National Curriculum in Primary Schools.* London: DES.

GREAT BRITAIN. DEPARTMENT OF EDUCATION AND SCIENCE (1990a). *Statistical Bulletin 7/90.* London: HMSO.

GREAT BRITAIN. DEPARTMENT OF EDUCATION AND SCIENCE (1990b). *Starting with Quality.* Report of Committee of Inquiry into the Quality of the Educational Experience Offered to 3- to 4-Year Olds, chaired by Angela Rumbold. London: DES.

GREAT BRITAIN. DEPARTMENT OF EDUCATION AND SCIENCE (1990c). *Grants for Education Support and Training (1991–2).* DES Circular. 20 July 1990. London: DES.

GREAT BRITAIN. DEPARTMENT OF EDUCATION AND SCIENCE (1990d). *Standards in Education 1988–89.* Annual Report of HM Senior Chief Inspector of Schools. London: DES.

HACKETT, G. and BLACKBURNE, L. (1989). 'Nurseries endangered by primary staff crisis', *Times Educational Supplement*, 14 July.

HOUSE OF COMMONS EDUCATION, SCIENCE AND ARTS COMMITTEE (1986). *Achievement in Primary Schools: Third Report,* Vol. 1. London: HMSO.

HOUSE OF COMMONS EDUCATION, SCIENCE AND ARTS COMMITTEE (1988). *Educational Provision for the Under-fives.* London: HMSO.

HURST, V. (1987). 'Parents and professionals: partnership in early childhood education'. In: BLENKIN, G. and KELLY, A. (Eds) *Early Childhood Education: A Developmental Curriculum.* London: Paul Chapman.

JOWETT, S. and BAGINSKY, M. (1988). 'Parents and education: a survey of their involvement and a discussion of some issues', *Educational Research*, 30, 1, 36–45.

KATZ, L. and CHARD, S. (1989). *Engaging Children's Minds. The Project Approach.* London: Ablex.

KERNIG, W. (1986). 'The infant looks at the world: some implications for the teacher'. In: DAVIS, R., GOLBY, M., KERNIG, W. and TAMBURRINI, J. (Eds) *The Infant School: Past, Present and Future.* London: Bedford Way Papers, No. 27.

LALLY, M. (1989). 'Curriculum for three to five year olds'. *Highlight No. 89.* London: National Children's Bureau.

McCAIL, G. (1989). *The Four Year Old in the Classroom.* British Association for Early Childhood Education.

MANNING, M. and HERRMANN, J. (1988). 'The relationships of problem children in nursery schools'. In: COHEN, A. and COHEN. L. (1988). *Early Childhood Education: The Pre-school Years.* London: Paul Chapman.

MANNING, K. and SHARP, A. (1977). *Structuring Play in the Early Years at School.* London: Ward Lock Educational.

MATTHEWS, J. (1987). 'The young child's early representation and drawing'. In: BLENKIN, G. and KELLY, A. (Eds) *Early Childhood Education.* London: Paul Chapman.

METZ, M. (1987). 'The development of mathematical understanding'. In: BLENKIN, G. and KELLY, A. (Eds) *Early Childhood Education.* London: Paul Chapman.

MOORE, E. and SYLVA, K. (1984). 'A survey of under-fives record-keeping in Great Britain', *Educational Research*, 26, 2, 115–20.

NASH, B.C. (1981). 'The effects of classroom spatial organisation on four- and five-year-old children's learning', *British Journal of Educational Psychology*, 51, 144–55.

NATIONAL CURRICULUM COUNCIL (1989). *A Framework for the Primary Curriculum.* York: National Curriculum Council.

NATIONAL NURSERY EXAMINATION BOARD (n.d.). *Role of the Nursery Nurse in Schools and Classes.* St Albans: NNEB.

NEILL, S.R. St J. (1982). 'Pre-school design and child behaviour', *Journal of Child Psychology and Psychiatry*, 23, 3, 309–18.

NEILL, S. (1982). 'Open plan or divided space in pre-school', *Education 3–13*, 10, 45–8.

PASCAL, C. (1989). 'What's all this fuss about the early years?', *Early Years*, 9, 2, 5–10.

POLLARD, B. (1989). *An Investigation into the Provision for Early Admission in Humberside Schools.* Humberside College of Higher Education and Humberside Local Education Authority.

POZZANI, J. (1989). Significant people, significant time: children and their teachers in the first term at school. Early years secondment report (unpublished).

PUGH, G. (1989). *Services for Under Fives: Developing a Co-ordinated Approach.* London: National Children's Bureau.

ROYALL, A. (1989). 'Awakening the senses', *Special Children*, 33, 27.

SCHWEINHART, L.J., WEIKART, D.P. and LARNER, M.B. (1986). 'Consequences of three preschool curriculum models through age 15', *Early Childhood Research Quarterly*, 1, 15–45.

SESTINI, E. (1987). 'The quality of learning experiences for four year olds in nursery and infant classes'. In: *Four Year Olds in School: Policy and Practice.* Slough: NFER/SCDC.

SHARP, A. (1989). 'Quality in the early years curriculum'. *Update: Current issues in Early Childhood*, No. 30. OMEP.

SHARP, C. (1988). 'Starting School at Four', *Research Papers in Education*, 3, 1, 64–90.

SMITH, P.K. and CONNOLLY, K.J. (1981). *The Ecology of Pre-school Behaviour.* Cambridge: Cambridge University Press.

STANILAND, B. (1986). Education and the early years. Paper presented to the NAHT conference. (unpublished).

STEVENSON, C. (1987). 'The young four year old in nursery and infant classes: challenges and constraints'. In: *Four Year Olds in School: Policy and Practice.* Slough: NFER/SCDC.

STEVENSON, C. (1988). *Focus on Four.* Stevenage: Area Advisory Centre.

SUTCLIFFE, M., BILLETT, S. and DUNCAN, J. (1987). 'Learning to move and moving to learn in the nursery years', *British Journal of Physical Education*, 18, 4, 157–9.

SYLVA, K., BRUNER, J.S. and GENOVA, P. (1976). 'The role of play in the problem-solving of children 3–5 years old'. In: BRUNER, J.S., JOLLY, A. and SYLVA, K. (Eds) (1976). *Play.* Harmondsworth: Penguin.

SYLVA, K. ROY, C. and PAINTER, M. (1980). *Child Watching at Playgroup and Nursery School.* London: Grant McIntyre.

TANN, S. (1990). 'Assessment-led schooling? Reflections on Term I of the National Curriculum', *Early Years*, 10, 2, 9–13.

TEACHER, THE (1989). 'Surprise change after Act', *Teacher*, 20 February, p. 7.

TIZARD, B. and HUGHES, M. (1984). *Young Children Learning: Talking and Thinking at Home and at School.* London: Fontana.

THOMAS, I. (1987). 'The Bedfordshire 4+ pilot scheme: some issues and implications'. In: *Four Year Olds in School: Policy and Practice.* Slough: NFER/SCDC.

TUDGE, J. and CARUSO, D. (1988). 'Co-operative problem-solving in the classroom: enhancing young children's cognitive development', *Young Children*, 44, 1, 46–52.

VAUSE, D. (1988). Educational provision for four year olds in primary schools in Lancashire. Paper given at the NFER conference *Four Year olds in School: Research and Practice* (unpublished).

VYGOTSKY, L. (1978). *Mind in Society.* Cambridge, MA: Harvard University Press.

WEIR, R. (1988). Paper presented to the NFER conference *Starting School at Four: Planning for the Future* (unpublished).

WELLS, G. (1985). *Language Development in the Pre-school Years.* Cambridge: Cambridge University Press.

WELLS, G. (1986). *The Meaning Makers – Children Learning Language and Using Language to Learn.* New Hampshire: Heinemann Educational.

WEST, A., BANFIELD, S. and VARLAAM, A. (1990). 'Evaluation of an early entry to infant school pilot exercise', *Research Papers in Education*, 5, 3, 229–50.

WILLES, M.J. (1983). *Children into Pupils*. London: Routledge and Kegan Paul.

WOLFENDALE, S. (1987). *All About Me* (revised edn). London: National Children's Bureau.

# Index

*Index compiled by Frank Pert.*